A Religion of Nature

A Religion of Nature

Donald A. Crosby

STATE UNIVERSITY OF NEW YORK PRESS

Published by
State University of New York Press, Albany

For information, address State University of New York Press,
90 State Street, Suite 700, Albany, NY 12207

Production, Laurie Searl
Marketing, Anne M. Valentine

Library of Congress Cataloging-in-Publication Data

Crosby, Donald A.
    A religion of nature / Donald A. Crosby.
      p. cm.
    Includes bibliographical references and index.
    ISBN 0-7914-5453-3 (alk. paper) — ISBN 0-7914-5454-1 (pbk. : alk. paper)
      1. Philosophy of nature. I. Title.

  BD581 .C69 2002
  113—dc21

                                                                  2002017734

10 9 8 7 6 5 4 3 2 1

For Pam

Where'er you walk, cool gales shall fan the glade,
Trees, where you sit, shall crowd into a shade;
Where'er you tread, the blushing flow'rs shall rise,
And all things flourish where you turn your eyes.

—Alexander Pope, "Summer"

. . . [T]he common *socius* [ally] of us all is the great universe whose children we are.

—William James, *A Pluralistic Universe*

The same stream of life that runs through my veins night and day runs through the world and dances in rhythmic measures.
It is the same life that shoots in joy through the dust of the earth in numberless blades of grass and breaks into tumultuous waves of leaves and flowers.

—Radindranath Tagore, *Gitanjali*

Contents

Preface

The beauty, sublimity, and wonder of nature have been justly celebrated in all of the religious traditions of the world, but usually these traditions have focused on beings or powers presumed to lie behind nature and to provide nature's ultimate explanation and meaning. Nature in these traditions is seen as pointing beyond itself to something more fundamental and important than itself, something that is assumed to be the proper object of religious devotion. In recent years, largely as a result of increasing attention being given to ecology and the natural environment, theological thought has tended to be much more concerned than before with the place of humans in nature and their responsibilities to nature. But what is still of primary religious importance in theology, as we would expect from the name for this discipline, is God, whether God be conceived theistically, pantheistically, or panentheistically. Also, many books and articles have been written of late on environmental ethics, but their principal concern is with ethics, not the *religious* significance and value of nature.

This book, in contrast, makes a sustained case for nature itself as a proper focus of religious commitment and concern. For it, nature—envisioned as without God, gods, or animating spirits of any kind—is religiously ultimate. It also argues that nature is metaphysically ultimate, that is, self-sustaining and requiring no explanation for its existence beyond itself. Moreover, humans are viewed as an integral part of nature, natural beings in the fullest sense of the term. They are at home in the natural world, their origin, nature, and destiny lie here and not in some transcendent realm, and their moral and religious responsibilities extend not only to one another and to the human community but to the whole of nature and to all living beings. This book urges us to grant to nature the kind of reverence, awe, love, and devotion we in the West have formerly reserved for God.

Part 1 is autobiographical and sketches stages in my journey from theistic faith to a religion of nature. Part 2 develops a concept of nature and of the place of humans in nature, discusses philosophical and scientific approaches to nature, examines the status of values in nature, and defends the metaphysical ultimacy of nature. Part 3 makes a case for the religious ultimacy of nature as nature is conceived in part 2. It first demonstrates that nature can be an appropriate focus of religious commitment and then goes on to show why it should be viewed as the most appropriate focus of that commitment. Chapters in part 3 also present and respond to six important objections to a religion of nature and show why nature, despite its moral ambiguity, can be viewed as the principal source of good for all of its creatures, including human beings.

My writing of this book was aided and enriched by colleagues, friends, and former students who either read and commented critically on parts of the manuscript or engaged me in informal conversations about some of the ideas incorporated in it. Among these are James Boyd, Delwin Brown, William Dean, Judy Naginey, Holmes Rolston III, and Joachim Viens. David Conner read the manuscript in its entirety and made many astute and helpful observations about it, both in writing and in conversation. My wife, Pamela Crosby, has read and reread the book in various stages of its development, helping me with her expertise as a teacher of English to avoid grammatical mistakes and infelicities of style, as well as pointing out from her thoughtful perspective as a fellow philosopher substantive issues in need of more adequate development. Ongoing and spirited conversations with her on a variety of topics stimulated me to think more deeply about the problems discussed here. Students in my graduate class "Philosophical Models of Nature," in my undergraduate classes in philosophy of religion, and in numerous other classes that I have taught over the years raised pertinent questions and made incisive critical observations about my emerging and often uncertain views about nature, the place of humans in nature, and a religion of nature. I am fortunate to have had these perceptive students in my classes. I am grateful for a grant from the Endowment Fund of the Department of Philosophy at Colorado State University that assisted me in completing this book. Finally, I wish to thank the three anonymous readers commissioned by the State University of New York Press, who made valuable suggestions for improving the manuscript and whose insightful questions about parts of it helped me present some of its ideas more clearly and, I hope, more convincingly.

Part 1

Introduction

1

From God to Nature: A Personal Odyssey

I enter a swamp as a sacred place—a sanctum sanctorum. There is
the strength, the marrow of Nature.
                              —Henry David Thoreau, "Walking"

I grew up in Bible-Belt northwest Florida (culturally indistinguishable from
southern Alabama). Religion there was pervasive, dogmatic, and real. My early
religious convictions were formed by the preaching of a large-hearted Scottish
minister with a musical brogue, a youth group skillfully orchestrated by a former missionary couple with exotic tokens of world travel in their home, and
summer church camps that continually urged us to make or reaffirm a Christian commitment. Often a new friendship with a special girl would grow up in
the near eternity of a week of church camp away from home, and this friendship's strange warmth would blend confusingly with emotions stirred by the
"friend we have in Jesus."

In my high school years I had a male best friend who, like myself, became
increasingly absorbed in a religious quest. We took long walks along Bayou
Texar and the deserted beaches of Escambia Bay, pondered books on developing our spiritual lives, attended services of worship three times a week, assumed
leadership roles in the youth group at church, and spent many evenings at his
house sipping coffee, lost in thought before a fire, and earnestly probing the
mysteries of religion. It did not occur to us to doubt that God exists or that the
Bible contains his definitive revelation, but there also was much that we did not
understand about God and the Bible and yearned to know. I remember being

in a car with my friend during one of our endless discussions and reaching into the glove compartment for a Bible to support a point I had just made. He remarked, "That's an interesting theological idea." I had never before heard the word *theological!* It sounded enigmatic and profound, whetting my appetite for more talk about the nature of God, his creation and governance of the world, and his purpose for human life—especially for my life.

My hometown, Pensacola, is a Navy town with an aviation training base the locals proudly call "The Annapolis of the Air." I was thirteen years old when World War II ended, and most of my late childhood games had related to war. Since my natural father had risen through the ranks to become a naval officer and had served with distinction on aircraft carriers in the pivotal battles of Midway and the Coral Sea, I thought that his record could help me wrangle an appointment to the Naval Academy, to prepare for a naval career. However, as my religious sensibilities deepened, I came to realize that I was more interested in studying for the ministry. Having finally made the decision to become a minister, after my high school graduation I traveled by Greyhound bus to Davidson College in North Carolina—a staunch, all-male Presbyterian liberal arts school—to prepare myself for what I now fervently believed to be my calling.

College opened up a vast new world. I began to grasp the multi-textured complexity of Western culture and to have the first glimmerings of cultures radically different from my own. I now sensed that my particular intellectual upbringing and outlook constituted just one sliver of a plenitude of possibilities. This upbringing and outlook were Protestant rather than Catholic or Eastern Orthodox, for example, and Christian rather than Buddhist or secular. They were not only American but reflected the rather provincial Americanism of the southeastern United States in the second quarter of the twentieth century. Also, I happened to have been born and reared white rather than black, a difference whose significance in the Deep South of that time was impressed upon me anew every summer when I came home from college to resume work with Arthur, "Junior," and "Bubba," the black men with whom I had labored since age twelve in my uncles' wholesale plumbing store. It had been unquestioningly assumed that I would go to college and that their children would not. Although I regarded these men as old friends, they lived in a world I had made little attempt to understand, and I was now being inducted into a world of rapidly expanding horizons I found increasingly impossible to explain to them.

All of this dawned on me rather slowly, however. I remember how startling it was, early in my college career, to come across an announcement in the student newspaper that someone was coming to the campus to argue for *atheism!* My shock was not much less than if the newspaper had announced the visit of an alien from a remote galaxy. A universe without God was inconceivable to me at that time. I dismissed the impending lecture from my mind and did not bother to attend; I wonder now what the effect on me would have been had I gone.

My junior year in college brought the first courses in philosophy. As I recall, that year we used textbooks and anthologies rather than reading major primary texts or exploring the intricacies of whole theories. The material was vaguely interesting but also elusively abstract—more informative than intellectually stimulating. In my senior year we read the philosophers themselves, and in some detail. I became aware for the first time of the astounding range and originality of philosophical positions and of the powerful aguments deployed in each position's defense. The fact that some of the greatest minds of Western history could come to such different conclusions on the many common problems they addressed—and that no closure had been reached on these problems, despite the concentrated efforts of these geniuses throughout their lifetimes—struck me with overwhelming force. I now recognized that no fundamental intellectual or spiritual outlook could be taken for granted; each had to be opened to critical scrutiny in the context of opposing points of view. This applied as much to my own outlook as to any other. Years later, I came across a statement that expressed exactly what I realized at this time: faith cannot simply be taken on faith; it has to be critically assessed if it is to give adequate support to a whole way of life. My days of unreflective credulity were coming to an end.

Once I had enrolled for ministerial studies at Princeton Theological Seminary in New Jersey, my attitudes toward Christianity became progressively more critical and informed. While my Christian faith remained strong, it was no longer unquestioned. I saw that there were few, if any, patent meanings of the scriptural texts that lay on their surfaces. What I had formerly thought to be the obvious meanings of these texts were debatable interpretations, filtered down to me through history. I learned to read the books of the Bible in their historical settings, in light of the latest theories of their historical development, and in their original languages. I came up against the fact of variant readings and different manuscripts. Even the oldest of the manuscripts dated from times much later than those of their original authorship. My reading of Albert Schweitzer's monumental study, *The Quest of the Historical Jesus*,[1] as well as other books on the New Testament showed how extremely difficult, if not impossible, it is to separate a Jesus of history from overlays of kerygmatic faith in the Gospels and the other New Testament writings.

As for the great creeds of the Church, I saw how these had been hammered out amidst raging controversy, that political as well as religious factors were involved, that the creeds were in some sense the outcomes of compromise, that a case could be made for each of the so-called heresies on the basis of vague or ambiguous biblical passages, and that the creeds were couched in the metaphysical categories of a period later than that of the New Testament and considerably different from the conceptualities of our own time. So once again there were no self-evident facts of the matter; it was interpretation all the way down. No external authority could settle the question of which of many possible construals was the best. I had to think for myself.

Up to now, my faith had developed in the isolation and introspective privacy of seven years as a student, first in college and then in seminary, but upon graduation from the seminary, I became the pastor of a small church in Delaware. I was twenty-four years old when I began my ministry, and I was now expected to be the spiritual advisor for my congregation, most of whom were much older than I. In planning worship services, preaching, pastoral visits, personal consultations, weddings, funerals, meetings, and other settings, I strove to articulate and exemplify a faith that not only made sense to me but could also do so for the persons who looked to me for spiritual guidance. My faith, formerly brooded upon in private, now had to be tested in this public arena.

I could try to impress these people with my learning, but I found that some of their queries and responses struck to the heart of my own emerging doubts about Christian theism, exposing a continuing ferment in my thought processes I could not ignore. To pose as the confident exponent of views I myself had begun to call into question became increasingly difficult. I felt that I needed a context where I could devote time to critical reflection and openly acknowledge and address my questions rather than try to be a specialist in answers. All of my role models of Christian ministers until that time had been eloquent proclaimers of a warm, utterly confident faith, strong shepherds of their flocks who spoke with authority and were readily able to counsel and discipline those who showed tendencies to stray from the fold. A different conception of the role of the minister would perhaps have enabled me to regard a more questioning, reflective, honest approach as appropriate where I was and even decidedly helpful to my congregation, but I did not have such a conception of the ministry at that time.

During my three-year period at the Delaware church, I decided to further my education by working on a master's degree in American church history at Princeton Seminary. I completed the degree in two years by attending classes each Monday, the minister's typical day off. This experience stimulated my appetite for further study and precipitated a change in my career goal. Instead of being a minister, I now concluded that I could make the best use of my academic interests and inquiring traits of mind as a teacher of religion in a college or university. Thus I enrolled in the joint Ph.D. program in religion of Union Theological Seminary and Columbia University in New York City.

Christian conviction was assumed in this seminary as it had been at Princeton, and I felt at home there, but the university was something else. Here for the first time I was thrown into the framework of a modern secular university, and one located in the heart of a huge city, itself a bastion of secular culture. Whereas before I had instinctively used the term *theology* as being synonymous with Protestant, Christian, and Trinitarian thought, my professors at Columbia now reminded me to employ the appropriate qualifying terms to set off this one form of theology from many others: Roman Catholic, Eastern Orthodox, Unitarian, Jewish, Islamic, Aristotelian, Neoplatonic, Stoic, Deistic, Monistic, Polytheistic, and so on.

I also was made strongly aware of the fact that there is such a thing as a dynamic secular culture, and that a religious approach to the problems of the modern world cannot simply be assumed. Some of my favorite teachers at the university were of Jewish, humanist, or other persuasions quite different from my own, in contrast with *all* of the teachers I had had in higher education until that time, including two graduate degree programs. In addition, I studied two fields in some depth in the program in which I finally enrolled: world religions and the history of Western philosophy. Both alerted me to layers of provincialism in my assumptions I had not realized were there.

Philosophy soon became my first love; I had originally enrolled in church history but changed my focus to philosophy at the beginning of my second year of doctoral studies. Moreover, I became increasingly fascinated with the teachings of the major religions of the world, and they continue to challenge and instruct me to this day. The study of Western philosophy and world religions opened up numerous fresh options for reflection, impelling me first to reassess my belief in the Incarnation and Trinity and later my belief in God. These investigations also helped lure me away from the exclusivistic religious absolutism, to which I had been unconsciously committed before, and in the direction of the position I now call *pluralism* or *convictional openness*.

Since the intended focus of this chapter is on my conversion from theism to a religion of nature, I will not discuss my struggles with the Incarnation, the Trinity, and other aspects of my former Christian commitment but will describe instead some of the thought processes that eventuated in the collapse of my faith in God.

Constantly drummed into us by the Barthian–Brunnerian[2] brand of Reformed theology that was normative at Princeton Theological Seminary when I was enrolled there was the necessity of being on guard against the snare of idolatry and the conviction that this snare was most closely associated with anthropomorphic conceptions of deity. While true that there was one sense in which God was "closer than hands or feet," there was another even more fundamental sense in which God was "totally other," radically distinct from his creation and his creatures, including human beings. Our professors taught us that the essence of paganism from Old Testament times to the present was identification of God with any of the things of this world. God was sovereign Lord of the universe; his providential rule over nature and events of human history was absolute and could in no way be questioned. He had created the world not out of some preexisting raw material or from his own substance but out of nothing.

After I received my degree from Columbia and began my teaching career, first at Centre College in Kentucky and then at Colorado State University, I began to realize that, for me at least, this doctrine of God was untenable. After being introduced to the writings of Alfred North Whitehead by Daniel Day Williams at Union Theological Seminary, I continued to study Whitehead and other process philosophers, especially William James. Whitehead's metaphysics emphasizes God's immanence rather than transcendendence and denies that God can or does exercise complete control over evil. It holds that God needs the world as much as the world needs God, and that God and the world are everlasting and develop together.[3] James insists that even God must have an environment and be limited by that environment, and that God is in time and "works out a history just like ourselves."[4] This radical finitizing of God was convincing to me, but I now see it as one important step toward my eventual rejection of all forms of theism.

My reading of Jewish theologian Richard Rubenstein's *After Auschwitz*[5] when it was first published in the mid-1960s, persuaded me that the conception of a God behind the stage of history, calmly and sovereignly directing its events for his own purposes—*including* the unimaginable horrors of the recent Nazi Holocaust—is indeed, as Rubenstein put it, too "obscene" to contemplate. I reread the Book of Job and was dissatisfied with the answer (or lack of answer) I found there to the theological (and existential) problem of evil. I could no longer be content with an appeal to God's transcendent majesty or with the soothing message that God knows what he is doing, however mysterious or even *criminal* his sovereign actions may often seem to us.

I also began to wonder what it could mean to have a nonanthropomorphic conception of God. I pored over the writings of Paul Tillich, who speaks of God not as a particular being among other beings but as "being-itself" or "the ground of being."[6] Tillich intends that these terms be understood existentially, as pointing to the power of being in human life that gives us courage to cope with nonbeing, that is, with such threats to self-affirmation as fate, death, guilt, and meaninglessness. But his conception of God is, in the last analysis, an impersonal one, however pervasively present and empowering being-itself might be thought to be. His "God above God"[7] avoids anthropomorphism but also skirts the borders of atheism, so far does it veer from traditional, personalistic theism. Given Tillich's rejection of a God "out there" in favor of something experienced in the depths of existence, I was later to wonder why the finite *had* to be viewed as pointing beyond itself toward an infinite in which it participates, as Tillich argues,[8] or why the power of being could not reside in nature itself rather than constitute some kind of "ground" behind or beyond nature.

On the other hand, to continue with traditional notions of God was to persist in thinking of God as "the Man upstairs" (the familiar terminology of common folk, encountered frequently in one's daily newspaper, usually after some disaster has been attributed to God's incomprehensible will) or as dictating "laws like a prince"[9] from a heavenly throne. The finite God of process theism was philosophically satisfying to me in many ways, and I saw it as a decided improvement over traditional theism, but I also found it even more anthropomorphic than the traditional conception of God and, most importantly, without religious power in my life.

Hence, I gradually began to suspect that Ludwig Feuerbach was right after all, and that the idea of God is the projection onto the heavens of the image of humanity[10] (and of the male portion of humanity at that, as feminist critiques of traditional theism have now made painfully apparent). One could with Tillich try to reconceive God in radically immanent, impersonal terms as the power of being-itself, or one could abandon the idea of God altogether as probably hopelessly anthropomorphic, a notion too limited in scope or persuasiveness to function effectively as the ground of a vast universe or as the focus of religious life. As much as I admired Tillich, the second of these alternatives came to be more and more persuasive for me. The writings of the "Death of God" theologians of the mid-1960s, such as Richard Rubenstein, made this alternative seem even more compelling.

My faith in God had begun to founder on two shoals: the theological problem of evil—made starkly evident by the Nazi atrocities against millions of Jews and other innocent human beings in the middle of the twentieth century and in the early years of my own life—and what now appeared to be an ineradicable and implausible anthropomorphism in both traditional and process conceptions of God. My resolve to reflect critically on these two issues, however unsettling that might prove to be, was undergirded by the educational experiences recounted above, by the probing questions of my honest parishioners in the Delaware church, and by the demanding give-and-take of daily classroom teaching in philosophy and religious studies at the secular state university where I have spent most of my teaching career.

In addition to my musings on the problem of evil and the seemingly incurable anthropomorphism of theism, two other factors crept to the forefront of my consciousness. With them, I experienced the final shipwreck of my theistic faith, but these four factors also have brought me to the unexpected landfall of a religion of nature whose character and significance I seek to clarify in this book.

The first of the latter two factors was my reading and rereading of the famous British Broadcasting Corporation (BBC) debate on the existence of God in the late 1940s between Bertrand Russell and Frederick Copleston. I have frequently assigned the published version of this debate[11] to my students, and while I first tended to side with Copleston's defense of theism, I was slowly won over by the force of Russell's arguments. Russell contends that it is unnecessary to ask for an explanation of the universe itself (he also asserts that it *makes no sense* to ask for such an explanation; I would not go so far). We can and do explain one thing in the universe in terms of another, but there is no compelling reason to believe that the concept of an explanatory cause must be applicable to the universe as a whole. Something has to be given, even for theists, so why can we not just say that the universe is given? In response to the classical question, posed again by Copleston, "Why something rather than nothing?" Russell suggests that there is no "Why"; things simply are what they are. In other words, the universe is its own ground; nothing beyond it need be posited.

I think that Russell is right in drawing this conclusion, but I take his reasoning in a different direction than he does. For me now, nature is that in which we "live and move and have our being" (Acts 17:28, Revised Standard Version; Paul quotes here from one of the ancient Greek theological poets, perhaps Epimenides). Or, to use Rudolf Otto's terminology, nature is an "aweful and fascinating mystery" (*mysterium tremendum et fascinans*) in its own right—fraught with the wonder, dread, overpoweringness, vitality, and blissfulness of which Otto speaks in his 1917 masterpiece, *The Idea of the Holy*.[12] We need not go any further than nature to probe the depths of our existence and the powers that sustain our being. Nature, then, is a fit object of religious concern. It is holy. Formerly, with thinkers such as Copleston, I assumed nature to be derivative, to require a support or an explanation beyond itself. Now I was learning to see nature and the associated powers of creation and destruction manifested in its ongoing transformations as ultimate.

The final principal factor bringing me to this faith in the ultimacy of nature, and thus to the present stage of my spiritual odyssey, was my reflections on the Darwinian theory of evolution and the closely related science of ecology. These two aspects of modern biology portray life as the historical outcome of processes ceaselessly working within nature, and they stress the entwined dependencies binding all forms of life together. It is a vision that includes human life as well.

Human beings, therefore, do not transcend nature in their essential being, as had traditionally been thought, and as I myself had long believed, but are the product and expression of its immanent powers. For a time I had been attracted to religious humanism as an alternative to theism, but now I began to realize that human beings, as one spin-off of the irrepressibly creative workings of nature, should not be regarded as religiously ultimate themselves but rather as evidencing, along with other forms of emergent life, the ultimacy of nature.

Furthermore, who is to say what other forms of life or intelligence, perhaps ranging far beyond the present capacities of human beings and human cultures, might evolve in the future? Or who can ignore the distinct possibility that such forms may already have emerged elsewhere in this universe of countless galactic systems? For me, then, an extension of the ideas of evolutionary origin and ecological order to human beings has come to mean that we neither stand at the apex of nature, as its obvious end point or goal, nor do we exist over against it as a separate order of being. Instead, we are just one of nature's multifarious creations, each special and wonderful in its own way, none merely subordinate to the other, and all finally subject to the ubiquitous natural powers that first gave them birth and now sustain them in complex patterns of mutual dependence.

I have made little attempt thus far to argue the case for a religion of nature or to consider objections to my present position or present ways of thinking. These tasks will be undertaken in the chapters to follow. Instead, I have provided a descriptive sketch of reflections that gradually brought me to a religion of nature, and I have related these reflections to some of the events of my life.

I also have not said much about the affective side of my odyssey, about what it *felt* like to experience these profound changes of religious outlook. What I have described is more of an intellectual map of the journey. Feelings of anxiety and misgiving, as well as of loss and regret, have occurred. One cannot set out in a new direction without leaving behind some (although not necessarily all) of what the old direction promised or provided. For example, I regret no longer being able to believe in a God who exercises providential care over the world, who has the power to transform our lives, and who communes with us in prayer—a God that Whitehead characterizes as the "fellow sufferer who understands."[13] Also, death for me has now a disturbing finality that contrasts with my former confidence that dying was like changing trains. I miss being part of a community of tradition and ritual whose faith is similar to my own: there is no First Church of Nature in my neighborhood.

However, there also have been feelings of liberation and relief, of finding an integrity and wholeness in my life that it seemed to lack before. Above all, the journey has brought a sense of rightness, of having come to terms with the being that I have perhaps always suspected myself to be, a being fully immersed in the natural world and sharing in the dependencies, limitations, and contingencies of its other creatures. My hope is in some ways more limited than before, but I see it as more realistic and firmly grounded.

The principal purpose of the remaining chapters of this book is to make a case for a religion of nature, filling in its details and dealing as forthrightly as I can with some of the philosophical and religious problems it poses. No faith's stance is immune to such problems; each must search continually for greater subtlety, adequacy, and depth.

Since a significant part of the task of making this case is clarifying the concept of nature upon which my religious outlook rests, part 2 addresses the topic of "the nature of nature." I conceive of this topic as metaphysical in character, as belonging to that part of philosophy that inquires into the most salient and general features of the experienced world and seeks a systematic understanding of how those features relate to one another. While I do not attempt to offer a full-blown metaphysics here, I devote a chapter each to subtopics relating to the nature of nature. Each chapter is intended to present an essential part of the philosophy of nature that informs my religious vision and to support the conclusion that nature thus conceived is *metaphysically* ultimate, meaning (1) that it is self-subsistent, requiring no explanation beyond its immanent powers for its sustenance or creativity, and (2) that it is all-encompassing, including within itself all that is or ever will be.

Hence, in my view, no separate realm of mind or spirit is set over against nature, nor does a transcendent supernatural being exist, such as that assumed by monotheists. Furthermore, this version of religious naturalism[14] makes no reference to any type of nature-pervading, nature-enveloping, or nature-personifying spirit or spirits, in contrast to pantheistic, panentheistic, mystical, polytheistic, or animistic traditions.

My outlook is, then, atheistic, but I remind the reader that the various forms of theism are all "anaturalistic" with respect to the type of religious naturalism that is the subject of this book. As logicians point out, the complement of any set is everything *not* contained in that set. While this is obviously the case, I see no need to refer to theistic traditions by focusing on what they are not, and I hope that a similar courtesy will be accorded to the religion of nature to be presented here. It is better to refrain from tocsin-sounding negative epithets and to concentrate, at least initially, on the *positive* content of each perspective.

Aspects of the philosophy of nature developed in part 2 are of critical importance in understanding how nature can be regarded as an appropriate object of religious concern. Once the metaphysical task is accomplished, I turn in part 3 to a defense of the *religious* ultimacy of nature. There I deal with religious themes and problems relating to a religion of nature, complementing the metaphysical discussions of part 2.[15]

Part 2

The Nature of Nature

2

Concept of Nature

. . . [T]hough nothing at all is present as a "whole" in experience, yet nature is present in every instance of experience and every process of experiencing.

—Justus Buchler, "Probing the Idea of Nature"

The purpose of this chapter is to lay out in a general, introductory manner the concept of nature that informs this book. My strategy in doing so is to respond to four questions that clamor for attention as soon as we begin to reflect philosophically on the nature of nature. (1) What does the term *nature* mean? (2) Is nature an in-itself reality, existing independently of human experience and conceptualization, or is it a human construct? (3) Is it one or many? (4) Is it fundamentally permanent or changing, pattern or process? Having addressed these questions, I will be in a position to explain, in a concluding section of this chapter, why I prefer to use the term *nature* rather than related terms such as *universe, cosmos,* or *world.*

THE PROBLEM OF MEANING

I indicated in the previous chapter that, for me, nothing lies behind, is the ground of, or is set over against nature. For example, there are no beings such as the *super*natural God, gods, spirits, angels, or demons envisioned in various cultures or religious traditions, and since I conceive of human beings as wholly immanent in nature, I do not regard them as having any aspect, such as an immaterial soul, that would place them even partially outside of nature or differentiate them in any way from nature. I also am unwilling, as will be seen in chapter 5, to separate human culture from nature.

But does such a view not signify that nature is simply everything that is? If that is so, will not attempted claims about it have to be so broad, diffuse, or vague as to lack any specific character? To talk of everything is not to talk about anything in particular, suggesting that we may be dealing with a vacuous abstraction. Moreover, if nature is everything, it appears that nothing can contrast with or be distinguished from it, making us wonder if this is not a pseudo concept devoid of content. Again, since we obviously cannot *experience* the totality of nature, encompassing everything that is and extending into the farthest reaches of space and time, as well as into the most minute, submicroscopic domains, how can we refer to that totality? If we cannot refer to it, how can our conception of it be meaningful? Finally, if Aristotle is right in claiming that nature (which he terms "the All") is literally nowhere, since, unlike particular entities, it exists in no place,[1] we are bound to puzzle over how we can make significant reference to something that, by definition, does not exist anywhere. Problems of this sort imply that the focal conception of a religion of nature, that of nature itself, may have no determinate content or meaning. If this claim is true, then the whole enterprise of this book—in both its metaphysical and religious aspects—must die aborning.

Let me respond to each of these issues in turn. First, to talk about the whole of reality is, admittedly, to talk abstractly, but it does not follow that the abstractness is necessarily vacuous. We use abstractions all of the time, and the more abstract our discourse, the less in immediate touch with particular things, events, or circumstances it is. This does not mean that abstract discourse is vacuous or useless—far from it; it is eminently useful, so much so that without abstractions, we could not think or talk at all. We certainly could not conduct investigations in philosophy, religion, or science without abstractions. The great abstractness or generality of mathematics, a principal means of investigation in the natural sciences, is a case in point.[2]

Second, far from there being nothing that contrasts with nature, *everything* else contrasts with it. That is, every particular occurrence or thing contrasts with nature as a whole. Nature contrasts even with the sum total of all particulars, if taken simply as an aggregation or a collection, for it is a dynamic system of complex relations among particulars, relations that affect the emergence, character, and functioning of those particulars in fundamental ways. While it is true that this system could not be comprehended apart from the particulars it encompasses, it also is true that elucidation of these particulars requires that they be viewed not in isolation but against the backdrop of the entire system of nature. The contrast between particular and whole, then, is essential to the understanding of either, and neither can simply be reduced to the other. Recognition of this contrast means that to speak of nature as a whole is not to speak of a meaningless abstraction. We also should notice that there is only one system of nature, whereas we can easily conceive of, and frequently experience, many particular existents of the same general kind within nature. There are many crabs, many orchids, many stars, many human beings, and so on. Nature contrasts with such particular things in that it is unique; there is only one member of the set "nature."[3] We will need to nuance this statement a bit, however, when we attend later in this chapter to the issue of whether nature is one or many.

Third, we cannot directly experience the wholeness of anything, including even our own selves. Experience is ineluctably partial and perspectival, and the possible perspectives on any thing that is experienced, no matter how seemingly trivial it might be, are inexhaustible. We could never exhaust the possible spatial outlooks on a penny, for example. It can be viewed from close up or from afar; from on edge, at an angle, or face on; right side up or upside down; directly, in a mirror, or in multiple mirrors. Thus the same penny can be seen as an undifferentiated mass of copper, a tiny dot, a line, an ellipse, a circle, a multiplicity of ever-reversing reflected objects, and so on. Moreover, we could never exhaust the possible ways of thinking about it. For instance, I can think about a penny, or think about myself thinking about it, or think about myself thinking about myself thinking about it, *ad infinitum*. I also can think of the penny in limitless contexts—as a type of currency, as a geometrical shape, as having a certain weight, as being made of copper, as having a certain date, as being manufactured in a particular mint, as contrasting with other coins in U.S. currency, as contrasting with coins of other nations in the present or past, as having a picture of Abraham Lincoln on its face, as ballast for a toy sailboat, as a shim for a wobbly table telephone, and so on. Every new moment of experience of the penny differs from every previous moment of experience of it, if for no other reason than in the new moment I have my fund of memories of all of the previous moments of experiencing it.

As for oneself, even though each of us has privileged access to his or her own consciousness, who can be said fully and completely to understand himself or herself—and who can exhaustively encompass the perspectives on oneself one has had in the past or might have in the future, to say nothing of the perspectives of others on oneself? Despite this inexhaustible perspectivity of all experience and awareness, however, we readily assume that meaningful reference can be made to objects or events in the world, to ourselves, and to other persons. We can speak of and refer to such things even though we can never directly experience their entirety. There is no compelling reason to think that the same does not hold true for discourse about and reference to the whole of nature. What we do, in fact, and I will have more to say about this later with reference to nature, is operate with a general *concept, model,* or *theory* of a subject matter and then interpret our particular experiences in accordance with it. We also may revise our general notion of a thing in light of our ongoing experiences of specific aspects of it.

Fourth, the problem we raised in connection with Aristotle, that the universe has no place, can be dealt with in this way. For him, *place* (Greek: *topos*) is defined as the immediate, unmoved limit or adjacent boundary of a surrounding body. Since the universe as a whole is bounded by the sphere of the fixed stars, and since that sphere itself has no immediate, unmoved limit, it follows that the universe occupies no place. In other words, the universe contains but is not contained. It encompasses all of the "wheres" it contains, but it has no "where" of its own. Admittedly, this is a difficult concept to grasp, but it is not devoid of sense. It stems from Aristotle's definition of *place* and his conception of the universe as extending no further than the sphere of the fixed stars. When we say that a thing is "nowhere" in common parlance, we typically mean that it is nonexistent. But Aristotle's notion of the universe's being nowhere does not imply its nonexistence, only its special character, a character that shows in one striking way its pronounced contrast with everything else, bringing us back to the first response above.

What, then, does the term *nature* mean? How can it be defined? We are not asking merely for a reportive or dictionary definition but for a philosophical one. A philosophical definition is generally to be understood in terms of a philosophical theory, and it can most usefully be seen as a shorthand designation for, or as a summation of, such a theory. Part 2 of this book is intended to provide the outlines of a theory of nature, so what I mean by the term *nature* can be fully understood only when the theory itself has been laid out. Nevertheless, I now want to offer a few general comments about the concept of nature I am assuming.

One essential part of this concept has been indicated in the first chapter: there is nothing beyond or behind nature, no supernatural being, presence, or power that transcends it or is required to account for its origins or its continuing existence. A second important and closely related point made there is that human beings are wholly immanent in nature. Another crucial observation about the nature of nature has been made in this chapter: nature is not just an aggregation of particular entities but the established, as well as the dynamically evolving, *system* of things and their relations (including the patterns, potencies, laws, and principles that are of special interest to the natural sciences)—a holistic system that enables particular entities to come into being and to pass out of being, that maintains them throughout their existences, and that makes possible their distinctive characters, capacities, and functionings.

This description is in keeping with the etymology of the word *nature*, from the Latin *nasci*, meaning "to be born," "to spring from," "to arise," "to be produced."[4] I also intend it to connect with the fact that we frequently speak, as did the Romans and the Greeks, of the orderly, regular, predictable characters and functionings of things as their "natures" or as their acting "by their natures." Nature, then, is the creative matrix from which all things arise and to which they return, the complexity of orders and powers by which these things are upheld and by which each of them, or each type of them, attains its own peculiar attributes and capabilities.

Nature also has a destructive side that we should not ignore. Each day's newspaper contains stories of the devastating effects of natural phenomena such as earthquakes, forest fires, floods, tornadoes, and hurricanes, wreaking havoc on plants, animals, and human beings. Destruction is the price often paid for nature's sustaining power and surging creativity. Creatures of one species are routinely consumed, for example, so that those of another can continue to live, and the process of biological evolution on earth is strewn with vast numbers of extinct species, left along the wayside in the march toward more diverse and complex organisms. I will have more to say about this darker side of nature in chapter 7, when I consider some objections to a religion of nature.

Finally, let me note that nature as such, as I conceive it, has no sentience, consciousness, or purpose, even though it provides for evolutionary emergence of at least some of these traits in many of its creatures, as we can witness here on earth. Neither this characterization nor nature's destructive side should be taken to mean, however, that nature itself is devoid of value or that whatever value it has must be conferred upon it by human or other sentient beings, a position that would hardly accord with my ascription of ultimate religious value to nature. I will address these issues in some detail in chapters 4 and 5 and return to them again in the chapters of part 3.

My preliminary answer to the question "What does the term *nature* mean?" can thus be summarized as follows:

1. Nature is the whole system of things and relations that continues to give rise to new particular things and types of things, maintains them in being as long as they exist, and makes possible their distinctive traits.

2. Nature is metaphysically ultimate, that is, there is nothing outside, beyond, or behind it. This statement includes human beings, who must be regarded as an integral part of nature.

3. Nature as such lacks purpose, sentience, or consciousness. Despite this fact, and despite its prominent destructive aspects, it is not devoid of value but is replete with value, including religious value.

In this section, I have dealt with some of the problems relating to the concept of nature, indicating how these problems can be resolved. I also have sketched some basic meanings I assign to the concept of nature, in anticipation of more detailed treatment of these and other meanings as our discussion proceeds. I turn next to the question raised in the beginning of this chapter about the *status* of nature. Is there really such a thing as nature? Is it an independent, in-itself reality existing in its own right, or is it only an imaginative construct of human beings?

THE STATUS OF NATURE

It may seem odd to ask whether there is such a thing as nature, but this is an important question about the metaphysical status of nature, that is, is it *real*, and if it is, *what sort* of reality can it be said to be? Closely connected to this metaphysical issue is the epistemological one of how or whether we can be said to know nature. If there is no way in which we can attain reliable knowledge of such a thing as nature, it is pointless to ask about its metaphysical status, since that will be unknowable as well. Conversely, if we *can* have knowledge of nature, our account of the character and scope of this knowledge is likely to have an important bearing on our view of the metaphysical status of what it is that we claim to know.

Two extreme positions can be taken, and have been taken, in the history of Western thought about the related issues of the status of nature and our knowledge of nature. One is that nature can be directly and transparently known, and that what is thereby known is a reality that exists entirely in its own right, independently of human thought and experience. This position of *direct realism* and of the complete *objectivity* of nature was taken, for example, by Aristotle. According to him, nature is a vast, interlocking system of entities with distinctive essences or entelechies (self-contained ends regularly attained by those entities), and the human mind is perfectly competent to understand these entities and their coordinated functionings. Thus the mind is equipped to understand the system of nature just as it is and just as it would remain were there no human beings to take cognizance of it.

The other extreme position is that nature has no knowable reality in its own right but is simply a product of human thought and imagination. This is the position of *radical constructivism* and of the complete *subjectivity* of nature. Take human beings away, with their distinctive experiences, languages, and cultures, and no system of nature would remain, because any and all systems of nature are whole-cloth inventions of human subjectivity with no objective status or reference. There is no intelligible nature as such, only numerous ideas of nature arbitrarily projected by the fertile minds of human beings. Jean-Paul Sartre is one thinker of our own time who has taken this extreme view in his influential book *Being and Nothingness*. This also is the outlook of Antoine Roquentin, the main character of Sartre's novel *Nausea*.[5] The position of radical constructivism is more recently reflected in this statement of gifted television writer and performer James Burke, in which he describes the role of conceptual structures in laying out the nature of reality for various peoples at various places and times:

> The structure or Gestalt controls all perceptions and all actions. It is a complete version of what reality is supposed to be. It must be so if the individual or group is to function as a decision-making entity. Each must have a valid structure of reality by which to live. All that can accurately be said about a man who thinks he is a poached egg is that he is in the minority.

> The structure therefore sets the values, bestows meaning, determines the morals, ethics, aims, limitations and purposes of life. It imposes on the external world the contemporary version of reality. The answer therefore to the question, "Which truth does science seek?" can only be, "The truth defined by the contemporary structure."[6]

Neither of these extreme positions does justice to our knowledge of nature or to the metaphysical status of nature. The first one, direct realism, fails because it ignores the fallibility and changeableness of all *interpretations* of nature, of those concepts, models, and theories required to guide and give intelligibility to our experiences of the world. Aristotle's conception of nature has been shown by the course of history in the West, for example, to be not privileged, final, or direct but highly debatable, as many of its features came to be called into question by subsequent religious and philosophical outlooks and, most particularly, by the Newtonian, Darwinian, and Einsteinian scientific outlooks of the past four centuries.

The second position, radical constructivism, fails to acknowledge the important role of *experience* in challenging and correcting particular interpretations of nature. Were these interpretations as arbitrary and unrooted as the constructivist position claims, the demonstrable role of ongoing experience in calling them into question would make no sense. For example, when Galileo saw craters on the moon through his telescope, his experience made him aware of the untenability of Aristotle's conviction that the heavenly bodies are perfect spheres. Similarly, a lifetime of field observations convinced Charles Lyell that the earth was much older than had been previously thought, paving the way for Charles Darwin's revolutionary theory of evolution, itself suggested and supported by Darwin's patient gathering of empirical data in his five-year voyage on the *Beagle* and elsewhere. A final example of the role of ongoing experience in imposing constraints on interpretations of nature, and in making clear the need for new and more adequate interpretations, is the fact that while Lord Kelvin was pronouncing, toward the end of the nineteenth century, that physical science was now basically complete, Marie Curie was burning her fingers on radiation.[7] Her experience, unanticipated and inexplicable by the natural science of her day, helped usher in a fundamentally different conception of the physical world from the Newtonian one that Kelvin so confidently endorsed.

Radical constructivism also fails to explain many incontestable facts of everyday life. One example is that the same barbed sticker plants that send sharp signals of pain when they lodge in my skin also cause my dog suddenly to limp on our daily walks. Another example is that I can be killed when run over by a speeding car just as surely in India as I can in the United States, despite the two countries' markedly different cultural traditions. It also is notable that not just any kind of paper airplane will fly; experience shows that some designs soar splendidly, while the trajectories of others exhibit little semblance of flight. This statement holds true anywhere on earth, and no matter what the respective belief systems, grand pianos are heavy, and hot stoves burn. Finally, people everywhere and at all times have basic emotions such as joy and sorrow, hope and despair, satisfaction and frustration, tranquility and fear, and basic needs such as food, shelter, community, and love.

These observations are not meant to deny the plasticity of much in human experience to different outlooks and interpretations, a plasticity to which cultural anthropology gives ample witness. But it is to take sharp issue with the notion that there are no common facts of experience that all outlooks and interpretations must somehow take into account. And it is to stress the likelihood that some interpretive schemes may take these stubborn facts into account more adequately than others, thus showing themselves to be something more than mere arbitrary constructions, inventions, or projections.

Without reference to, rootage in, and responsibility toward ongoing experience, concepts of nature are useless abstractions, an arbitrary glass bead game of the mind; and without conceptual interpretations of our experiences, changeable and fallible though history has shown such interpretations to be, reflections on the nature of nature cannot even begin. The dictum of Immanuel Kant must be taken to heart, then, that concepts without percepts are empty, and percepts without concepts are blind. We have no compelling reason, on the one hand, to conclude that concepts of nature must be projected willy-nilly upon a chaotic world entirely devoid of structure or meaning. Nor, on the other hand, are we compelled to believe that we can directly perceive the world just as it is, with no need for mediating hypotheses—bold creations of the speculative imagination such as Isaac Newton's theory of universal gravitation, Darwin's theory of natural selection, or Albert Einstein's special and general theories of relativity—to direct and order our inquiries and to be subjected to empirical tests.[8]

Therefore, our epistemologies and metaphysics must deal with two sorts or aspects of nature. One is *experienced* nature, and the other is *conceptualized* nature, the nature portrayed in postulated models, analogies, metaphors, and theories. Neither is ever wholly or sharply separate from the other, but neither can be simply identified with the other. The two often meld together indistinguishably in our minds, but one can challenge the other in unexpected ways. New theoretical models may prompt us to question hitherto unanalyzed attitudes regarding experience or alert us to new avenues of experience, just as new experiences, perhaps aided by new technologies, may lead us to revise or abandon established theories.

There is an undeniable obduracy of long-held theories but also an obduracy of ever-unfolding experiences. The two obduracies must be kept in dialectical tension, meaning that we must always be open to the possible revision of assumptions about either in light of the other. There are no finalities, no absolute certainties in our visions of the natural world. The best we can hope for are tentative and yet significantly testable hypotheses. The hypotheses about nature in which we are entitled to repose considerable though never unquestioned confidence are those that continue to meet tests such as adequacy to experience and continuing empirical confirmation, internal consistency, coherence with well-established beliefs in a given context of inquiry, fruitfulness for fresh and sustained lines of investigation within that context and possibly others as well, and general usefulness for thought and life. We see the world ineluctably through the lens of theory, and to this extent the constructionists are right, but that lens need not be a mere silvered surface reflecting back arbitrary, purely subjective projections. The theoretical lens can enable us to interact meaningfully with the world and to explore the intricacies of our relationships to it.

The above is at least the general sort of answer I propose to the question "Is nature an in-itself reality, existing independently of human experience and conceptualization, or is it a human construct?" The nature we encounter is a nature *for us*, for our experiences and conceptualizations. It is never an in-itself nature, a nature *out of relation* to our experiences, beliefs, and inquiries. I have no idea what nature in the second sense would be like. Encountering it would be analogous to seeing something with no specific angle of vision or physical conditions, and with a total absence of expectations and suppositions, a concept of seeing that contradicts everything in our experience. It also would be like conceiving of an object of thought with no need for debatable interpretive perspectives or structures, a notion of conceiving for which there is no precedent or analogue anywhere in human history. All seeing is seeing-as, and all conceiving is accomplished by means of and against the background of assumptions, models, and strategies required to give focus and significance to our thought. Moreover, perceiving and conceiving constantly work together.

The need for this working together can be especially appreciated when it comes to concepts of nature. We obviously do not experience nature as a whole; all of our experiences of it are partial and fragmentary at best, but the abstractions of broad-ranging conceptual schemes can help fill in the gaps, as it were, yielding what John Dewey calls "the mysterious totality of being the imagination calls the universe."[9] Even when experience and conceptualization work together in optimal fashion, however, the accent must be placed on the two words "mysterious" and "imagination." For as Dewey reminds us:

> The idea of a whole, whether of the whole personal being or of the world, is an imaginative and not a literal idea. The limited world of our observation and reflection becomes the Universe only through imaginative extension. It cannot be apprehended in knowledge nor realized in reflection.[10]

As we shall see in the next section, the already elusive notion of the totality of nature is made even more complex and mysterious when we reflect on the extent to which the world is not merely a universe but also a pluriverse or multiverse, an order pervaded by volatile forces of diversity, discontinuity, and disorder.

I present in this book, then, outlines of a conceptual and imaginative model of nature intended to order and elucidate important aspects of our experience of nature. The model is incomplete and no doubt inadequate in many other respects, but it is at least a start, and the sketch of a general concept of nature presented in this chapter and throughout part 2 will help provide specificity and detail to the religious vision of nature that is the subject of part 3.

UNITY AND DIVERSITY

We count on the unity or uniformity of nature every time we make a prediction about the future, and we make predictions about the future every moment of our lives. Sometimes we make them unconsciously, as when we assume without thinking that the chairs we were just sitting on will support us when we plop down on them again, or when we take our next breaths, confident that the atmosphere will still be breathable. Sometimes we make these predictions consciously, as when we lay out plans for the future based on our experiences of the past. Were there no uniformity of nature, we could never execute our choices, because we would have no idea about what to expect in the way of necessary conditions for those choices. However, we successfully execute our choices moment by moment and day by day. When we classify something or give it a name, we do so because we believe that it will exhibit a continuity of character in the future. Without this premise, language, which is among other things an elaborate system of classifications and references, could have no intelligibility.

The natural sciences are based on a precise predictability of the future and thus on an assumed order of nature. A scientific theory is said to be empirically confirmed when it can be subjected to repeated experimental tests, tests that assume the persistence of natural processes from one experiment to the next. Scientific laws are formulations of regularities in nature that count on the continuity of cause-effect relations over time.

Nature is one in the sense that it is pervaded by predictable patterns and regularities that make all forms of life possible and support the simplest and the most elaborate technologies. Farmers throughout the earth rely on such patterns and regularities when they plant their crops, and space engineers trust them when they send their sophisticated vehicles into the outer reaches of our solar system. The fact that we speak of planets in the vicinity of the sun as a "system," and regard that system as having a place within a certain galactic system, and go on to speak of galactic systems as existing within an overall system of the universe exhibiting a common set of constituents, principles, and laws, tells the story of an assumed uniformity of nature.

However, that story is only part of the whole story of nature, for in addition to its predictable uniformity of functioning, its general order and regularity, there also is an impressive amount of intractable diversity in the world and an openness to creativity and change that defies complete prediction. Every planet and star is different from every other one in some significant respect. No two flowers or leaves are exactly alike. Every person has distinctive traits of biological makeup, appearance, behavior, and character that mark off him or her from every other person. An astounding variety of biological species has existed on earth in the past, an equally impressive abundance of species exists today, and scientists fully expect that if terrestrial nature is left to do its thing without catastrophic interference from human beings, myriad new forms of life will emerge in the future that we have no way to predict.

I spoke above of the importance of the uniformity of nature for the execution of our choices, but we also should note that were there nothing but a uniformity of cause-effect relations, choice would be impossible. Genuine choice requires an open future, a future in which the realization of more than one option can take place. To choose is to select among a set of possible alternatives, any one of which can be made actual. Our choices are made within a causal context, but the causal context does not solely determine what the choice will turn out to be. The context is a necessary, but not sufficient, condition for explaining the choice. Another part of a choice's explanation lies in the freedom to select from available alternatives in light of reasons. These reasons are considerations that can provide justification and rationale for our choices and that can lead us to decide against strong bodily urges or narrow self-interests. Not everything about our choices is predictable in principle, because more than causal explanations are required fully to account for them.

Our sense of moral responsibility turns on our possession of such freedom, as does our ability to theorize meaningfully about anything, including the topic of freedom itself. If only one realizable alternative were truly before us, we could neither weigh nor choose in light of the reasons for making one moral choice rather than another, nor could we weigh or choose in light of the reasons for one theoretical outlook over against another. We would be predetermined to make the choices we make in either context. The concepts of moral responsibility and theoretical inquiry would be damaged beyond repair.

It would make no sense to hold persons morally responsible for their choices if, in every causal context, there were only one possible choice they could have made in that context and no way for them to have altered the context. A determinist might respond, "They could have changed the present context by acting differently earlier on," but then they could not have changed the context of that previous action, and changing any actions earlier than that context would only have been possible if they had changed even earlier ones. Thus, for determinism, in no given situation are persons ever free to act in a manner that departs even in the slightest degree from efficient causes operative in a situation; those causes are, *ex hypothesi*, sufficient to produce and account for the action. To say that "Jones did x, but she ought to have done y" can have no meaning, because in the causal context in which she found herself—a context that was itself determined by previous contexts, those by even earlier contexts, and so on—Jones had no alternative to doing x. How, then, could we hold her *morally responsible* for choosing x and not choosing y?

The case is similar when it comes to the concept of theoretical inquiry. If I ask Smith "Why do you believe p?" he might respond by explaining that his family would be deeply offended if he did not believe it, but there are two things wrong with this answer. First, it might explain why he *claims* to believe p around his family, without indicating whether or why he *actually* believes p, but it is his actual belief in which I am interested. Second, even if the influence of his family did give him strong causal *motivation* to believe p and provided *causal explanation* for his belief in it, that would not mean that he is *justified* in believing p or can support his belief with plausible reasons. I want to understand the reasons he has for believing in p. I have posed an epistemological question to him, not a question about psychological motivation.

The concept of theoretical inquiry presupposes this crucial distinction between motivations and reasons. Theoretical inquiry is an epistemological activity, not merely a psychological one. When I ask "Is p true?" I am not asking "Do I personally have strong motivations to believe it?" Instead I am asking "Are there good reasons for anyone to believe it, no matter what her or his psychological motivations may be?"

For example, a scientist may have a good chance to win a coveted prize if she can successfully defend a disputed theory. She is no doubt intensely motivated to defend the theory and will try every way she can think of to do so, but her *wanting* to believe the theory and successfully defend it is different from her being able to offer convincing *justification* for its truth. Such justification also is independent of whether or not others might want to accept the theory. The defender of a different theory would have strong motivation not to accept a rival's theory, for example, but if theoretical inquiry is really possible, there must be a capacity to evaluate contending theories in light of the reasons given in their defense, no matter how strong the personal psychological motivations may be to accept or reject those theories.

Can causal determinism uphold this crucial distinction between reasons and motivations, between theoretical justifications and causal explanations? It cannot, because, according to it, we always act in accordance with our causal motivations. This includes our acts of believing or not believing. If I am causally determined to believe p, I will believe p, and if you are causally determined not to believe it, you will not believe it. What might look like shared inquiry into a theoretical question, turning on the indispensable distinction between reasons and motivations, cannot be so. It is just the confrontation of one pattern of causal motivations with another. All we can ever expect to get in the way of honest response to the question "Why do you believe p?" is the answer "Because I am strongly motivated to do so." Whatever reasons are offered in defense of or against a given belief are in fact just disguised efficient causal motivations.

If the foregoing critique of causal determinism and view of genuine freedom are cogent,[11] then nature must allow for such freedom. It must have enough latitude or indeterminacy to permit its exercise.

Nature also must permit the creativity and change to which scientists give testimony when they speak of cosmic, geological, and biological evolution.

There must then be, in addition to causal order, a significant place for the workings of chance, a volatility, looseness, and creativity in the world that can account for the continuing emergence of new kinds of being and new forms of life.

Some thinkers argue that if we had sufficient information about the efficient causes underlying such phenomena, we could completely explain them in terms of the causes, but this is only a statement of faith. We do not have such information with which to test the disputable hypothesis of the *in-principle* predictability of everything, and there is much that has occurred in the universe that would not have been predictable *in fact*. This claim holds true for the incredible diversity of life-forms and impressive varieties of human linguistic and cultural systems familiar to us here on earth. I can therefore find no strong reason to believe that each and every event or action must be exhaustibly explicable by its causes. Chance and an open future have their important roles to play.

Chance is not just "a word for our ignorance," Charles Hartshorne shrewdly notes; "the supposition that there is always a precise reason for what happens is itself only ignorance passing as knowledge."[12] For "precise reason" in his statement we can substitute "sufficient efficient causal explanation," and the point still stands. Moreover, our everyday experience of what certainly feels like freedom of action and thought, and the demonstrable need to assume the reality of such freedom in order to salvage such crucial conceptions for daily life as those of moral choice and theoretical inquiry, provide convincing evidence against the theory of causal determinism.

Nature must be characterized, then, as both one and many. It contains palpable aspects of order and disorder. It exhibits a teeming diversity of things that are nevertheless sustained in their being by complex networks of interrelation and interdependence. In living beings, both cooperation and competition exist. Nature also combines massive continuity with unrelenting change. While predictable in countless ways, it is not so in all ways. It is a seething cauldron of overbrimming creativity and emergent diversity, not just a smoothly running, routinely functioning machine. It is an open arena for the exercise of freedom and the workings of chance, not just an iron cage of causal necessity.

We can approach this issue of nature as one or many from another direction. Nature, as I view it, is a complex blend of things and relations. Neither is prior to the other, for neither could exist without the other. Moreover, the relations in which things stand are both internal and external. An internal relation is one that is essential for a thing being what it is, while an external relation is not, but we must be careful here. While a thing could not exist without the *specific* set of internal relations in which it stands, it also could not exist as an individual thing without *some sorts* of external relations. Both kinds of relation are therefore necessary *in general* for its being the thing it is, but while its external relations can vary widely without affecting its identity or integrity as an individual, its internal relations cannot. They must remain what they are for it to remain what it is.

I am internally related to my mother, because my being her son is necessary for my being what I am genetically. She is only externally related to me in that regard, because her genetic makeup does not depend on mine. She was what she was genetically before I came into being and remained such after I was born. I also am internally related to the hemoglobin in my bloodstream; were it to cease to be there, I would cease to exist, but if I have a glass of wine at a cocktail party and get a certain amount of alcohol in my blood, I am only externally related to the alcohol. Whether it is there or not, I continue to exist. Of course, if I get too much of it in my bloodstream, I might cease to exist, but that is a different story.

Another example of the difference between internal and external relations is that my present moment of experience is internally related to the past moment, while the past moment of experience is only externally related to the present one. The past moment would remain what it was even if the present moment had been different, or if it had not occurred at all. The present moment, in contrast, could not have occurred as it did had this past moment not been there to provide for it specific content, context, and impetus. I have argued that the past is always necessary but not always sufficient to explain the present; here I am emphasizing its role as a necessary condition.

However, the idea that the past is only necessary and not sufficient to explain the present also implies that the present moment cannot be simply reduced to the past moment. A present event has something in it of its own; it is a novel upsurge of reality that does not merely replicate the past, so its internal relatedness to that past does not wholly account for what it is; there is something about it that is external to the past, not determined or explicable by the past. Without this integrity of the present moment that differentiates it from the past as well as from the future—an integrity dependent on the reality of external relations—there would be no *experience* of time, because there would be no recognizable present to demarcate the difference between the past and future. There also would be no time *as such* without something novel or distinctive in the present; the putative present would simply collapse into the past. Here we can clearly see the incoherence of causal determinism, which makes occurrences in the past both necessary *and sufficient* to explain those in the present, thereby making unintelligible the very notion of a novel present as the locus of differentiation between past and future.

The view that not all relations affect the being of a thing means that it can have an independence and integrity in the context of the whole pattern of relationships that it otherwise could not have. For example, I can move a book to the right or to the left of a lamp without affecting the persistent being of either the book or lamp, and I can destroy either one without affecting the other. The two remain what they are in the context of widely varying external relations, but on the other hand, what they are is not wholly independent of patterns of relationship in which they are found. Some relations are essential to their being what they are, for example, their relations to persistent functionings of temporal process and natural law that allow them to exist as stable beings over time. Such internal relations contribute to the uniformity of nature, while the presence of external relations helps to account for its diversity.

Were all relations internal, there would be persistence and uniformity but no change or plurality in the world; the world would be like Benedict Spinoza's model of the universe in which only one thing truly exists, a universe of intricately woven internal relations, and that one thing is fixed and unchanging forever. Diversity and change would be mere illusions in such a world.

Were all relations external, as they are assumed to be in the worldview of David Hume, the opposite would at first appear to be the case. It would seem that there would be ample diversity but no unity, no system or order of nature, no predictable, stable relations of cause and effect, but actually this interpretation is not quite right. It is true that there would be no unity of nature, and its absence is the ground of Hume's skepticism about efficient causality and inductive reasoning. But it is equally true that there would be no diverse beings of any order of complexity. Internal relations are necessary for such beings to be what they distinctively are. The being of an atom, a molecule, or a cell, for example, requires an intricate and essential interrelatedness of its constituent aspects. If all relations were external, there would be none of the particular things of our experience,[13] and hence no diversity of such things. There also would be no change in a Humean world, for change combines novelty with continuity, an intermingling of external and internal relations. Did something not persist through a process of change, as Aristotle wisely observed, we could not speak meaningfully of anything undergoing change.

Nothing in the universe exists outside of relations, whether internal or external. Each event or thing is conditioned and at least partially defined by its relations to other events or things, but it also is the case that each event or thing has an integrity and individuality belonging to it alone, something about it that cannot be simply subsumed under a system of nature as a whole. While there are pervasive uniformities in nature, it also is replete with stubborn, irreducible particulars.

You and I are examples of such particulars, as is every fresh moment of our respective experiencing. Each quantum of energy, each grain of sand, each microbe, each plant or animal also is an irreducible particular within an overarching but not all-absorbing system of nature, so once again we see that nature must be characterized as both one and many. The interrelations and interdependencies of the many constitute the oneness of the world; the irreducible integrity and independence of each particular event or thing constitute the world's plurality.

Therefore, the oneness of nature is not a through-and-through, all-encompassing oneness. We should not think of nature as a super entity ordering and monitoring all other entities and systems, or even as containing them like subsets; it is not like an organism or a nested set of Russian dolls. This point suggests yet another way of understanding the world's irreducible plurality. To speak of nature or a system of nature is to speak inclusively of all of the entities and relations there are, but we should be careful not to assume that this requires us to think of it as something that brings those entities and relations into final integration or unity. There really is no such thing as "the" order of nature; we need to think instead in terms of multiple orders of nature and to preserve a keen sense of the incommensurabilities among those orders. For all its uniformity and interrelatedness, nature displays an ineradicable amount of disunity, disorder, and diversity. It is universe-pluriverse, a melding of continuity and novelty, predictability and unpredictability, unity and multiplicity, cosmos and chaos.

PROCCESS AND PATTERN

We noted in the preceding section that nature exhibits massive uniformities, that it is suffused and underlain by persistent patterns and regularities. Its most general traits seem to have remained impressively stable over vast stretches of time. But is the current system of nature everlasting? Has it always existed, or will it exist forever?

The fourth question posed at the beginning of the present chapter speaks to this issue: Is nature fundamentally permanent or changing, pattern or process? There are three possible answers to the question: that nature is fundamentally permanent, that it is fundamentally changing, or that it contains important aspects of permanence and change, but neither is prior to the other. We have already seen that nature does indeed exhibit pervasive aspects of both permanence and change, but we have not yet tried to determine whether one of the two aspects is more basic than the other.

I shall critically weigh reasons that can be given in support of each answer and explain why I finally opt for the second answer, that nature must be characterized as fundamentally changing, despite all of its stable structures and patterns. To adopt for a moment the familiar medieval terminology, I shall argue that nature is most adequately characterized as *natura naturans* ("nature naturating") rather than as *natura naturata* ("nature naturated"). All of its patterns are the outcomes of its processes, and its present patterns will eventually be eroded and overridden by continuing change, just as previous patterns have been in the past. Therefore, the only thing that is truly everlasting about nature is the unrelentingness of change.

As part of my defense of this thesis, I shall critically consider arguments that might be presented in support of the other two views and indicate why I do not regard those arguments as convincing. We will consider first an argument for the priority of permanence to change. It runs in general as follows: without some basic structures, laws, or principles remaining the same through all of the changes that nature undergoes, those changes could not occur; hence, the former are prior to and more fundamental than the latter.

One version of this argument is implicit in certain dialogues of Plato, where it is alleged that there is a fixed, unchanging domain of essences or forms that forever defines what changes are possible. All change takes place within this structure of possibility; it itself does not and cannot change. A basic reason for this position is that actualities are judged to be actualizations of antecedent possibility: there must first be the possibility for something to occur before it can occur. Its occurrence is therefore dependent on that prior possibility.

Moreover, it is assumed in this argument that possibilities do not change; only actualities do. It is possible at this moment that there are dinosaurs, even though they are currently extinct. It is possible today that an athlete could run a two-minute mile, or that the earth could begin to orbit around the moon instead of the sun, although neither of these events has any likelihood of occurring under current physical conditions. The realm of possibilities is thus a timeless one, logically prior to all temporal change and wholly independent of present circumstances.

This timeless structure of possibility, we can further infer, firmly defines and delimits transformations in or of the world. That structure is the requisite "nature," so to speak, of all changes within or of nature, the eternal, defining essence of nature in all of its guises. Nature fundamentally understood, then, is just this permanent umbrella of possibility within which its changes take place.

A variation on this Platonic theme is Alfred North Whitehead's distinction in part 1 of his metaphysical treatise *Process and Reality* between "generic notions" and "derivative notions." The former and their specified interconnections constitute the "categoreal scheme" of the work, Whitehead's vision of the metaphysical structure that defines any possible universe. The latter are notions consistent with the categoreal scheme but not required by it. The derivative notions happen to be pervasive traits of what Whitehead calls the present "cosmic epoch," which he construes as only one of a succession of such epochs, each with its own distinctive characteristics, principles, and laws, which have emerged in the past and will continue to do so in the future. Since all of these different epochs must instantiate the generic notions, and since these notions do not undergo change but are eternal, they are the preconditions for any and all transformations of nature. So once again, pattern is prior to process, and nature in all of its forms must instantiate that basic pattern. The pattern is the persistent essence of any cosmos—past, present, or future.

Another argument for the priority of pattern to process in nature reasons that there must be fundamental scientific laws that forever regulate or describe what changes are possible and how those changes shall occur. The first and second laws of thermodynamics, for example, can be regarded as such laws. According to the first law, there is a constant amount of energy in the universe that is always conserved, and according to the second law, the amount of *usable* energy in the universe is being continually depleted, as changes—all of which must involve some kind of energy-expending "work"—take place within it. No matter what happens, these two laws will remain in effect. They constitute, therefore, a precondition for all change. The second law, furthermore, points toward an inevitable cessation of change. When no usable energy is left, no more work can be done, and no more changes can occur. Whatever structure remains in the universe after the last gasp of change will then presumably endure forever—the final triumph of pattern over process.

However, there are problems with each of these arguments in support of the priority of structure over process. A difficulty with the Platonic argument, as Aristotle clearly saw, is that it too sharply separates the forms from particular existents, assigning the forms to a transcendent, superior realm and consigning the particulars to an inferior, shadow-like status in the sensible world. This view leaves entirely mysterious why there should be any such thing as a separate realm of sensible reality, since the forms already exist splendidly in their own right in the Platonic vision, and in what manner the chasm between the wholly distinct worlds of forms and particulars could be bridged. A closely related question is, how could the transcendent universal forms be the traits of particular things in an inferior, sensible realm? Vague metaphors of "participation" of particulars in the transcendent forms or of pale "imitation" of them to be found in various Platonic dialogues do not resolve but only accentuate the mystery.[14]

Aristotle's alternative model is that the forms reside in, and are posed as possibilities by, sensible actualities rather than lording over them from a transcendent, self-subsistent realm. Forms reside in particulars as the present traits and relations of those particulars, and they are posed by those same particulars as relevant forms of possible realization made available for the future by their existing traits and relations. The existing traits of a human child and her or his relations to things in the environment, for example, make possible the child's maturation and education as an adult human being. Thus, for Aristotle, there is no free-floating realm of sheer possibility to be contrasted with a realm of factual entities; there are only those possibilities for change implicit in current facts.

If we apply his view of possibility to the three examples of so-called transcendent, timeless possibility mentioned earlier, we find that it is not really possible that an extinct species of dinosaur will reappear in the next moment, or that a human being, in even the most outstanding physical shape, will run a two-minute mile at a track meet this afternoon, or that the earth will suddenly begin oribiting the moon. These are abstract logical possibilities, possible only in the sense that they do not violate the logical law of noncontradiction, but they are not possibilities for current actualization. Traits and relations of particulars existing at the present time do not support their occurrence. Hence, these are not timeless but time-bound possibilities. That so-called timeless possibilities can be found in domains of language, formal systems, and conceptualization does not entail their existence as unchanging structures of nature. As traits and relations of particulars in nature change, so do possibilities for actualization change. This is the empirical, down-to-earth view of the character and status of possibility to be found in Aristotle's philosophy, as contrasted with Plato's, a view that is highly persuasive.

For Aristotle, of course, the basic facts of nature do not change; such change as there is occurs in the context of or is simply an instance of persistently recurring facts. Nature always has been and will forever be what it now is. There is no such thing as cosmic, terrestrial, or biological evolution in Aristotle's system. But if we retain his view of possibilities as implicit in actualities, rather than having a separate existence as the defining essence of the universe or of all possible universes, and build in the idea of evolution that is so fundamental in current scientific cosmology, then there is no longer any convincing reason to affirm a priority of structure to process, such as exists in Plato's thought.[15] Possibilities can change, just as actualities change, or more accurately, possibilities *have to change* as actualities change, since actualities are for Aristotle the locus of possibilities. At the very least, then, the two are of equal, correlative importance, although I shall try to show later why we should regard process as more fundamental than any kinds of structures, including structures of possibility.

Whitehead's distinction between generic and derivative notions, which also implies a priority of pattern to process, is vulnerable to at least two basic criticisms. In the first place, it is unempirical, and in the second place, it is inconsistent with the most fundamental part of Whitehead's own metaphysics, his "category of the ultimate." The distinction is unempirical because it purports to lay down a structure for all possible universes, past, present, and future, but the only universe we have to work with is the one we presently have, the one available, directly or indirectly, to experience. The best we can do is seek generic traits of this universe, that is, the most general features and interrelations of those features implicit in all that we experience. This observation implies that all of our notions must be "derivative" as long as we restrict our interpretations to the experienced or experienceable world.

It is conceivable that there could be a succession of cosmic epochs, each with its own defining traits, principles, and laws, but we have no empirical way of ascertaining what those distinctive traits, principles, and laws have been or will be. We can vaguely entertain their possibility but not specify their character. We cannot even specify a most general common character of those other epochs, because there is no empirical way to determine whether or not certain features and relations must persist through all time, through all transformations of worlds. We can try to extrapolate such features and relations from our own experienced world, as Whitehead does, but such extrapolations are suspect and may well be mistaken. In fact, it is highly likely that these extrapolations will be mistaken if the epochs are to be as different from one another as he allows. Only a rationalist can repose confidence in notions thought to be purely generic and wholly nonderivative, because a rationalist can hold such notions to be *a priori* and thus necessary and universal. Whitehead, however, claims to root his metaphysical interpretations in experience, not in *a priori* principles. Because I strongly endorse his empiricist program, I take issue with his distinction between generic and derivative notions and with the precedence of pattern over change that it implies.

The second objection to this Whiteheadian distinction is that it flies in the face of what he himself announces to be the ultimate principle of his metaphysics, creativity.[16] This principle means that the many things of the world are continuously being brought into the unifications of events that exhibit widely varying degrees of novelty but are never entirely devoid of novelty. As befits a process philosopher like Whitehead, this principle would seem to underwrite a final priority of process to pattern, the view of nature that I shall defend later.

The principle, however, also seems to be in sharp conflict with Whitehead's conviction that a single, most general metaphysical pattern must obtain through all of the transformations of nature. Why should such a pattern itself be immune to the novel intrusions of ongoing creativity? Whitehead seeks to resolve the apparent conflict with his theory of the primordial nature of God. According to this theory, God eternally envisages the eternal objects (pure universals, pure potentials) and timelessly orders them into an integrated realm of logical possibility. This realm then serves as the unchanging background or context for all change. It also is the subject matter of metaphysical speculation, for the generic notions sought in that speculation are, by Whitehead's reasoning, the conditions for any possible world.

How, then, can creativity, a principle of ongoing transformation and change that finally explains why even a cosmos cannot last forever, still be said to be ultimate? Whitehead's answer—a rather weak one, in my judgment—is that God's primordial envisagement is the "aboriginal instance" of creativity,[17] a timeless bringing of the many eternal objects into the unity of the divine envisagement. A timeless creativity, though, is an odd sort of creativity, one that only sustains an order and never brings about a change, an alleged creativity without emergent novelty.

It also is a kind of creativity with no purchase in experience, for our experience is never merely repetitive or continuous but combines elements of continuity and novelty. And the workings of creativity to which experience gives abundant testimony always take place in time or have a temporal character. This appeal to experience brings us back to the first objection to Whitehead's distinction between generic and derivative notions. A parade of cosmic epochs accords well with Whitehead's claim to the ultimacy of creativity, as I shall argue in more detail later. The idea that all such epochs must exhibit the same generic pattern does not.

The third argument for the primacy of pattern, at least to the extent that it rests on the two laws of thermodynamics but probably in general as well, assumes close analogies between nature as a whole and events within nature. The argument may, therefore, be guilty of a fallacy of composition, uncritically reasoning from traits of the parts to traits of the whole. Because energy is conserved in observed closed systems within nature, it is assumed that it must be conserved as a finite amount in nature as a whole, and because usable energy is progressively depleted when work is done in those observed closed systems, it is assumed that usable energy must be progressively depleted in nature as a whole. Is nature, however, simply an aggregation of its parts? Is it itself a closed system? Does it have the tight coherence and unity of such systems? Must it forever exhibit the same lawlike regularities exhibited by those systems?

Our observations in the previous section raise serious doubts about giving affirmative answers to these questions. We saw there that nature must be seen as universe-pluriverse rather than as a completely unitary, orderly system. We saw that it blends the regular workings of cause-effect relations with operations of chance (as well as of purposive freedom in the case of human beings and other highly developed organisms on earth and perhaps elsewhere in the universe) that are unpredictable in principle. Nature, then, may not be restricted to any specific overall pattern but may well come to assume different patterns as causal continuity combines with innovations brought about by chance and as shifting relations among its diverse, partly incommensurate constituents develop in novel ways.

These observations strongly suggest that everything about nature needs to be viewed as ultimately dynamic and open rather than fixed and closed, meaning that traits of its remote past and distant future cannot simply be inferred from its contemporary character or, more specifically, from currently observed operations of isolated systems. Regularities and interrelations that obtain today may not obtain tomorrow; there is no sure way to tell empirically what a future not predictable in every detail might bring.

We need to remind ourselves again that we do not experience nature as a whole. Talk about the whole of nature always involves models presented by and to the imagination. Viewing nature through the lens of the first and second laws of thermodynamics is one such imaginative projection; it has important rootage in observations of closed systems and deserves to be taken seriously. But the processive, open-ended vision of nature that I am proposing here also has significant empirical warrant and is tied to notions of cosmic, terrestrial, and biological evolution that play such a prominent role in today's thinking about nature.

This vision augments or qualifies those evolutionary accounts in three ways. First, it accords a prominent metaphysical role to chance or novelty, insisting on an in-principle unpredictability of important aspects of evolutionary change. Second, it extends the notion of evolutionary change to the basic laws of nature as currently experienced and conceived, arguing that all of these laws without exception are subject to evolution and thus to significant, unpredictable alterations over vast periods of time. Third, it endorses Whitehead's striking idea of multiple successive universes, world upon world without beginning or end. Thus while this universe may have had a beginning similar to that of the standard Big Bang theory of contemporary physics, and though it may someday come to an end, perhaps in a Big Crunch, such as that envisioned by physicists John Archibald Wheeler and Andrei Linde, we need not regard ours as the only universe there ever has been or ever will be.[18]

I certainly do not want to argue that nature, for any significant length of time, has lacked or will lack dominant patterns of traits, principles, and laws, but I deny that it must forever have exactly the same set of traits, principles, and laws, no matter how fundamental or inviolable a given set may seem to be at a given time. Hence, I take issue with the claim to the permanence or unalterability of the first and second laws of thermodynamics, as well as with any other putatively necessary, permanent laws of nature. All such laws, in my view, are ultimately outcomes of, rather than preconditions for, innovative and destructive processes of nature that never cease.

Someone could object to this view, however, by arguing that neither process nor pattern is prior. Both work together, each requiring and depending on the other. Let me first sketch how such an argument might go, and then I will indicate why I disagree with it and continue to uphold the priority of process to pattern.

A defender of process and pattern as correlative principles would observe that all experienced process or change is a transformation of existing structures. There is no such thing as sheer, *de novo* change. Instead, all change is change of existing structures, of something already there to undergo change; hence, structure and change are correlative—neither is prior to the other. This argument is a version of Aristotle's insistence, noted earlier, that something must persist through any process of change. If it did not, the very notion of change would be unintelligible. Aristotle thought that this insistence meant that his concept of substance (*ousia*) was required as the basis for an adequate metaphysics. The argument under consideration, however, need not assume a concept of substance. It is enough that some pattern or something that does not change persists through all process. The conclusion drawn from the argument is that, since some pattern must continue through any meaningful change, there must be a constant pattern of some kind that continues through all the changes in or of nature as a whole.

I have no quarrel with most of this argument. I have already stated that all process and the very nature of time itself involve both continuity and novelty. My disagreement is with the argument's conclusion, which does not seem to follow from its premises. To note, correctly, that *some* pattern must persist through any process is not the same thing as concluding that *one identical* pattern must continue through *all* processes. It is enough that there is a pattern; what is not required is that the pattern must be the same forever. A pattern that serves as the context for change at one time need not be the pattern that serves as the context for change at an earlier or a later time.

Transformative processes in nature can therefore work, gradually and steadily (with sometimes abrupt effects), to produce new basic patterns (e.g., new fundamental principles and laws) that will provide a stable setting for later processes of transformation. But not only *can* they do so, they *must* do so. Once we have seen why this is the case, the argument for the priority of process to pattern will be complete.

New fundamental patterns must eventually emerge from the processes of nature, because the cumulative effects of chance and novelty are unrelenting. Given enough time, they are bound to alter any existing order. Chance and novelty, the inevitable ingredients of all change, are like the tiny drippings of water on the granite wall of a mountain. No matter how adamant the surface of the wall and how minuscule the force of that dripping, the surface will eventually erode. In the same way, chance and novelty are bound eventually to erode any existing structure, pattern, or law that provides context for their operation. This is the logic of Whitehead's affirming the ultimacy of creativity and of his envisioning an unending procession of cosmic epochs. It also is the logic of my conviction that nature is best characterized as process rather than pattern, as *natura naturans* instead of *natura naturata*. While its present patterns are of inestimable importance, so obviously important that I would not be here thinking and writing about nature if they had not been sustained over eons, its inexorable processes of change are even more fundamental and should be given full recognition in any adequate concept of nature.

A NOTE ON TERMINOLOGY

At the beginning of this chapter I indicated that I wanted to conclude it by saying something about why I prefer to use the term *nature* in this book, over similar terms such as *universe, cosmos,* or *world*. The reader already will have noted that I have used the latter terms in discussing the book's basic subject matter, but for me the preferred term is *nature*. Several reasons support this preference. *Universe* has too much of the connotation of unrestricted unity and order; it fails to do justice to the irreducible plurality and diversity of things in nature or to the inexorable, disruptive workings of chance and novelty.

World and *cosmos* are in some ways fit terms for a given cosmic epoch with its distinctive order (i.e., its defining traits, principles, and laws) but not for the endless succession of radically different cosmic epochs spun off by nature in its fundamental role of *natura naturans*. Even with this more restricted application, these two terms tend to place the accent too much on uniformity, regularity, and pattern in a particular state of *natura naturata* and not enough on its turbulent undercurrents of change. Nature, as we presently experience it, is a volatile tension between aspects of cosmos and chaos, and it is not just a serenely ordered cosmos (cf. the Greek word *kosmos*, meaning "order," "harmony," "arrangement"). The ultimacy of what Whitehead calls *creativity*, and what I have termed *chance* and *novelty*, ensures that any state of nature will exhibit this tension, though perhaps with varying degrees of relative cosmos or chaos among successive cosmic epochs or at different stages in the development of a particular epoch. So just as we earlier labled nature as universe-pluriverse, we also ought to describe it as cosmos-chaos, and we need to conceive of it not just as a world but also as a process of world-making and world-unmaking.

Finally, the etymology of the term *nature,* discussed earlier, suggests a dynamic, restless energy of growth, nurture, productivity, and change. It points to nature as the fruitful womb of all that is, has been, or ever will be. This etymology even hints at the wondrous power of nature to produce and sustain myriad forms of life, here on earth, in all likelihood in other regions of space, and probably in other epochs. These aspects of the concept of nature are for me the ones that are most definitive, awesome, and compelling.

3

Science and Nature

An unflinching determination to take the whole evidence into account is the only method of preservation against the fluctuating extremes of fashionable opinion. This advice seems so easy, and is in fact so difficult to follow.

—Alfred North Whitehead, *Science and the Modern World*

Since the scientific revolution of the seventeenth century, developments in the natural sciences have continued to have deep effects upon concepts of nature. In the preceding chapters I noted the influence on my own thinking of developments in the sciences of geology and biology in the nineteenth century with their emphasis on terrestrial and biological evolution and their implicit endorsement of a dynamic, processive conception of nature.

Scientific developments in the twentieth century helped give credence to the notion of the evolution of the universe itself. Although current cosmological thought among scientists tends to argue for the evolution of only one cosmos rather than for a succession of cosmic epochs—from a promordial Big Bang to the formation of heavier elements, stars, planets, and galaxies and to an ever-accelerating expansion of interstellar space—the door to multiple successive universes is still left ajar. An accordion-like succession of Big Bangs and Big Crunches would mean an unending generation and destruction of cosmic systems, assuming that there was enough mass in each system to cause the gravitational collapse of it upon itself once it had reached its limit of possible expansion.

It is even scientifically conceivable that the chaotic upheavals and unimaginably violent churnings of these cosmic implosions could give rise to universes with fundamentally different constituents and laws from universes that pre-ceded them[1] (though at least some sort of gravitational law would have to remain constant for this particular model of successive universes to work). If the majority of today's physicists are reluctant to stretch the evolutionary idea this far and are led by their researches and theoretical assumptions to favor something like the more traditional Western notion of an absolute beginning and ending of one world, the evolutionary idea itself is so well established in this and other areas of their outlook as still to provide marked contrast with the static view of nature that tended to be taken for granted in the West before the nineteenth century.[2]

Another striking respect in which the natural sciences have fundamentally challenged earlier views about the nature of nature is the ways in which they have jolted us away from the cozy earth-centered and human-centered outlook of medieval thought to concepts of nature in which human beings and the planet on which they live are no longer accorded a central, dominant role. Nicholas Copernicus in the sixteenth century, William Herschel and his son, John, in the seventeenth and eighteenth centuries, and Charles Darwin in the nineteenth century contributed, each in his own way, to this altered vision, as did pioneering ecologists of the twentieth century such as Frederick Clements and Aldo Leopold.

Copernicus placed the sun rather than the earth at the center of things. Patient observations of the heavens with new, more powerful telescopes by the Herschels helped inspire and provide evidence for the idea of countless galaxies or "island universes" at vast distances from our own solar system and the Milky Way, thus making our own earth seem like a tiny speck in the enormous reaches of intergalactic space. Darwin saw human beings as just one of a myriad species of biological organisms, all interconnected by an evolutionary history that continues to unfold. Clements and Leopold stressed the delicate and precarious dependence of all biological species, including our own, upon one another and upon nonliving components of their natural environments. These developments in natural science have helped make increasingly untenable the older vision of humans as the privileged, singular beings for whose sake the whole of nature exists and around whose terrestrial home it revolves, a nature of which they are not essentially a part and on which they do not ultimately depend, a nature that they are entitled and even divinely commanded routinely to subjugate for their own uses.

My reflections in these pages on outlines of a metaphysics of nature are deeply informed by these broad implications of the scientific view of the world. They are only two of many examples that could be cited in support of the rather obvious thesis that developments in the natural sciences have had crucial and sometimes even revolutionary impacts on our thinking about nature and the place of humans in nature, and that they will continue to do so. Scientists have provided not only general theories of sweeping scope such as the theory of natural selection, the special and general theories of relativity, quantum theory, Big Bang theory, DNA and RNA theory, and ecological theory that focuses on the diverse ways in which complexly interrelated organisms utilize the energy of the sun. They also have devoted themselves to the discovery and precise formulation of more specific natural laws, principles, and relations. These include Johannes Kepler's three laws of planetary motion, Isaac Newton's three laws of motion and law of gravity, the first and second laws of thermodynamics, the ideal gas law, Gregor Mendel's laws of biological inheritance, Clerk Maxwell's equations of the electromagnetic field, Einstein's famous $E = mc^2$, the uncertainty principle of Werner Heisenberg, the wave equations of Erwin Schrödinger, and John Bell's theorem.

In addition, scientists working in many different fields of investigation bring to the study of nature detailed observations of all types of natural phenomena and the design of finely tuned instruments for detecting and analyzing these phenomena. Finally, the methodologies of the various natural sciences give expression to an ideal of disciplined objectivity in the study of nature, of the search for hypotheses that not only commend themselves to exacting demands of the rational mind but also interpret our experience and predict empirical outcomes that can be brought repeatedly to the test of the five senses. Thus, for example, the daring speculation of Einstein's general theory of relativity about the curvature of paths of light in the vicinity of massive objects was subjected to an empirical test during a solar eclipse in 1919, and Alain Aspect and his scientific colleagues in Paris in the 1980s devised ingenious experiments to assess and give support to the calculations of Bell's theorem and the Copenhagen interpretation of quantum theory.

Past and continuing contributions of the natural sciences to our understanding of nature are thus of immense, indispensable importance and ought always to be taken into account in philosophical reflections about nature. As important as these contributions are, however, we cannot rely on the methodologies and findings of the natural sciences alone to give us a comprehensive vision of nature or of ourselves as natural beings. The main purpose of this chapter is to show why this is so.

I argue that while the natural sciences can provide us with exemplary models of disciplined objectivity in the study of nature, models of objective inquiry from other fields need to be noted and emulated as well; that the metaphysical perspective on nature being sought in part 2 of this book must be different in significant respects from a scientific one; and that an adequate comprehension of nature and of ourselves as part of nature requires a focus on *lived* nature in all of its dimensions, not just on those aspects of nature most amenable to scientific investigation.

OBJECTIVITY AND THE STUDY OF NATURE

One thing the "second scientific revolution" (the radical changes in physical theory introduced by physicists such as Max Planck, Einstein, Heisenberg, and Niels Bohr early in the twentieth century) has helped teach us is that even the supposedly hardest of "hard" natural sciences is a fallible, historically conditioned human undertaking, subject to unexpected basic shifts and discontinuities. If scientific thinking changed so fundamentally from the late nineteenth century to the early twentieth,[3] it is quite conceivable that it can change as much or even more in the future.

Instead of progressively reading from the "book of nature" (the revealing metaphor of early science) structures, laws, and principles residing there ready to be deciphered, scientists, we now more fully realize, must have recourse to tentative, changeable models, metaphors, images, analogies, and hypotheses produced by the free play of their imaginations and tied to numerous background assumptions not directly subject to scientific assessment, assumptions of which practicing scientists themselves often are not clearly aware.

Also, as scientific theories become more complex and more intricately meshed with networks of other highly complex theories and assumptions underlying those theories, and as they come to require ever more elaborate, sophisticated types of instrumentation for their testing (particle accelerators are a good example), the connections between the theories and sensate experiences claimed to give evidence of their truth become less obvious and direct.[4] Hence, a perception of risk and alterability is attached to the assertions of scientists today that was not generally associated with their pronouncements in the heyday of the Newtonian era.

The import of these observations is not that natural scientists can no longer lay claim to objectivity but rather that the objectivity of their findings can no longer be regarded as absolute and must be reinterpreted in a manner consistent with recent awakenings to the fallibilistic character of science and to sometimes startlingly abrupt, unpredictable changes in its basic theories. This contemporary perspective on natural science also implies that it is no longer plausible to view science as the sole guardian of objectivity or as the exclusive source of reliable knowledge, a view uncritically propounded by the Logical Positivists early in the twentieth century. The moral of the story for our own purposes is that we must be careful not to exaggerate or misinterpret the objectivity of the natural sciences or their construals of the natural world, even as we seek to give due recognition to the undeniable importance of these sciences for a metaphysics of nature.

A second thing to note about the various natural sciences is that they do not exemplify the same type of objectivity. The objectivity of particle physics is different from the objectivity to be found or expected in taxonomic biology, for example. While both combine elements of conceptual construction with modes of empirical testing in their respective formulations, there are also at least two important differences between the two fields. First, the constructions of particle physicists are typically couched in a language and approach that are highly mathematical, while those of taxonomic biologists are not. Second, the kinds of instrumentation required for experimentation in particle physics are generally inapplicable to taxonomic biology; the two fields appeal to markedly different sorts of evidence.

Is not mathematical physics, however, the most rigorously objective of all of the sciences? Should not the other sciences try to approximate its modes of analysis as closely as they can? Finally, are these other sciences not, or should they not ideally be, reducible to physics as the most basic of sciences? Although an affirmative answer to these three questions often has been assumed, I do not think it is warranted. Given the range and variety of problems with which sciences such as meteorology, hydrology, vulcanology, paleontology, neurobiology, immunology, and weed science must deal, there is no reason to think that all of them should be held to the standard of only one kind of objective inquiry, or that they should all be reducible to the one science of mathematical physics. Moreover, there is no reason to believe that physics is the most rigorously objective of the sciences. It is more plausible to think of each of the special sciences as representing, or aspiring to represent, canons of objectivity appropriate to its subject area and type of research.

Just as I argued earlier for irreducible pluralism in nature, I am now affirming an irreducible pluralism in natural science. Each of the sciences has its distinctive role to play in interpreting nature, and while there are numerous overlaps among them, this fact does not imply an ideal of final unity. The sciences are unified in a common goal of understanding nature, but they remain conspicuously diverse in their ways of seeking that understanding.

Such interrelations as can be found among the sciences should of course be brought into view and developed, but it should be no cause for regret to conclude that each scientific field has important things to contribute from its own perspective that the others do not and cannot. The point, then, is that not even in the natural sciences do we encounter a single, most basic, or most exemplary kind of disciplined objectivity. Instead, we discover an impressive variety of distinctive approaches to that general ideal. As John Dupré reminds us, there is a "remarkable particularity of the actual practice of science in specific research programs."[5]

A third thing to note, as we continue to address the topic of types of objectivity, is that there are no obvious, clearly discernible lines of demarcation between the natural sciences, on the one hand, and all other kinds of thought, on the other hand. This point is closely related to the second one, for the latter implies that we cannot expect to determine whether or not something is scientific by appealing to a single methodology thought to characterize all genuine science or to a particular area within the natural sciences considered the paradigm of objective scientific research. The way is left open, then, to significant overlaps among at least some fields commonly regarded as scientific and others not so regarded.

If a particular field is believed to represent a form of disciplined objectivity because it is seen as a science, then there is no good reason to deny objectivity to one or more nonscientific fields that may be similar to it in method and approach. For example, evolutionary biologists base accounts of evolutionary history partly on the available fossil evidence, and this practice is similar to a historian's basing his or her accounts of human history on extant documents and artifacts. If the first qualifies as an example of disciplined objectivity, on what basis can we deny this characterization to the second?

Approaching the matter more directly, and this is my fourth point in relation to the theme of objectivity, disciplines other than the natural sciences have their own standards and sorts of objectivity. So outcomes of their endeavors need to be taken as seriously as those of the natural sciences. With specific reference to the concerns of this book, this means that we should make every effort to draw upon the nonscientific fields as sources for understanding nature with the realization that they can provide perspectives of vital importance for comprehending nature in its multiple dimensions.

Poets and painters can tell us things about the complexity, diversity, and fullness of our experiences of nature that physicists cannot, and these can be essential things to take into account in our thinking about nature. For example, Camille Pissaro and Robert Frost awaken us by eye and ear to a poignantly beautiful, awesomely powerful natural world of which we humans are an integral, absolutely dependent part. What we learn about the natural world from these two sources has a concrete immediacy it does not have when taught by evolutionary biologists or ecologists, although the scientists' more abstract ways of describing that world also are important. So the same lesson is taught from different angles of vision, with different kinds of insight. Neither the artistic nor the scientific way of conveying that lesson is adequate by itself; each interprets and enriches a momentous truth in its own distinctive fashion.

The basic claim I am making in this section is that as we move from one scientific field to another, or as we move from the natural sciences as a whole to the social sciences, humanities, or arts, we should not think in terms of different *degrees* of objectivity (or subjectivity) but rather in terms of different *types* of objectivity. I do not deny that distinguishing degrees of objectivity is important. For example, some theories in physics will be more coherent, complete, and elegant or more firmly based on replicable experiments than others, and some works of literature will illumine aspects of character, situation, or life more powerfully and convincingly than others. I am proposing though that this distinction is not made simply by comparing one scientific field to another (where physics, for instance, is assumed to be the most objective of the sciences and botany the least), or by comparing the natural sciences to literature or painting and concluding that while scientific investigations of nature are objective, those of literature and painting must be regarded as subjective. To the contrary, Leo Tolstoy's *War and Peace* is every bit as much an example of rigorously disciplined objectivity in its own manner and with its own subject matter, as is Einstein's special theory of relativity.[6] Both are singular achievements of human creativity with a compelling inner logic, and both are deeply responsive to the relevant empirical evidence.

However, in making this point, do I not use the important term *empirical* too carelessly and loosely? The evidences on whose basis scientific theories are tested, a critic might object, are distinct, replicable, public data of one or more of the five senses, while those to which works of literature appeal or on which they can be said to rest are vague, inward, and emotional. Surely the first sort of evidence is more objective than the second. This criticism brings me to the fifth point I make in connection with the topic of types of objectivity.

This point is that we need to construe experience as broadly as possible in order to take into account everything of which it gives evidence, as far as the nature of nature and our relations to nature are concerned. The fact that some modes of experience are more distinct and replicable and others are more vague and elusive does not in itself mean that the former are more objective or crucial for inquiry, especially if our search is for an understanding of all of the important aspects of our experience of nature.

One of the enduring contributions of William James, John Dewey, and Alfred North Whitehead to philosophy is their insistence that a wide range of modes of experience is relevant in assessing philosophical claims and theories. In addition to experiences of the five senses, we have experiences of memory and anticipation; of causal efficacy and the "withness" of the body; of aim, purpose, freedom, and novelty; of spatial location and the flow of time; of moral obligation, aesthetic sensibility, and religious yearning; of felt unity with one another, with other sentient beings, and with the entire natural world; and so on. Subtleties of feeling, mood, assumption, attitude, orientation, valuation, and intimation inform all of our experience, including our sensate experiences, and we should not ignore these subtleties when reflecting on what experience can tell us about nature and our place within nature.

How to take sufficiently into account all of these aspects of experience without falling into patent nonsense in our claims about nature is no doubt a problem, but if we are not willing to take that risk, then we can all too easily succumb to an eviscerated, one-sided view of things, a view that does not dare move beyond what can be understood from a single angle of vision. If we construe objectivity too narrowly, we end up with the untenable constrictions of logical positivism; if we construe it too broadly, objective investigation itself goes by the board. What is needed is a delicate balance, one we must struggle constantly to maintain. The philosophical writings of James, Dewey, and Whitehead are exemplary in their devotion to this ideal.

Distinctions among the various types of objective inquiry are of course important. A sixth point, therefore, is that we should be careful not to confuse one type with another or to assume that one type can stand in the stead of another. I would not want a symphonic composer to design the automobile in which I drive at high speeds on the highway; its design should incorporate the most reliable research and theories of automotive engineering, but by the same token, I would not generally care to attend performances of symphonies whose scores had been created by automotive engineers.

I once served on the graduate committee of a student who was a promising poet. After my reading the fine collection of poems that was to serve as her graduate thesis and discussing these poems at some length with her, she suggested that I try my hand at writing a poem. I did so and thought I had done a decent job. When she read the result, her only comment was, "It's the sort of thing I would expect a philosopher to write." With this statement she was gently informing me that I had little gift or competence for the sort of objectivity that poets work to achieve, an objectivity for which a typical philosopher's musings—even in poetic meter—are no substitute. Despite the fact that symphonic composers, engineers, poets, and philosophers reflect on aspects of a world that we all experience in common, each of their forms of inquiry is capable of making distinctive, irreplaceable contributions to elucidation of that world. So inexhaustibly mysterious is nature and so mutifarious its guises that we need a great variety of methodologies, perspectives, and modes of expression for probing its depths.

METAPHYSICS AND THE NATURAL SCIENCES

An important theme of the previous section is that when we use the term *natural science,* we should think of it as a convenient, if somewhat misleading, umbrella term for numerous sciences, research programs, or areas of investigation that are quite different from one another and that cannot be reduced to any single methodology or discipline. Despite the diversity of fields within the general area of natural science, each of the special sciences and all of them taken together can be meaningfully, although not absolutely, contrasted with the branch of philosophy called metaphysics (which, of course, has ample diversity of its own, as even a cursory survey of the history of metaphysical systems will show). I indicated previously that part 2 of this book is a sketch of some outlines of a metaphysics of nature. The present section can help give methodological context to this sketch by explaining my interpretation of the task of metaphysics and its relations to the work of the natural sciences.

A good way to begin reflecting on the task of metaphysics is to acknowledge and weigh the implications of John Dewey's observation that "selective emphasis, with accompanying omission and rejection, is the heart-beat of mental life."[7] This means that all modes of inquiry are necessarily partial and selective, including metaphysics. Dewey goes on to insist that what is *left out* with each selective emphasis in order that its distinctive area of concern can be brought to the fore "is just as real and important in its own characteristic context."[8] What is real and important, then, for metaphysics that the natural sciences fail to include, and what is real and important for the natural sciences that metaphysics fails to include? An answer to this question will help us see how the two compare and contrast with one another.

What is included in each of the natural sciences is a complexity of detail characterizing a special subject matter, but at the price of throwing into the background subject matters that are the concerns of other sciences and of non-scientific modes of inquiry. What is inquired into by metaphysics, in contrast, is commonalities and relations that bind all of the modes of inquiry. Here richness of detail is necessarily sacrificed for the sake of a more inclusive vision. If the metaphysics is intentionally empirical, as is that of philosophers such as James, Dewey, and Whitehead, and as my own metaphysical reflections are meant to be, then the search will be for general traits and relationships that characterize experience in all of its manifestations, not just the aspects of experience that might be the particular concern of a special science or some other special field such as archaeology, painting, politics, or religious studies.

The contrast, then, is between detail and comprehensiveness, specificity and generality. When claims to the broadest possible comprehensiveness and generality are being made and the express concern is to leave out no dimension of experience but to include and systematically order all of its salient aspects, then we have at least an attempt at an empirical metaphysics.

But of course metaphysics should not and cannot generalize or integrate in a vacuum. It must draw upon the special sciences and other special fields for its data, for detailed examinations of particular sorts of experience that are essential in bringing the common, integrative traits and relations of all forms of experience more plainly into view. Metaphysical systems try to provide the broadest possible context within which each of the distinctive modes of experience, and each dimension of inquiry, is accorded its appropriate place. These systems seek a general perspective or overview within which the contributions and role of each type of experience—for example, sensate, desiderative, aversive, recollective, anticipatory, aspirational, inward, outward, reflective, active, frustrating, fulfilling, sorrowful, joyful—and of each special area of investigation—for example, aesthetic, moral, religious, psychological, historical, social, economic, technological—can be interpreted, interrelated, and understood.

This conception of the task of metaphysics is in solid agreement with Dewey's conviction that "all modes of experiencing are ways in which some genuine traits of nature come to manifest realization."[9] Proponents of this conception are anxious to avoid slighting or omitting any part of the wholeness of life as it searches for a vision of the world in which each mode is given its due. Their guiding concern is to work for a vision of nature sufficiently lavish and encompassing to incorporate the diverse ways in which nature makes itself known.

It may help us understand the task of metaphysics and its relations to the natural sciences if we return to a topic of the previous chapter, where we began our explorations into a metaphysics of nature. That topic was chance, novelty, and freedom in relation to the causal connections of nature. Scientists need not critically inquire into this topic in order to conduct their inquiries. They can simply accept the reality of both causality and chance, for example, without the need systematically to explore the metaphysical possibility of each or its relations to the other. They can assume the reality of time without puzzling about the interrelations of continuity and novelty implicit in the experience of time. They can take for granted the possibility of theoretical inquiry, even if also supposing universal causality, without taking notice of the problem raised in chapter 2 that theoretical inquiry—including inquiry into the metaphysical issue of free will and determinism itself—would seem to require genuine freedom if it is to be intelligible. They can repose trust in an intelligible causal order of the world without worrying about its persistent aspects of disorder and unpredictability.

The endeavors of the natural sciences, therefore, rest upon metaphysical assumptions but do not usually require active inquiry into those assumptions or into daunting questions of how they can be conceptually related to one another, or to the most pervasive traits of the experienced world. The findings of the natural sciences often are replete with metaphysical import, but their metaphysical implications usually are left unnoticed and unanalyzed in scientific theory.

Metaphysics, in contrast, makes explicit what is only implicit in these sciences. It boldly tackles the question of how the multiple dimensions of experience can be brought into coherent, meaningful relation to one another. Its task, unlike that of a special science, is not concerted analysis of some particular domain while leaving all other domains in the background. Its job is to understand how all of the domains fit together, how each relates to and informs the other. Metaphysics wants to leave no loose threads dangling but to weave them all together into a tapestry of nature as a whole. Such a tapestry can only be woven, of course, from the gossamer threads of high generalization. Since it cannot hope to assimilate the minute detail of each special area of investigation, metaphysics must be content to leave behind most of the distinctive contents and concerns of the special sciences and other disciplines as it aspires toward more inclusive understanding.

Having presented this brief background on my understanding of the task of metaphysics and its relations to the work of the natural sciences, I hasten to add that I make no attempt in these pages to develop anything like a complete metaphysical system but only to lay out themes of a metaphysics of nature that bear on the religion of nature, to be discussed in part 3.

LIVED NATURE

The nature that is the concern of these pages, then, is not merely that presented in the various natural sciences, although the contributions of these sciences to our understanding of it are certainly important. We are interested, for example, not merely in physical, chemical, or biological phenomena but in the presence in nature of conscious, purposive, questioning physicists, chemists, and biologists who identify and inquire into those phenomena. Our concern is not just with nature as the subject of scientific theorizing but also with nature as *lived*, as encountered in the concreteness and immediacy of everyday experience. This nature includes us; we are not apart from it but a part of it. We are not disembodied spirits but fully embodied beings, one of earth's biological species among an incredible number and variety of others.[10] We are not outside of nature looking in but inside of nature looking around, responding with bodily sensation, feeling, and thought to the capacious architecture of our ancestral home. Our cultural achievements, marvelous and distinctive as they are, are actualizations of inherent powers of nature, not something imported into it from another realm. All of nature's profuse nonhuman aspects and manifestations are included in the scope of our concern here as well, all of nature that is not us and definitely not centered on us but that is integral to the nature to which we ourselves also belong.

What Thomas Berry rightly insists upon with regard to the planet Earth applies to nature as a whole: "[A]ny adequate description must include its every aspect." He elaborates the point as follows:

> The simpler elements are not known fully until their integration into more comprehensive modes of being is recognized. Later complex unities are not fully intelligible until their component parts are understood. We would not know the real capacities of hydrogen, carbon, oxygen, and nitrogen were it not for their later expression in cellular life and indeed in the entire world of living beings, including the remarkable world of human consciousness. So with consciousness: the thoughts and emotions, the social forms and rituals of the human community, are as much "earth" as the soil and the rocks and the trees and the flowers. We can reduce the flowers to the atoms or the atoms to the flowers. There are no atoms that are just atoms, no flowers that are just flowers.[11]

A poet or painter might "reduce . . . the atoms to the flowers," just as a physicist might "reduce the flowers to the atoms," but Berry is reminding us that neither account tells the whole or privileged story of nature. Both flowers and atoms can come within the range of our experience, although atoms tend to come into it more indirectly than directly. Neither has greater absolute importance than the other, but either may be given exclusive attention in a particular context of expression or inquiry. Each is a distinctive and nonreducible aspect of a many-splendored nature, a nature that can be encountered, experienced, and contemplated in countless ways.

It is nature that sustains my body as I write these words. It is nature that provided my morning's breakfast, supplies oxygen to my lungs and tissues, and wards off infectious invaders. It is nature that allowed my species to evolve, that facilitated the emergence of human language, culture, and history, and that accounts for my existence as an individual being. It is my natural body with its large brain that permits me to reason, to read, and to reflect, and that body also enables me to have felt motivations and purposes for carrying through the project of writing this book. The book itself, whatever its worth, will itself be a product of nature. Humans write books just as mule deer prepare beds in pine straw for the night. Each of these two kinds of natural creatures is doing its own thing. The life that I live day by day, whether spent brushing my teeth, eating lunch, reading a book, playing with our cat, visiting our two daughters and their families, raising a linguistic or philosophical question with our son, teaching a class at the university, participating in a professional conference, volunteering at a thrift store, puzzling over a philosophical question with my wife, having a discussion with a friend, or just settling down to sleep at night, is a manifestation of nature's multifarious character and inexhaustible creativity. All such aspects of everyday lived experience must necessarily be included in any conception of nature that strives for comprehensiveness and adequacy. The importance of this basic assumption will become increasingly evident in the chapters to come.

4

Values in Nature

Value ... cannot be grounded in humankind, for to do so is to catch
ourselves in an infinite regress: human value exists only in context....
We do not impose value on a valueless cosmos; rather, we are sensitive registers of values created through the unfolding of time.
—Max Oelschlaeger, *The Idea of Wilderness*

This chapter is concerned with the metaphysical status of values attributed to
nature, or to specific aspects of nature. Are values inherent in nature? If so,
what does it mean to conceive of them as inherent? If values are present in
nature, what basic sorts of values are these? If values exist in nature, do *disvalues* exist there as well, and if so, what basic sorts of disvalues are these? If both
values and disvalues exist in nature, how do the two relate to one another? Or
alternatively, do values exist only in human consciousness and then get projected onto a nature that is itself devoid of value? On what basis might it be
concluded, or has it been concluded in the past, that nature is devoid of value?
These are some of the questions to be considered in this chapter. Our interest
here shall be mainly in the *nonhuman* rather than human aspect of nature. We
shall focus on the human side of nature and make reference to the values
involved there in chapter 5.

Let us begin with the view that nature has no inherent values (or disvalues), that the locus of values is solely in needs, desires, and imaginings of
human beings, or in their subjective responses to processes or aspects of
nature that have no value in themselves. The wholesale denial of values to
nature, and the radical subjectivizing of the metaphysical status of value, is one
of the strangest and least plausible legacies of the rise of the modern era in

the West in the seventeenth and eighteenth centuries. Yet this view of values is widespread and considered axiomatic by many in our own time. We need to have some understanding of why this attitude persists. This is a large topic, and we can only make a brief foray into it here. Doing so will provide background for presentation of my own view of the matter, namely, that values do inhere in nature and that if we peel away some of the dubious assumptions on which the denial of their presence in the natural world rests we can readily acknowledge the truth of this assertion. To specify an appropriate meaning of the terms *inherent* and *inhere* is extremely important, however, to ensure that we do not fall into the trap of a purely external, nonrelational, "in-itself" view of nature—with its inevitable drift toward rigid dualisms of body and mind, nature and culture. I shall have more to say about these matters as the chapter proceeds.

ARGUMENTS FOR DENYING VALUES TO NATURE

Perhaps the most significant factor that has led many thinkers of the modern era to deny values to nature is their unquestioning, uncritical confidence in the competence of the natural sciences, and especially physics as the assumed queen of the sciences, to give a *complete* account of nature. Accordingly, these thinkers have come to regard the responsible and reliable study of the natural world as the exclusive province of natural science. But scientific description and understanding are restricted to the "what" and "how" of natural processes; they attempt to set forth a purely factual world of cause-effect relations and lawful processes, a world of sheer mathematical and mechanical goings-on. In this world, there is no place or role for values.

Exclusive reliance on the natural sciences for our understanding of nature leaves us with a nature devoid of values. We can outline the argument in support of this conclusion in the following way. Standard methods of scientific investigation provide no way of adjudicating, that is, criticizing or justifying, claims to value. Only claims that can be scientifically adjudicated, and in that manner found to be true, can be relied upon as true of nature. Therefore, nature is devoid of inherent value. Whatever values nature might have been thought to have before the age of science—aesthetic, moral, religious, existential, or practical—must now be seen as imposed upon it from without by the subjective feelings and responses of human beings.

Many modern thinkers envision the austere world of scientific descriptions and explanations, with its blank indifference to considerations of value, as the only "objectively real" world, the reality that would remain if human beings and the crucial valuative dimensions of their experiences, lives, and cultures were to be removed. Values lack status or support in a scientifically described nature, and for these thinkers this is nature as it truly is in and of itself. Nature is thus set over against the consciousness and culture of human beings as a separate, foreign domain that gives no sanction or response to their experiences of beauty, worth, and reverence, or to their deepest aspirations and goals.[1]

A second route to the conclusion that nature has no inherent value focuses on the alleged inconclusiveness of disputes concerning value in contrast to statements of a factual character. According to this argument, facts of nature such as the law of gravity, the stages of development of an embryo, the structure of the carbon atom, or the composition of the atmosphere of the planet Venus can be ascertained and agreed upon, but differing assessments of value are endlessly debated and debatable and seem never to be settled. These assessments seem to vary widely from person to person, culture to culture, and time to time. At an earlier period, for example, most Europeans living in the vicinity of the Swiss Alps thought that they were horrible and terrifying, while today the Alps are seen as majestic, serene, and beautiful. Some people love living in the desert and cherish its life-forms, while others regard the desert as empty, hot, and inhospitable. Snakes and spiders fascinate some folks, who see them as exquisite and wonderful, while others fear and despise these creatures. Safari hunters take delight in killing large "trophy animals" they regard as "game," while others are repelled by the idea of killing such creatures for fun. One segment of society looks at nature as a collection of "natural resources" to be exploited whenever possible to satisfy human beings. For them, nature has only instrumental value; it is simply a repository of means to be employed for the sake of economic, technological, recreational, and other kinds of human wants and needs. For others, nature has precious value in itself. Humans are entitled to find their appropriate place within it, as one sort of natural creature among others, but the emphasis should be on the well-being of nature as a whole, not merely that of human beings.

How could such disagreements and disputes about values or disvalues in nature ever be settled? How could correct answers to the valuative questions posed in these disputes ever be found? Scientific factual and explanatory claims can be formulated with a high degree of exactitude and put to the test of critical experiments. In this way, we can arrive at a justified consensus about the facts of nature, but there is no way, or so the argument goes, to achieve such a warranted consensus in the realm of values. The clear implication would seem to be that differing claims about natural values are at bottom personal, private, and subjective, with no dependable reference to nature as it is in and of itself, while contending claims about natural facts can continue to be addressed and resolved in an impersonal, public, and objective manner, giving us an ever-enlarging store of knowledge about real traits of nature.

A third line of argument for denuding nature of value is based on propositions such as the following. Feeling and intellect can be sharply distinguished. Feelings are notoriously vague, imprecise, and inconstant, whereas intellect allows for a precision and stability of thought, reaching its zenith in pure mathematics and mathematical physics. Furthermore, feelings by their very nature are concrete, participatory, and engaged. They tend to center on and be confined to particular situations. Responsible intellectual apprehension, on the other hand, requires and allows abstraction and critical distance, that is, universality rather than particularity, a dispassionate, analytical, and cool detachment from that which it seeks to understand.

In light of these two fundamental differences, it is clear to those who argue in this way that intellectual apprehensions can have cognitive significance but that feelings cannot. That is, our intellects equip us to address general issues of truth and falsity; our feelings, in contrast, can only express particular personal preferences, predilections, aversions, reactions, and the like. This line of reasoning holds, finally, that valuative utterances and commitments are rooted in our feelings and manifest our feelings, and that they do not involve our intellects in any significant way. It follows from all of these allegations that claims to value in nature must lack cognitivity and cannot really be claims at all but only expressions of subjective feelings. Feelings of value or disvalue evoked by encounters with nature may be powerful and compelling, but they give us no warrant for attributing inherent values to nature.

I now want to present some lines of criticism of each of these three arguments for denying values to nature or, more specifically, to the nonhuman side of nature. Later in the chapter I argue more directly for the position, not only that values are present in nature but that nature's valuative features are every bit as prevalent and important as its factual ones.

THE FIRST ARGUMENT:
SCIENCE THE SOLE ARBITER OF CLAIMS ABOUT NATURE

I have already dealt with the first argument in chapter 3, where I argued that scientific claims about nature tell only part of the story about it. Scientific accounts of nature are, as I indicated there, selectively abstract, focusing intensively on some aspects of what is being studied but at the price of ignoring, either deliberately or unconsciously, other important aspects or possible aspects. One thing these accounts exclude from attention, and therefore do not decide one way or another, is the question of values in nature. The silence of the natural sciences on this question has, therefore, *no relevance whatsoever* to how it should be answered. To think otherwise would be similar to concluding that ultraviolet rays do not exist in nature, because we take no notice of them with ordinary vision, thus ignoring the possibility that they might be detected in some other manner. Scientific inquiry is not the appropriate kind of inquiry to rely upon if we want to determine whether or not values inhere in nature.

We also should note that practitioners of various disciplines within the natural sciences often are heard to speak of their love for nature, their enchantment with its beauty, their fascination with the intricacy of its workings, their delight in its diverse forms of being, and their intense concern to respect and preserve the integrity of these forms. These are all statements about perceptions of value in nature. Moreover, there would be no such thing as natural science if scientists did not greatly value the enterprise of interpreting and explaining natural phenomena, valuing it so much, in fact, as to devote their lives to it. Finally, scientists take for granted in their inquiries and methods values such as respect for logical, mathematical, and empirical reasoning; following the path of truth wherever it might lead; patience in pursuing answers to demanding questions in the face of frustrating setbacks and difficulties; exactitude and honesty in conducting and reporting on the results of their research; and trust in the carefulness, truthfulness, and dedication of their scientific colleagues. But the natural sciences as such typically offer no way of either justifying or criticizing scientists' recognitions of values in nature, their lifelong dedication to the value of the scientific enterprise, or their assumption of the methodological and moral values that make that enterprise possible.[2]

Such values have obvious crucial importance for scientists, but they cannot be criticized or defended in a purely scientific manner, partly because the disciplines of the natural sciences are not equipped to deal with issues relating to the status and significance of values, but also because commitment to certain values must be *presupposed* by the scientific disciplines. All of the values mentioned above lie within a more encompassing domain of human beliefs, attitudes, activities, purposes, and endeavors of which the natural sciences are only a part. Similarly, the question of whether or not values inhere in nature is not one to be resolved by the scientific study of nature alone. It is a question of primary importance for the metaphysics of nature, which, as we saw earlier, is concerned with the wholeness and concreteness of nature as *lived*, not just with those aspects of it amenable to standard techniques of scientific interpretation and explanation.

THE SECOND ARGUMENT:
VALUATIVE DISCOURSE TOO VAGUE TO BE OBJECTIVE

The second argument for denying values to nature can be criticized in several ways. We should notice first that putative facts assumed by scientists also have changed over time, and within the relatively brief history of the natural sciences in the modern period. For example, up until the late nineteenth century, physicists thought that such conceptions as a luminiferous ether, absolute space and time, a sharp distinction between matter and energy, and irreducible material atoms were fundamental facts of nature, but the physics of today has rejected them all. Notions such as those of "caloric" and "phlogiston," once identified by responsible scientists as types of material substance, have vanished from the scientific lexicon. Prior to the development of non-Euclidian geometries in the nineteenth century, scientists took for granted that space must be Euclidian, largely because no one had thought of conceiving of it differently, whereas today, following on the work of Albert Einstein, a Riemannian curvature of space-time is widely assumed.

Secondly, disputes have gone on among reputable scientists in the recent past and continue to do so today, and the established methods of scientific investigation do not seem easily able to resolve these disputes. A familiar example is the disagreement between Einstein and Niels Bohr over whether there is such a thing as an in-principle quantum indeterminacy, as Bohr was inclined to believe, or whether causality and determinism continue to reign at the subatomic level, as Einstein insisted throughout his life. Another example is the debate among evolutionary biologists over the standard view of evolutionary change as steady and continuous, and a newer view called "punctuated equilibria," propounded by paleontologists Stephen Jay Gould and Niles Eldridge. A third example is the vigorous debate among quantum physicists over local and nonlocal reality theories, a debate stimulated by the theoretical and experimental work of David Bohm, John Bell, Alain Aspect, and others from the mid-1950s to the early 1980s.[3]

Someone might object that the examples I have cited are all disputes about *theories*, not facts, but this objection helps make the third point I wish to elaborate in response to those who accept the second argument for denying values to nature. The point is that no absolutely sharp distinction can be made in the natural sciences between theories and facts; the two are closely conjoined. This observation recalls our discussion in chapter 2 about the necessary interpenetrations of experience and theory construction in conceptions of nature. Even the etymology of the term *fact* (from *factum*, a past participle of the Latin verb *facere*, "to make" or "to do") suggests that a fact is something that is, at least in part, made or constructed within a network of already established beliefs. I do not want to argue that fact and theory are the same thing. More often than not, there is enough distinction between the two for theories to give significance to experienced facts, and for facts to be meaningfully employed for the testing of theories.[4] I do want to insist, however, that facts do not come to be recognized as such in a vacuum. We identify something as a fact in the context of antecedent patterns of interpretation, expectation, and habituation.[5] The fact may call some aspects of these patterns into question, but it cannot overthrow all of those aspects at once and still retain significance as a fact. Once established, a fact is always subject to change, partly as theoretical beliefs that inform it change and partly as new facts come into view. The identification of facts is a fallible enterprise, both within and outside the natural sciences.

Philosopher Charles Sanders Peirce argues convincingly that even the simplest sensate perceptions are *mediated* by inferences or habits of inference, usually unconscious, rather than being direct, unmediated recognitions of objects in the world. Such perceptual inference links a "monadic" experience of sheer quality with a "dyadic" experience of force or resistance (dyadic in that the perceiver is in relation to something felt as over against or in addition to himself or herself). Peirce asserts that this process of inference is "triadic," that is, on a third, mediating level in relation to the experience of quality and that of force or resistance.[6] Alfred North Whitehead later came to a similar conclusion, arguing that a sensate perception is a rather complicated "symbolic reference" joining clear and distinct experiences of "presentational immediacy" (sensible qualities) with more vague experiences of "causal efficacy" (feelings of relatedness to the past and of being influenced by the past).[7]

If particular perceptual facts are inferences, then surely the more large-scale findings of the natural sciences, commonly regarded at a given time as facts of nature, are inferences as well. As such, they are far from being immune to significant disagreement. We also should note that the wider, more pervasive *scale* of an assumed scientific fact, the more vulnerable it is to possible questioning, as shown by the examples cited above. A scientific fact is thus born within a matrix of assumptions and theories, or at the very least it is tinctured with elements of antecedent belief. As such, it is never completely beyond the pale of reasonable debate.

The upshot of this discussion is that factual assertions of the natural sciences are not fixed in place forever. They, like affirmations about values, can and do vary over time and with the differing contexts of changing scientific theories. Such variation usually is not taken to be proof that scientific facts are purely subjective, or that they have the character of arbitrary constructions of the mind with no credible claim to ontological status. In similar fashion, observations about continuing disagreements regarding assertions of value or about variations of such assertions over time should not be taken as proof that valuative assertions have no basis in reality. It could even be argued, although I shall not try to do so in any detail here, that fundamental moral principles in Western culture have endured longer and, on balance, have varied less over a period of nearly 2,000 years than have basic principles in the natural sciences in the past 400 years. We tend to exaggerate the extent of disagreement about such moral principles.[8]

Fourthly, just as we should not try to draw too sharp a distinction between facts and theories, especially when we are thinking of large-scale putative facts assumed or propounded in the natural sciences, so we also should be wary of drawing too sharp of a distinction between facts and values. These two also are interlinked in various ways. The intelligibility of nature, for example, is not only a fact but also a good. It is a good partly because without it we could have little hope of surviving and also because our understanding of various aspects of nature's functioning enables us to thrive as a species. In addition, this intelligibility may, if used wisely, enable us to help other species survive and thrive as well. Nature's intelligibility is good for still another reason. Humans value and cherish knowledge for its own sake, not just for its practical uses. We delight in the pursuit of a fuller understanding of ourselves and our world.

Furthermore, for someone to identify something as a fact is already to value it. It is selected as being something important, in the context of some sort of inquiry or experience. Any act of focusing or giving attention is thus at one and the same time an act of valuation; it is valuing a selected aspect of experience in general or of a particular experience, over all of the other aspects that might have been attended to instead. Facts have value as ways of testing our hypotheses about the world or suggesting the possibility of new theories about the world. Facts further responsible inquiry, and in that respect they are not simply facts but something to be valued as good.

Values also pervade our experiences of the world, showing those experiences to be not merely informative or matter-of-fact but valuative as well. I walk in a park on a warm summer's day and observe flowers, grass, trees, birds, squirrels, and a lake. If I am in a receptive mood, I apprehend these features of the park not only as facts but as values, as factors in an overall experience of refreshment, beauty, and repose. I tell my friend to look for an automobile of exquisite design in the parking lot, and he is able to find the car I had in mind without further description. I walk across the campus of my university and continually make unconscious judgments about aesthetic traits of buildings I see, landscapes through which I pass, and people I encounter. I also make more or less unconscious moral judgments about the way motorists drive as I cruise down the highway or about the way check-out clerks behave in a grocery store. And I instinctively experience moral sorrow and regret when I witness the ravaging of a mountain side and the despoliation of its adjacent wetlands and streams by the extensive mining of a company that has now ceased its operations in an area of the Rocky Mountains. In other words, aesthetic evaluations are not confined to art museums or concerts; we make them instinctively and all of the time. And moral judgments are not restricted to special circumstances. Both kinds of judgment tend to be pervasive features of everyday life. The same thing might be said about valuative experiences of a more distinctively religious character. We can be powerfully stirred with feelings of awe and reverence as we behold a vista of rugged, snow-draped mountains stretching to the horizon, a soon-to-be mother bird's patient, almost fastidious building of her nest, or the face and figure of a newborn child. The facts are taken into account in such experiences, but overtones of value surround these facts. In nature as lived, facts and values are mixed together; our experiences are of facts in contexts of value, and values in contexts of facts. To see where the one leaves off and the other begins is not always easy.

We can add two more considerations to what has already been said about the interpenetration of facts and values. The first is that some things are made true by our choices. For example, it is now a fact that human beings can routinely fly through the air, because some people in the past chose to develop the science of aeronautics by trying to build airplanes. Since choices are guided by values, it follows that some facts flow from acts of valuation. The second consideration is that assessments of the relevant facts are necessary if our attempts to realize values in practice are to be successful. Some things that we might desire to do we cannot do, because the facts do not permit the realization of our desire. In other cases, intimate knowledge of the facts is requisite to our achieving a goal or an ideal.

In light of observations such as the ones presented above, some philosophers have even been so bold as to contend that every experience of fact is inseparably linked to an experience of value, in other words, that the two are never separated from one another in the concreteness of our relations to other humans and to the nonhuman world. This linkage is always present, even though we can separate the two abstractly and analytically. Whitehead, for example, builds this notion into the heart of his metaphysics, claiming that achievements of the value of their own unique self-realizations are an essential part of the coming into being of actual entities, the fundamental realities of his system. To become a fact is also, therefore, to become an attainment of value, the value of this unique new being and whatever it can offer to the world. The new being can also, of course, be a disvalue to the extent that it introduces unwarranted discord and disruption or inteferes with the optimal self-realizations of future beings within their patterns of interrelatedness.[9] Philosopher William James, for his part, insists that "truth is *one species of good*, and not, as is usually supposed, a category distinct from good." His reason for this initially rather startling assertion is his conviction as a pragmatist that ideas are factual or true to the extent that they contribute something of profit or importance to our lives and help *"us to get into satisfactory relations with other parts of our experience."*[10] These laudable goals confer goodness upon truth and upon the search for truth. Even if we might not wish to go quite as far as Whitehead and James do in linking ascertainments or attainments of fact with realizations of values, we still can acknowledge that their systems of thought make provocative suggestions in this regard that stimulate us to reflect critically on an assumed sharp separation of fact from value.

The fifth and last criticism I want to make of the second argument for denying values to nature centers on the sharp contrast drawn in the argument between a supposed exactitude of scientific claims and their confirmations, on the one hand, and an alleged vagueness and looseness of valuative assertions and judgments, on the other hand, that are said to bar the latter from any sort of rational adjudication and doom them to a purely subjective status. My criticism of the denigration of valuative judgments and the consequent denial of values to nature based on this assumed contrast rests on two points. First, the argument under discussion fails to take into account the price that must be paid for exactitude in the natural sciences and elsewhere. As a consequence, it also fails to grasp both the necessity and the cognitive significance of a certain amount of inexactitude and vagueness in all of our interpretations of the world, scientific or otherwise, factual or valuative. These two points together imply that the radical distinction between scientific and valuative judgments taken for granted in the second argument is exaggerated and overblown.

Exactitude in the natural sciences is typically achieved at a level of abstraction where unavoidable variations in the analysis or measurement of the particular details of a given empirical situation are either deliberately or unconsciously ignored. The troublesome variations, in other words, are not *valued so much* as the smooth consistency that can be achieved in a more abstract portrayal. For example, two researchers at Princeton University found that in developing computer simulations of a northeastern forest in Connecticut, it was a mistake to try to include data detailing the exact location of every tree, the exact amount of light and shade each one gets, and other factors. So much detail, they soon discovered, magnifies the slightest errors in the gathering and assessment of empirical data and interferes in a fundamental way with the predictive and explanatory power the simulation can otherwise achieve. The professors concluded that they should seek more simplified models that could capture what they judged to be the essential features of a system, models that did not get bogged down in too much detail.[11] Of course, this conclusion means that exactitude of prediction and explanation, in this case as in so many cases of routine scientific research, is achieved at the price of neglecting many of the empirical details of the situation under study. The computer simulation is no doubt useful as an overall, aggregate representation of the forest, but it cannot pretend to capture the functioning of the forest in its every fine and variable detail. The simulation is highly exact, but its exactitude masks the inexactitude and fuzziness of the empirical situation. Hence, it is correctly regarded as only a "simulation" of and approximation to the particularities of that situation.

Scientists generally deem such a gap between theory formulation and theory testing, on the one hand, and the concreteness of experience, on the other hand, as unimportant in comparison to what can be gained, but recognition of the gap reveals the price that usually must be paid for a high degree of exactitude. Their regular and usually unthinking acceptance of the gap also shows scientists to be in the business of according greater *value* to those aspects of empirical situations that give support to their theories, over the stubborn aspects that do not. We can add this observation to what has already been said by showing that there are significant senses in which putative scientific facts are not only theory-laden but value-laden as well.

The highest degree of exactitude in the realm of thought is achieved in pure mathematics and formal logic, but this observation remains true only as long as no empirical interpretations or applications are made of these systems. Once experience is brought in, a situation similar to that of the study of the northeastern forest is introduced. The mathematical or logical systems become models or simulations whose exactitude contrasts with the relative vagueness and variability of the concrete experiences they interpret. As Robert T. Pennock notes,

> scientific claims are almost always to be understood in terms of approximation. That is, when scientists claim that a law is true what they mean is not that it is perfectly precise, but that it is accurate to within some stated limits of tolerance. However, being careful and explicit about margins of error and not claiming absolute precision is one of the strengths of science.[12]

Scientific principles and laws are thus to some significant extent idealizations of experience, not completely accurate descriptions of it. No two experiments or sets of empirical data (e.g., measurements) are ever exactly alike, but repeated experiments can rightly be deemed *alike enough* for researchers to regard them as continuing confirmations of scientific theories.

That there will always be aspects of the empirical situation that resist the neat categories and formulations of scientific theories, especially theories of a highly exact logical or mathematical character, becomes especially evident when we recall that any particular experience takes place in the context of a massive network of interrelated experiences and assumptions. The relative clarity and distinctness of the recognition of a finite fact, as Whitehead observes, can only be achieved against a background of something that cannot in its very nature be made clear and distinct, an encompassing "environment which, in its totality, we are unable to define." "The finite focus of clarity," he observes in another place, "fades into an environment of vagueness stretching into the darkness of what is merely beyond." Whitehead's conclusion is that "[t]he notion of a mere fact is the triumph of the abstractive intellect."[13] The notion of an exact fact has undoubted value and importance for all levels of human inquiry and practice, including those of the natural sciences, but the price paid for this notion is abstraction from the underlying, informing complexity and detail of lived experience. The old adage that the truth lies in the details is only partly correct. A significant amount of the whole truth also lies in the more general, vague, suffusing contexts presupposed in the clarity and precision of particular facts.

This observation leads directly to the next point I want to make in connection with my fifth criticism of the second argument for refusing to attribute values to nature. The point is that some aspects of our experience stubbornly resist the kinds of exact formulation that characterize certain scientific theories, but that this fact does not in itself imply that assertions or judgments about these aspects must be deemed purely subjective, or even that they are less objective than those to which we can give more precise expression. Some important features of the experienced world *require* the accommodation of vagueness in our thought and discourse if we are even to begin to do them justice. It sometimes turns out to be the case that the more pervasive or fundamental a feature of experience is, the less able we are to achieve completely clear conceptual interpretations of it. Importance and objectivity, on the one hand, and precision of formulation or confirmation, on the other hand, are thus on some occasions in tension with one another. The two do not necessarily go together. The second argument for denying values to nature assumes without question that they do.

An appropriate amount of vagueness in relation to some subject matters can be a virtue. Vagueness is not always a vice to be avoided at all costs as we aspire toward a more comprehensive understanding of the world. Hence, even if it could be shown that discourse about values tends generally to be more vague than discourse about putative scientific facts, or that consensus on valuative issues tends to be more difficult to achieve than consensus on scientific descriptions and explanations, it would not follow that valuative discourse is merely subjective. The status of values in nature would remain an open question, and it is worth reminding ourselves that the importance of values, at least in the human part of nature, is undeniable.

Peirce has two comments about these matters that are worth evoking. In one place in his writings he makes the point that

> [a]n opinion that something is *universally* true clearly goes further than experience can warrant. An opinion that something is necessarily true (that is, not merely is true in the existing state of things, but would be true in every state of things) equally goes further than experience will warrant. . . . I may add that whatever is held to be precisely true goes further than experience can possibly warrant.[14]

His statement is another reminder of the gap between the precision of certain concepts and the imprecision of experiences those concepts are used to interpret, a gap that we earlier identified as the price of exactitude. Peirce remarks in another place that "some of the most important [concepts] for everyday use are extremely vague," and he cites as an example the common belief, operative at the most basic level in the natural sciences as well as in ordinary human affairs, that there is order in the universe. He then goes on to ask:

> Could any laboratory experiments render that proposition more certain than instinct or common sense leaves it? It is ridiculous to broach such a question. But when anybody undertakes to say *precisely* what that order consists in, he will quickly find he outruns all logical warrant. Men who are given to defining too much inevitably run themselves into confusion in dealing with the vague concepts of common sense.[15]

Another example of such vagueness entering into the deliberations of natural scientists and others would be the most fundamental principles of reasoning that must be assumed in the construction of any logical, mathematical, or other carefully reasoned system of thought. Whatever precision we are able to attain in such systems is made possible by the unquestioning reliance we place on these principles. We can perhaps in some cases precisely state them, but we cannot always do so. We also cannot, without vicious circularity, justify our reliance on them.

Something similar could be said about natural scientists' belief in the reliability of the five senses, their assumption of the possibility of providing causal explanations for the occurrences of events, and their confidence in successful prediction as a test of truth. We should also note in this connection scientists' dependence on values such as those indicated earlier. The whole enterprise of scientific investigation rests on these values, but scientists *qua* scientists do not critically analyze them or seek to confirm their metaphysical status, so we can see that exactitude and vagueness are not necessarily antithetical to one another. They frequently go together, because exactitude in one area of our thought is made possible by vagueness in another. To associate objectivity exclusively with what can be precisely articulated and confirmed, and therefore to relegate everything else to the realm of mere subjectivity, is to have a narrow, uninformed conception of objective knowledge.

THE THIRD ARGUMENT:
VALUES ROOTED IN FEELING RATHER THAN INTELLECT

We can begin a critical response to the third argument for separating values from nature by observing that, contrary to the argument, feelings in many situations do have cognitive import. A physician asks a patient, "Where does it hurt?" She does so because she is seeking information based on a feeling of pain that can be put to use in the treatment of the patient's injury or illness. When a detective investigating an alleged suicide says, "I have a hunch that there is something amiss here; something just does not feel right about this case," he is taking seriously his feeling state as a starting point of inquiry, an inquiry that eventually may lead to his gathering sufficient evidence to charge someone with murder. In similar fashion, a philosopher may find herself initially responding to a seemingly persuasive argument with a gnawing feeling that it is deficient in some way, although she cannot quite, at this moment, say why. She then proceeds to develop a line of criticism that exposes the argument's faults as she comes more clearly to articulate and understand them. Feelings—even quite vague or jumbled feelings—often can be rendered into distinctive claims, and these claims can be tested for their truth or falsity by evidence and argument. Commonplace examples such as these imply that feeling and intellect are not as opposed to one another or as distinct from one another as the third argument assumes. Feelings can be an important ingredient in cognitive judgments.

The hard-and-fast distinction between feeling and intellect assumed in the third argument can be countered from another direction with the recognition that all thought, factual or valuative, scientific as well as aesthetic, moral, or religious, rests in the final analysis on something closely akin to feeling, in James' sense of "a *that* which is not yet any definite *what*, tho' ready to be all sorts of whats,"[16] a relatively amorphous field of experience waiting to be sorted out, abstracted from, conceptualized, and understood. Here there is not yet critical detachment but absorption, oneness with the flow of undifferentiated, complexly interwoven aspects of experience. The form of the sortings, abstractings, and conceptualizings will vary depending on the purpose or point of view. This purpose or point of view may be (1) the search for accurate descriptions and explanations of phenomena; (2) the need to determine a course of action; or (3) the endeavor conceptually to articulate and critically to assess intimations of value. These purposes and points of view also may intermingle, to the extent that each is seen to have relevance to the others in a given context.

The main point to notice is that there is no compelling reason to think that inquiry into the valuative dimensions of experience, (3) above, is any more (or less) dependent on a background of feeling than are the other two types of inquiry, (1) and (2) above. In all three cases, appropriate universes of discourse exist, a wealth of relevant conceptual categories and relations developed over the course of human history and cultural development into which as yet unconceptualized experiences can be drawn for elucidations of their meaning. In all three cases, therefore, the means for attaining generality and critical distance lie ready at hand, and cognitive judgments can be made. Judgments about questions of value, no less than those about fact and explanation or courses of action, can be based on the discernment of relevant features of a situation and thoughtful consideration of alternative possibilities posed by the situation. With long habituation, modes of conceptualization and interpretation tend to become second nature; this point holds true as much for judgments of value as it does for judgments of the other two sorts. Given the complexity and volatility of experience—to say nothing about continuing innovations in conceptual schemes stemming from irrepressible human inventiveness and imagination—there also is room for differing interpretations in the three areas of experience and thought. No absolute, final, indisputable truths or resolutions are to be found in any of these domains. At best, putative truths or resolutions will be probable or generally reliable.

John Dewey warns against the vice of an "arbitrary 'intellectualism'" that restricts nature or reality to what is (or can be made) entirely distinct and explicit, forgetting that "[w]hat is really 'in' experience extends much further than that which at any time is *known*." Behind the distinct and evident, rightly to be prized for the clarity of understanding they can provide, lie "the dark and twilight" of what is not and cannot be captured in clear conceptualizations at any given time, the "vague and unrevealed" background of "primary experience" in all of its mystery and depth. Dewey also notes that "cognitive experience must originate within that of a noncognitive sort," and that the "intellectual and cognitive," in relation to the fullness of concrete experience, are "secondary and derived." To identify truth about the world only with that which is clear and distinct is to ignore the bulk of its reality as presented in experience. It is to forget "that context of non-cognitive but experienced subject-matter which gives what is *known* its import." Hence, it is not just articulations of value but identifications and explanations of fact as well that depend crucially upon a suffusing context of what we here term *feeling*, the indistinct, dense, undiscriminated "primary experience" that Dewey associates most closely with the ordinary, day-to-day experiences of the human organism as it seeks continually to adjust itself to its natural and social environment.[17]

It is not at all surprising that there should be this intimate dependence of theoretical thought, as well as of judgments concerning action and value upon feeling, when we reflect on the fact that we are not free-floating intellects but *embodied* beings with profound feelings of interconnection and interaction with the surrounding world. These feelings are prior to our articulations and understandings of them, and they are the final tests of the adequacy of those articulations and understandings. What we seek to achieve in our metaphysical inquiries into the nature of nature is an understanding of the world as it presents itself to us in our experience. Since this experience is shot through with apprehensions and responses that persistently pose issues of value—needs, desires, anxieties, aspirations, enjoyments, loves, hates, attractions, repulsions, satisfactions, regrets, sorrows, struggles, pains, terrors, inspirations, and the like— our attempts at adequate understanding must strive to take fully into account these dimensions of experience and their valuative implications.

These modes of experience are about ourselves, to be sure, but they are about more than ourselves. They are about the world in which we are embodied and embedded as one sort of natural species among others. It is beyond dispute that such aspects of experience are vital and indispensable in our everyday lives. To insist that they relate only to ourselves and to values we conjure up wholly within ourselves, and that they imply nothing of importance about values in a nature that includes us but also extends beyond us, is to sunder what is of central significance in our lives from the wider world of which we are a part. This approach requires disconnection of one domain of the experienced world—the one that relates most closely to issues of value—from its other domains. Such an abrupt breach within the field of experience is arbitrary, forced, and untenable.

However, as Dewey properly reminds us, feelings are not by themselves values. They are only candidates for value—*problematic goods*, he terms them— that to be finally judged as such must be put to the test of experience, reflection, criticism, and judgment. To feel strong desire for some object, for example, is not the same thing as recognizing that object as morally desirable or according it positive value in some other sense. The fact of something's "being desired only raises the *question* of its desirability; it does not settle it."[18] Similarly, to experience rapture in contemplating a work of art is not automatically to certify it as a great work, nor does a work's proven ability to evoke profound feelings of any sort suffice to make it such. More than feelings are at stake in such matters, although feelings are certainly involved.

A feeling in itself counts no more as a significant value than a bare sensation constitutes a significant fact about the world. Responsible value judgments must interweave feelings, sensations, conceptual categories, and intellectual appraisals just as responsible factual judgments must. To act from blind feeling with no constraint of thought is the source of much deplorable evil in the world. Feeling alone hardly constitutes the essence of moral value or of any other kind of value. Our feelings must be brought before the court of reason and appraised in the context of other aspects of experience, anticipated as well as recollected, before they can hope to qualify as reliable guides to thought and action.

Impartiality and critical distance are of great importance in this process of critical reflection. It is not unusual for critical assessment of values to require that we judge or act in ways that *run counter to* our most intimate and compelling feelings, the feelings in which we may be most directly and immediately absorbed. A soldier in battle must struggle to act against his instinctive dread of injury or death in order to carry out faithfully what he rationally judges to be his duty. A person in desperate financial straits may have a powerful yearning to embezzle funds but also may have to conclude in light of reasons, and not just other, conflicting feelings, that to give in to this yearning would be a serious wrong. Such conflicts between feelings and values are commonplaces of the moral life, showing that projecting our thinking beyond the immediate situation and beyond attitudes or beliefs toward which we may at a given moment be emotionally inclined, is as incumbent upon us when we weigh questions concerning moral value as when we consider questions about fact. The same point can be made with respect to questions about aesthetic or religious value.

The third argument for the separation of values from nature fails to take into account the need for critical distance or dispassionate inquiry in making value judgments. More fundamentally, it does not even recognize the role of *judgments* in the domain of values, regarding valuative utterances as no more than simple expressions or evocations of feeling. Dewey's analysis of the relation of values to feelings is more adequate and convincing:

> Values . . . may be connected inherently with liking, and yet not with *every* liking but only with those that judgment has approved, after examination of the relation upon which the object liked depends. A casual liking is one that happens without knowledge of how it occurs nor to what effect. The difference

between it and one which is sought because of a judgment that it is worth having and is to be striven for, makes just the difference between enjoyments which are accidental and enjoyments that have value and hence a claim upon our attitude and conduct.[19]

The point holds for assessments of values in the nonhuman parts of nature just as it does for valuative judgments about human social relations, artistic creations, or religious outlooks and practices. In none of these cases is there persuasive reason for thinking that values depend *exclusively* on such feelings as those of desire or repulsion, like or dislike, approval or disapproval, pleasure or pain.

THE STATUS OF NATURAL VALUES

We have critically examined three influential arguments for the claim that values are projected upon nature by human subjects rather than being present in nature. Each of the arguments has been shown to be flawed in basic respects, and thus each is unpersuasive. The way is now clear for a positive case to be made for the presence of values in nature. If values have status in nature itself and are therefore in some sense objective, what is that sense? If values inhere in nature, how should we interpret this inherence?

In what follows, I sketch a *relational* view of natural values intended to show that values are present in the *interactions* of subjects and objects rather than located in either aspect by itself. This relational or interactional view implies, as we shall see, that it is just as much of a mistake to think of values as objective in a strictly antecedent, in-itself sense as it is to think of them, after the fashion of the three arguments discussed above, as purely subjective. The new mistake would lie in regarding natural values as being complete and self-contained, prior to and independent of all acts of interpretation, *simply out there in the world waiting to be passively identified by perceiving subjects.* Such a construal of the status of values in nature is closely akin to the direct realism attributed to Aristotle in chapter 2 and shown there to be untenable. This type of realism, with its assumption that knowledge consists in a simple, unmediated correspondence between ideas in the mind and traits of nature—whether associated with facts, descriptions, or explanations, on the one hand, or with values, on the other hand—stands in sharp contrast to the empirical-constructive approach to the nature of nature endorsed and defended in that chapter.

Values in nature are neither passively identified nor sheerly constructed. They are not merely in nature, nor are they merely in us. Recognition of specific values results from active interpretations of aspects of experience that contain implications for valuative judgments and commitments. A potential value is felt, contemplated, and responded to here, but as located there. We do the interpreting, but we are interpreting something that presents itself in experience as belonging to the world. The experience does not automatically sort itself out into types of value, nor does it judge by itself the relative importance of its various demands for valuational response. We do the judging and sorting but with the stimulation of and constant reference to what is experienced.

The valuative aspects of experience have a persistence and a compellingness that cry out for interpretive reactions. When those reactions are made, conceptual constructions are brought into play, and when we allow our continuing thought and ongoing experience to test and refine these constructions, we are in the process of making responsible judgments about values in nature. Thus reliable claims about values in nature emerge from interactions between the compulsions and constraints of experience and imaginative conjectures about the world, just as reliable factual, descriptive, and explanatory claims about natural phenomena do.

From the perspective of this relational view of the status of values in the world, it is entirely correct to say that were there no valuers, there would be no values. But it is equally correct to say, on the basis of the empirical-constructive approach to the nature of nature discussed earlier, that were there no seekers for facts, there would be no such things as facts. Neither of these observations implies subjectivism. Both call attention to an unavoidable relational character of all judgments about the world and of all putative truths about the world. This relational character does not strip judgments concerning truths or values of their possible objectivity; it only requires that objectivity be conceived of in a different way from the traditional notion of an antecedent, ready-made world waiting to be passively described.

Self, no less than world, is a construction or interpretation of the dense plenum of experience that selects out aspects of experience and gives them a distinctive character. A human baby is not initially aware of itself experiencing or even of itself as such, yet it experiences, continuously and persistently, only gradually learning to separate itself from a surrounding world within the field of that experience. Throughout life, self and world continue to be differentiated within this field of experience. To determine boundaries between the two is not always easy, since they interfuse one another, and their borders are sometimes fuzzy and indistinct. Thus self, or the concept of an experiencer, presupposes experience, not the other way around.[20] Self has meaning only as set in contrast with world, showing the two conceptions to be correlative rather than separate.

Recognition of these truths enables us to avoid the subjectivist turn of the modern era, an approach reflected in the radical subjectivizing of natural values that persists into our own time. This recognition also enables us to see through the illusion of a purely objective world devoid of interpretation and perspective, a world just as it is in and of itself, apart from all experience and conceptualization. Such a world is by definition inaccessible and unknowable; to try to imagine it is pointless, and it is even more pointless to insist upon its reality.

The world for us, the lived world, is the world of experience and conceptualization; there is not and cannot be for us any other world. The notion of an in-itself world is not only problematic, it is inherently contradictory. It is so because this would be a world experienced from no perspective or combination of perspectives, hence, not experienced at all. The very notion of "world" is itself perspectival, the outcome of a point of view, a way of interpreting and arranging the complexities of experience.

This is a world that exists only in relation to its perceivers and conceivers,[21] and its values, no more or less than its factual truths, have their being only in and through this relation. To be, in any meaningful sense of the term, is to be in relation, just as to be true or valuable is to be such in relation. Facts do not just drift in a sea of absolute reality. They are outcomes of inquiry and hence exist only in relation to or in the contexts of the processes of testing and affirming that give birth to and sustain them.[22] Values also exist in relation to those who value, those who search for satisfactory ways to articulate or respond to dimensions of value pervading experience.

The upshot of the relational view, as I have outlined it so far, comes to this. Take self away, and world collapses. Take world away, and self collapses. Each requires and depends upon the other, and both are inferences from dim but insistent awareness of a teeming, suffusing field of experience that forever eludes full understanding or complete conceptualization. There is thus no such thing as pure, self-contained object or pure, self-contained subject, and there is no absolute demarcation between the two. There is no prospect of a final fathoming of the mysteries of the world, because all knowing is perspectival and therefore partial, because there can be no such thing as an absolute, all-encompassing perspective. This observation holds true because a perspectiveless perspective is an obvious contradiction, and an absolute perspective or ensemble of all perspectives would have to be a perspectiveless perspective. Further evidence of the truth of the observation is that there is an inexhaustible infinitude of possible perspectives on even the most trivial features of experience, as we noted in chapter 2.[23]

Finally, and most importantly for the themes of the present chapter, there is no privileging of facts over values in this outlook; each is the outcome of processes of inquiry into aspects of experience that are of interest or importance for that inquiry. To attribute values to nature in a relational sense of that attribution, or to say that values "inhere" in nature in that sense, is no more perplexing or problematic than to attribute facts to the world or to claim that scientific laws, theories, and explanations pertain to the real world—in the same relational manner.

So far we have dwelt on values in nature as viewed from the standpoint of human experience and conceptualization. What if humans were removed from the world? In that event, it is obvious that values specific to the human part of nature would cease to exist. For example, no values pertaining specifically to interactions of human beings with one another would exist, because there would be no human beings to interact with one another. There also would be no values stemming from or pertaining to human traditions, institutions, or creations of human cultures in general. And there would be no issues of value concerning interactions of human beings with the rest of nature. But would any natural values at all then exist? Would not the relational view of the status of values outlined above require that they disappear? My answer is that natural values would still exist and be prevalent in the world, because they would be present in the relations of all of the nonhuman valuers or searchers for value to their natural environments.

Animals also respond to their experiences by constructing their world, both with respect to important facts and interrelations of facts in that world and with respect to issues of value in that world. They crave and plan; they fear and avoid. They usually cherish their young, and they have their favorite foods. Many of them give every indication of taking delight in the sport of play and in the celebration of their lives. They may not construct conceptually, lacking the resources of language and complex cultures and the capacities of large, highly developed brains, but they do construct in some sense, carving out for themselves a sense of the world and of its opportunities, threats, and demands. Values exist, then, from their perspectives or contexts of relation to the world, since they not only have feelings of pleasure and pain, preference and aversion, serenity and fear, and the like but also make judgments and decisions about appropriate responses to those feelings. These judgments and decisions may be made only instinctively in the cases of most kinds of animals, but they are nonetheless made.

Even plants, in their own characteristic ways, can be said to attribute, from their own perspectives, a relational status to values in the world, a status independent of human beings. A plant carves out an environment for itself by the pressure of its roots and the insistent growth of its branches. It may move in the direction of the circuiting sun, array itself splendidly for pollination by insects, protect itself from predators by special secretions, or have means for sheltering itself from the cold. There are things in the world it responds to as having value and other things it responds to as having disvalue. It does not conceptualize, and its experience of the world, if we can refer to it as that, is presumably devoid of even the slightest amount of consciousness. So it does not differentiate itself from the world in any but the most primitive and minimal ways. Nevertheless, it sustains values in a relational fashion through its construction of a world and its responses to that world.

We humans can try, with empathetic imagination, to enter into the world as seen from the perspectives of nonhuman organisms. We can strive to think what it would be like to live the life of a fish in the depths of a sunless sea, of a plant probing for water and minerals in the soil, of a hawk riding currents of the air while in search of its prey, of an ant making its home in a rotting log, of a black bear pawing that ant into its mouth, of a fly that alights on our window screen, or of a bacterium in another organism's gut. However, there is much that must remain forever strange here, despite the intersections of our perspectives with those of other creatures on earth. There are delight, mystery, and sometimes dread in our encounters with this multiple otherness of perspectives, as well as fascination in musing on what we seem to share with the myriad nonhuman forms of life. To restrict the variegated realm of values to ourselves alone seems arrogant and presumptuous in the extreme. My thesis is that there are no such things as nonrelational, nonperspectival, noncontextual values, but also that valuative relations, perspectives, and contexts are to be found throughout the biosphere. They are not confined to human beings.

EXAMPLES OF VALUES IN NATURE

If, as is assumed throughout this book, humans are an integral part of nature, it follows from that fact alone that nature contains values. Valuative convictions, commitments, and concerns are fundamental features of human cultures in all places and at all times. They play a central role in the day-to-day lives of individual human beings and in their interactions with one another. Moral, legal, religious, and aesthetic creations and institutions give decisive evidence of the importance of values in human thought and practice and thus in the human part of nature. The natural sciences also would not exist without specific kinds of assumed values, as we saw earlier in this chapter, and developments of technology from earliest times have posed numerous possibilities and problems of value (including the current ecological crisis) with which human beings have had to grapple. The prominence of valuative concerns in human life is not at all surprising in light of the attribution of purposive freedom to human beings, argued for in chapter 2. Purposive freedom is the power of choice among alternatives in light of reasons, and this power allows for, and indeed requires, consideration of the relative values of the alternatives available for choice in any given situation.

Our main concern in this chapter, however, is not with the values that permeate human cultures, institutions, and creations but with those that can be ascribed to the nonhuman part of nature. We have seen that there are no persuasive reasons to deny inherent, nonsubjective values to nature and good reasons to ascribe such values to it, at least in the relational fashion that has been characterized and defended. Our discussion of this issue so far, however, has been extremely general. Let us now try to make it more specific by considering some examples of the kinds of value that can be found in the nonhuman part of nature. This is a large topic, and I do not pretend to do justice to it here, but a brief consideration of a few examples can at least suggest the variety and range of the natural values whose metaphysical status has been the principal theme of this chapter. I shall have more to say about values in nature when I make a case for a religion of nature in part 3.

The first example of values in nature is *life*, not just human life but the life of all of the creatures on earth. Our lives are of obvious and instinctive value to us, and we can surmise that the same is true for other organisms. Paul Tillich notes that organisms accept "want, toil, insecurity, pain, possible destruction" for the sake of remaining alive and for the sake of the lives of their progeny. He calls this organic self-affirmation in the face of adversity and danger "vitality," and he emphasizes its close analogy to human courage.[24] The persistent affirmation of life by biological organisms implies the value of their lives to these organisms, as a similar self-affirmation implies the value of our lives to us. Since the affirmation of life is pervasive in the biosphere, we can conclude that the value of life also is pervasive there.

Second, *biological species* have value. It was mentioned above that part of the story of the affirmation of life that is pervasive on earth is the effort that organisms expend to ensure the survival of their progeny. These progeny or future generations of organisms have value because they are valued by their parents, valued so their own particular species of organisms may continue to survive. We can recognize the implied value of progeny, and thus of species, from another angle by noting the large amount of time and effort expended in nature by sexually reproducing organisms to find and mate with suitable partners of the opposite sex. And of course without ongoing progeny, new individuals of a given species would cease to exist, and the value of the lives of those individuals would vanish from nature.

Third, if life is valuable throughout the biosphere, then the conditions necessary for maintenance of the diverse forms of life also must be valuable. These conditions include not only the other organisms that make their distinctive and necessary contributions to the life of any particular organism but also the nonorganic features of the environment that are constantly relied upon and utilized by organisms. There is value, in other words, in the *particular ecological systems* whose various components work conjointly to carve out places for and to contribute to the maintenance of all of the life-forms within those systems. Not only are individual lives valuable then, but the specific ecosystems that contain and sustain those ecosystems have value. This is thus another example of natural values.

Fourth, particular ecosystems are dependent on other ecosystems for their viability, and ultimately they are all bound by their complex interdependencies with one another and by common conditions of the nonbiological constituents of the earth on which they rely (e.g., the energy of the sun on which all organisms finally depend; the availability of carbon dioxide, oxygen, and water; the quality of air, soil, and water). So the *biosphere* as a whole can be said to have crucial value and to constitute a fourth kind of value in nature. Humans, as well as all other organic species, must be able to count on the biosphere's continuing health and vitality for their own survival and flourishing. This inescapable fact lies at the heart of ecological science and ethics.

However, is not the basic reasoning behind the claims for these four values in nature open to a fundamental criticism? From the mere fact that something is valued, it does not follow necessarily that something is a value. Granted that life is pervasively valued in nature, this fact does not in itself establish life as a value. A similar point was made earlier in discussing Dewey's response to the question of whether values can be said to derive directly from feelings such as those of need, desire, or preference. Dewey argues that they cannot, because judgments about the implications for value of such feelings must be brought into play. Feelings present candidates for values, but they cannot by themselves establish values. Similarly, acts of valuing also present candidates for values, but values cannot be said to follow directly from those acts of valuing. Let us accept Dewey's challenge then and see if there is a way to arrive at the more considered judgment that life in all of its diverse forms on earth has value. If the challenge can be met, then we will have established that the presence of the various forms of life on earth, the continuation of these forms through successive generations, and the necessary conditions for the presence and continuation of these forms are all natural values.

My response to the challenge is relatively simple but, I think, convincing. I have already argued that values, as well as facts, are relational, perspectival, or contextual. Were there no life-forms, there would be no values, because only half of the valuational equation would exist. We would have a "there" but no "here," no angle of experience or vision from which assessments of potential values could be made. In a deeper sense, not even a "there" would exist, because "there" has meaning only in contrast with "here." The notion or impression of a world is, as argued earlier, itself perspectival or relational. To be is to be in relation, just as to be true or valuable is to be such in relation. Organisms can be said to make assessments of value and disvalue in their ongoing lives, some of which are borne out in their experiences and others of which are not. Usually these assessments are unconscious and instinctive, but they still must meet such tests as compatibility with patterns of the past or suitability for new circumstances. Living beings, then, are preconditions for values, since in order for values to exist, there must be valuers or assessers of value. Living beings are of incontrovertible importance and value, because they are the necessary basis for the existence of all other values. If anything else is to be of value, life must be of value.

I cannot imagine a more fundamental argument for the value of life than the one just offered, but perhaps such arguments are unnecessary. All assessments of value have to rest at some point on something intuitively seen to be of value, otherwise we would have an infinite regress of such arguments. Nothing seems to me to be more obviously of value than life itself. Of course, a certain quality of life also is assumed in the recognition of life as valuable. Not every conceivable form of life would be of inherent value at all times. For example, a life wracked by endless, excruciating, irremediable pain, suffering, and misery might cease to have positive inherent value for a person, and that person might be justified in reqesting that his or her life not be prolonged by medical measures.[25]

It could now be objected that these observations about the value of life would hold even if there were only one type of life on earth. Why must there be so many? Why should we value the incredible profusion of forms of life on earth? Posed here is the question of whether *diversity of life-forms* is a value. I believe strongly that it is, and I propose that it be considered a fifth kind of natural value. It ought to be considered such, because life on earth is made possible by the interdependence of a large number of different biological species. A single form of life could not exist without the network of other forms on which its life depends. Air-breathing animals could not exist, for example, without the oxygen contributed to the atmosphere by plants, nor could they exist without other animals or plants to eat; beavers could not live as they do without twigs and bark to eat or logs with which to build their dams and lodges; and so on. The life of each organism is made possible by the occupational niche provided for it in a complicated ecosystem made up of many other organisms.

However, an abundance of life-forms is not only of value because of its being essential to the maintenance of each type of organic life within a complex, interdependent ecosystem. It is also of value because it promotes a sixth kind of natural value: *creativity*. Not only individuals and species are diverse in nature. There also is diversity within the genes of individuals within species. This diversity is not static but continues to develop through mutations. In this way, there is variability within species that allows for the natural selection of variations of genetic makeup best suited for adaptation and survival within changing ecosystems. This selection process is the secret of the continuous generation of new species of organisms and thus of biological evolution. It also accounts for the diversity of life-forms providing the complex ecological niches that allow particular life-forms to flourish. So if life is valuable, it follows that the diversity of life is valuable, and that the creativity that produces that diversity also is valuable.

At this point, another objection could be raised. If life is so valuable, why is it so commonly squandered on earth? Organisms must prey on one another to remain alive: this is a large part of what the ecological interdependence touted above comes down to. I shall make one brief response to this objection here. Most of my response to this important question is reserved for chapter 7, where I consider some major objections to a religion of nature. It is true that the vitality of the predator can hardly be seen as a positive value from the perspective of the prey animal,[26] and that we ourselves could not long survive without sacrificing the lives of other organisms on a daily basis. Death is the price paid for life, in this as in other ways (e.g., the extinction of organisms of one species that makes way for the proliferation of organisms of another species), but the need to sacrifice one form of life for another does not negate the value of the life that is sacrificed. Such sacrifice must be seen as a conflict of goods. The life that is given up remains a value, even as it is given up so that another kind of life may be sustained.

So far we have found reasons to affirm six basic values in the nonhuman part of nature: life itself, the enduring species to which individual lives belong, the particular ecosystems in which these individuals and their species make their livings, the whole biosphere on earth in which all of these particular ecosystems are conjoined, the teeming diversity of forms of life, and the creativity that gave rise to that diversity and continues to generate new types of life.

I want to mention other values in nature in addition to these six that cluster around the fundamental value of life. *Splendor* is a seventh value. Under the category of splendor I include nature's vastness, complexity, power, and beauty. The vastness of nature is beyond imagination, consisting as it does of countless galaxies traversing reaches of space remote from our tiny solar system, places to which we could not travel in many lifetimes, even if we could achieve velocities approaching the speed of light. This vastness also includes ranges of the incredibly small, far below the scope or ken of ordinary human experience.

Nature's complexity of organization and functioning is endlessly intriguing, and it is being made more evident by continuing new discoveries.

Nature's power to create or destroy is astounding, as seen in the continuing saga of cosmic, geological, and biological evolution, the emergence of varied human languages and cultures, the extinction of most past species, or the impacts of earthquakes, floods, and fires. Finally, the sheer beauty of nature's vistas, its plays of light and shadow, its textures, tastes, sounds, and smells, its alterations of day and night and changes of seasons, its mountains, hills, oceans, bays, and rivers, its grasses, flowers, trees, and profusion of other kinds of creatures, is haunting and overwhelming. The fact that we are not always fully aware of nature's power and beauty can be attributed to deficiency of attention, to a mind dulled by long familiarity with what, experienced for the first time, would be so miraculous and dumbfounding as to defy belief.

These four features of nature—its vastness, complexity, power, and beauty—singly or in combination, have immense aesthetic significance and value. We know from a long history of human cultures that they can evoke profound and diverse aesthetic responses in us. There may be ways in which one or more of them do so for other creatures as well. The Western Meadowlark, for example, seems to revel in the cool beauty of a dawning spring day, making its own contribution to the morning's loveliness with the exuberance of its lilting song. And the female peacock is invited to be a critic of the variously patterned, gorgeously colored tail feathers of potential mates, proudly displayed for her appraisal like works of art in a gallery. Is it all just sex and territoriality? Perhaps not. Perhaps something akin to our own aesthetic sensibilities also is involved. At the very least, there is strong warrant for affirming that although the aesthetic experiences of nature we know at firsthand are human, they are not just about us but about a world beyond ourselves that includes us and all of our achievements as mere samplings of its inexhaustible splendor.

An eighth type of value inherent in nature is its *practical* value. Nature's principles, laws, operations, and entities have the practical value of nurturing and sustaining life by allowing the regularity of functioning to the bodies of organisms, providing organisms with food and shelter, giving them various means of protection from danger, and contributing in other ways to the zest and quality of their lives. This value is already implicit in the values of ecosystems and the biosphere, mentioned earlier, but it deserves mention as a significant type of value in its own right. When some aspect of nature has practical value for some other, the former aspect can be said to be of instrumental value for the latter. But something's being of instrumental value in one context does not preclude its also being of intrinsic value (i.e., value in and of itself) in another. Implicit in what I have already said about the fundamental value of life is that all forms of life have intrinsic value, but these forms can have, and often do have, instrumental value for other life-forms. The most obvious examples are when one form of life is used as food or as shelter for another.

Let me now make more explicit the distinctions among intrinsic, instrumental, and inherent values that I have been assuming. The practical or instrumental values now under discussion are not, as such, intrinsic values. That is, while they have great value as a means to valuative ends, they are not valuative ends in themselves. Nevertheless, practical values are inherent in nature, because they are fundamental to the ways in which it works. If practical values did not inhere in nature, the intrinsic values that also are inherent in it would not exist. Nature is an interweaving of means and ends, and both have ineluctable value, so both intrinsic and instrumental values are inherent in the sense of being aspects of the real world, not something artificially imposed upon it from without by the whims of human subjectivity.

It also should be noted that human beings, conceiving of the world as providing a storehouse of "natural resources" for their use does not necessarily mean that they must be bent upon ruthless exploitation of the natural environment—even though exploitation has sadly and all too often been their tendency. There is considerable truth (as well as danger) in the concept of natural resources, for it implies the recognition of a basic type of value present throughout nature, a type of value upon which we, no less than other biological species, crucially depend.

All of the aforementioned values have moral import because, as fundamental types of value, they imply urgent obligation on the part of humans to recognize, respect, and seek to preserve them. Thus nature also can be said to possess a ninth type of value, *moral* value. As creatures gifted with the powers of rational deliberation, calculation of consequences, and freedom to choose among alternative courses of action, ours is a grave moral obligation to ensure that our human enterprises are and continue to be in harmony with what goes on elsewhere in nature and with the well-being and flourishing of all of its other creatures. We are part of a much larger community of beings that includes human communities but extends far beyond them.

As citizens of this larger community, we have rights and privileges, but we also have serious responsibilities. Our responsibilities to the nonhuman dimensions of nature stem partly from the indisputable fact that we are part of the earth's biosphere and cannot survive without its continuing health and vitality. But more fundamentally, they flow from such values in nature as its diverse, ever-evolving, subtly entwined varieties of life and its majestic, commanding splendor, as well as from the practical values of everything in nature supporting, subserving, and making possible its other values. Among the nonhuman part of nature's bedrock values, then, are its moral values, the numerous ways in which it commends itself to our moral consideration and concern.

A tenth and final type of natural value that can illustrate the presence of inherent values in nature is *religious* values. Explication and defense of these religious values constitute the principal burden of this book and will be our main concern in part 3, so I need not say anything further about them here but shall only mention them in passing. In summary, we have seen that nature exhibits at least ten types of inherent value: life, species, ecosystems, biosphere, diversity, creativity, and splendor, and its practical, moral, and religious values. In addition to these positive values, however, there also are negative values or disvalues in nature, and to them we must now briefly turn our attention.

DISVALUES IN NATURE

To think of nature as possessing only positive values would be as wrong as to assume it to be devoid of values. Disvalues as well as values exist in nature, and it is essential that we recognize both. We have seen that values in nature are relational, perspectival, or contextual. The same holds true for disvalues. There are perspectives from which a feature of nature can rightly be seen as a value, and perspectives from which that same feature can rightly be seen as a disvalue.

For example, life is a value to the being that possesses it, and it is not just that the lives of animals and other organisms justifiably matter to them. Their lives can be of great value to us as well. We can experience fascination and enjoyment in watching animals, insects, and plants work to survive and flourish. We can applaud and seek to conserve the manifold shrewd and stubborn strategems they have developed for sustaining their lives. We can generally be glad that they persist in being alive, just as we are glad that we are alive. Their lives are good to them and generally can be good to us as well.[27] However, the ecological interdependence of organisms requires that the lives of some must be forfeited in order to sustain the lives of others. I noted earlier that the forfeited life remains good, even though it must be sacrificed for the sake of the life of another. From this reasoning it follows that the forfeiture of life, so prevalent throughout nature, is a disvalue as well as a value. It is a value from the perspective of organisms it allows to flourish, but it is a disvalue from the perspective of organisms whose lives must be given up.

More generally, death is the disvalue that must be present throughout nature so that life itself might exist. The pervasiveness of death is required by the way nature's system of ecological interdependence, or more specifically its so-called food chain, works. The feeding of organisms on one another is the chief way in which the energy of the sun is made available to nurture the diversity of organisms on earth. We also should acknowledge that it is not just the death of particular organisms that is commonplace in nature, but that whole species also have frequently become extinct due to natural causes. The death of individuals and the loss of species then are widespread disvalues in nature.

Not all organisms are able to find sufficient food to survive, so starvation is another kind of disvalue often found in nature. It also is part of the process of selection by which biological evolution functions. Starvation helps filter out those less fit to survive, those less resourceful in finding food for themselves and their young. In some circumstances, it may pave the way for genetic variants to take hold in the population of a species and eventually allow the emergence of a new species in place of the old one. Thus starvation is a disvalue that can help make possible the good of greater diversity. Starvation can be of practical or instrumental value, even as it is an intrinsic disvalue. That some organisms must starve in nature is deeply regrettable and sad. The statement remains implacably true, even though starvation also may sometimes subserve ends that are good.

Another kind of disvalue in nature is suffering and pain. Starvation causes suffering and pain, as predation often does, at least for organisms with sufficiently developed nervous systems to experience pain. Injuries resulting from accidents, which are not infrequent in nature, also cause suffering and pain. Once again, these phenomena may serve good purposes. They may help keep animals alert and on guard against danger and enable them to learn other valuable lessons from their experience, but no matter what their instrumental uses, suffering and pain are intrinsic disvalues from the standpoint of the organisms experiencing them. The truth of this statement is brought home to us when we recall how much we ourselves want to avoid suffering and pain whenever we can, and with good reason. We also confirm its truth when we remember how morally wrong it would be to wantonly or needlessly inflict suffering or pain on any creature. Death, starvation, suffering, and pain are not just imputed by humans as disvalues to nature—these disvalues are pervasive characteristics of nature itself.

Disease is still another disvalue, one that may wipe out whole groups of organisms or cause them much suffering and pain. It is notable that disease usually can be attributed to microorganisms seeking to maintain their lives in the world, so disease is yet another way in which the flourishing of some creatures is at cross-purposes with that of others, at least in the short run. Loss of mates and progeny and the deterioration of habitats are still other kinds of disvalues, as is the overpopulation of one or more species at the expense of others. Nature is a dynamic, volatile system, as we have seen. Its various aspects are radically dependent on one another, and all are therefore made highly vulnerable to change. The future is not always dependable for nature's creatures and can bring them severe frustrations, setbacks, and losses. Whatever interferes with a creature's *telos* or characteristic mode of developing and flourishing is a disvalue in nature, and there is much such interference in the natural world, quite apart from any role that human beings might play in it. Nature is not all good then but a mixture of majesty and tragedy, of good and evil, of light and shadow, and of value and disvalue. Does this fact disqualify it from being a suitable focus of religious commitment and concern? It might appear so, but I argue in part 3 that it does not.

Is nature wasteful, and is that one of its disvalues? Is it cruel, and is that another? Can it be said to be indifferent to its creatures, and is this indifference yet another disvalue? If nature as a whole is devoid of purpose, is that a disvalue? These questions also will be addressed in part 3. For now, the examples cited of disvalues in nature, along with those highlighted earlier to illustrate its values, will suffice to show that nature is not just a bare collection of facts or relations of facts but a system rich in valuative significance.

My focus in this chapter has been on the nonhuman part of nature. My main task has been to show that there are values and disvalues that inhere in this aspect of nature, and that they are not just projected onto it by human subjects. The next chapter reflects on the human part of nature. It envisions human beings entirely as creatures of nature, that is, as one species among others, but it also emphasizes potentialities, traits, and achievements that are distinctively their own. Acknowledging the commonalities of humans with the nonhuman part of nature and their close dependence on it, as well as the many significant respects in which they differ from the rest of nature, raises the question of how to conceive of the place of human beings within their natural home. This question will figure prominently in the discussions to come.

5

Humans and Nature

Though distinct in my own way, I yet belong, deeply, within the harmony of nature. There is no experiential given more primordial than that.

—Erazim Kohák, *The Embers and the Stars*

Human beings are an integral part of nature, one biological species among an extraordinary profusion of such species across the face of the earth. Every species has something distinctive and special about it; that is, of course, what warrants its identification as a species. Some species, however, are more distinctive than others, and none is more astoundingly different from other kinds of organisms in its behavior, history, and accomplishments than the human species. In this chapter, we discuss the place of human beings in nature, giving due attention to traits they share with all organisms, traits that provide compelling evidence for their immanence in nature and their character as natural beings, in the fullest sense of that term. We also shall examine the traits and capacities of human beings that set them in sharp contrast to other natural beings. These special features imply a unique role and responsibility for humans in their relations to other organisms and to the environments providing habitation and nurture for those organisms. Recognition of this unique role and responsibility has crucial significance, as we shall see, for a religion of nature.

HUMANS AS NATURAL BEINGS

The most obvious and incontrovertible evidence of the immersion of human beings in nature is the fact that, like all other living beings, they have bodies and exhibit capacities and limitations of embodied beings. As embodied beings, they must eat to survive. They have to have oxygen to breathe and must drink water to slake their thirst. They cannot long endure extremes of cold or heat without protective shelter or clothing. They experience physical suffering and pain. They need rest and must spend a certain amount of time in sleep. They produce wastes. They are distinguished into two sexes and must copulate to produce progeny. They experience disease, old age, and death. They are vulnerable to predators and must learn how to ward them off or defend themselves against them. There are certain things that they must refrain from eating and drinking, or else be subject to illness or death. The well-being of their bodies is crucially dependent upon a favorable physical environment and upon the vitality and richness of surrounding ecosystems.

In addition, these bodies give humans the capability of moving about, and of hearing, tasting, smelling, feeling, and seeing. They protect against parasites, heal injuries, and, in normal functioning, sustain robustness and health. Their bodies give humans the ability to interact with their natural environments, to fashion and use tools, to experience and express feelings, and to execute their choices. Because they are physical beings, humans are enabled fully to participate in a physical world. Their bodies limit and condition them but also support and facilitate the living of their lives.

The bodily existence of humans is their most evident and intimate link to other living creatures of earth. It also links them to the inorganic parts of the earth, since the bodies of humans are made up of physical elements and are subject to the same natural laws that pertain to physical objects throughout the universe. Alfred North Whitehead highlights the close relationship to nature implicit in our having bodies when he remarks that

> the body is part of the external world, continuous with it. In fact, it is just as much part of nature as anything else there—a river, or a mountain, or a cloud. Also, if we are fussily exact, we cannot define where a body begins and where external nature ends.
>
> Consider one definite molecule. It is part of nature. It has moved about for millions of years. Perhaps it started from a distant nebula. It enters the body; it may be as a factor in some edible vegetable; or it passes into the lungs as part of the air. At what exact point as it enters the mouth, or as it is absorbed through the skin, is it part of the body? At what exact moment, later on, does it cease to be part of the body? Exactness is out of the question. It can only be obtained by some trivial convention.[1]

Acknowledging the central importance of the embodiment of humans guards against exaggerated accounts of the differences between them and other life-forms. And it counters the tendency—so long prevalent in Western thought—

to place humans outside of the natural order and to view them as somehow exempt, in their essential character, from provisions, conditions, and constraints of that order that apply inexorably to every other earthly creature.

Their evolutionary origin is a second kind of evidence showing that humans are natural beings. Since the revolutionary work of Darwin and Wallace in the mid-nineteenth century, we have become accustomed to viewing the human species as having come into being through a process of biological evolution operating in accordance with the principle of natural selection. Humans are thus tied to all other biological organisms by their participation in a history of origin and development in which more complex forms of life have arisen from the substrate of less complex ones, a history that has resulted in an incredible diversity of species, including the various primate species of which the human species is one example.

Humans are animals, then, and they and other types of animals are interwoven with all other forms of life in an immense network of evolving species that stretches back into pre-Cambrian time, nearly 4 billion years ago. E. O. Wilson notes that although most of the species of the past are now extinct, more are alive today than at any time in the past. The resolution for this apparent paradox is that any given species typically has given rise to new species before it became extinct, and these new species, in their turn, have produced additional species prior to their demise.[2] Human beings are an offshoot of this profligacy of species production over past eons and share with all earthly organisms a common biological heritage.

A third way in which humans are intimately related to nature is through the central role played by DNA (deoxyribonucleic acid) molecules in the cells of their bodies and the bodies of all cellular organisms. DNA is the template that controls the genetic makeup and reproductive process of each species, from the simplest kinds of unicellular life to the most complex, highly organized types of multicellular organism. It directs the life of each many-celled biological individual from origination to maturity by providing the complicated information necessary for the development and functioning of the numerous specialized cells of its body, and for the coordinated relationships of all of those distinctive kinds of cells with one another.

Perhaps the most striking evidence of this close genetic connection between humans and other species is the fact that we share with our nearest biological relative, the chimpanzee, 98.4 percent of our nuclear DNA. Even this small difference of 1.6 percent may be too large if taken as an unqualified expression of the genetic difference between humans and chimpanzees, since the figure includes both coding and noncoding regions of the genome. To cite a second example of our genetic closeness to another primate relative 93 percent of the human DNA, is identical to the DNA of monkeys.[3] DNA is the master thread that runs through the whole process of organic evolution and directs the biological program of each individual organism. It binds all species, despite their many fundamental differences from one another.

A fourth kind of evidence for the intimate relation of humans to nature is the fact that humans are social beings and in this respect resemble many other natural species. Unlike spiders and leopards, for example, who for most of their existence live and hunt in independent solitude, humans live in groups and greatly rely on one another for their survival and the maintenance of their distinctive mode of life. In this respect, they are more like ants, bees, monkeys, dolphins, wolves, and the many other species that are social by nature. Their social character means that humans must live together and interact with one another in ways that contribute to their mutual benefit, and this means, in turn, that they must have conventions or norms that guide their interactions and ensure their survival both as individuals and groups. The roots of human moral and legal systems lie here, but these roots are not confined to human beings. They extend deeply into the behaviors and forms of life of other social species as well, showing the close linkage of this aspect of human life to the lives of other natural beings.

Frans De Waal, a zoologist and ethologist who specializes in the study of primate behavior, notes in his book *Good Natured: The Origins of Right and Wrong in Humans and Other Animals* that "[i]nsofar as the interests of different individuals overlap" in monkey and ape groups, "community concern is a collective matter."[4] He defines community concern as "the stake each individual has in promoting those characteristics of the community or group that increase the benefits derived from living in it by that individual and its kin," and he goes on to say that "this definition does not hinge on conscious motives and intentions; it merely postulates benefits associated with particular behavior."[5]

Out of this community concern among monkey and ape groups grow practices and rituals of sharing, tolerance, alliance, hierarchy, reciprocity, sympathy, conflict resolution, reconciliation, punishment, reward, and the like, as De Waal shows in detail throughout his book, based on his extensive research on the behaviors of these groups. In these primate practices and rituals we can observe something akin to human moral and legal conceptions and conventions. This observation remains true, De Waal insists, even if animals do not deliberate in the ways that we do, weigh their individual interests against the rights of others, develop a vision of the greater good of society, or feel guilt about something that they should not have done.[6] The lesson of this story for our purposes is that community concern is by no means exclusive to human beings but is fundamental and widespread among social animals and other social beings, even if it is only implicit in their behaviors and not consciously envisaged by them. It is this same community concern, now explicit and conscious, that lies, in De Waal's words, "at the heart of human morality."[7]

Humans share with social animals not just community concern and its moral import but also culture, or at least something closely resembling culture, in at least two important aspects. This is a fifth respect in which humans can be identified as natural beings and not as beings wholly set apart from nature. Culture, in its most basic manifestation, can be defined as patterns of behavior that are not just biologically programmed and determined and would consequently be invariant for all normal members of a particular species but (1) are *learned* and in that manner transmitted through the generations, and (2) can and do *vary* in notable respects from the members of one group within a species to another group within that same species. With this conception of culture in mind, De Waal notes that "group specific signals and habits have been documented in bonobos as well as chimpanzees," and he adds that, "[i]ncreasingly, primatologists explain these differences as learned traditions handed down from one generation to the next."[8] Thus bonobos and chimpanzees can be said to have a kind of learned culture; their behavior is not just "instinctive."

In another part of his book De Waal shows how a group of rhesus monkeys learned to make up after fights more easily after having lived with a group of stumped-tailed monkeys. By being put in the same housing with a group of stump-tails for a period of five consecutive months, the rhesus monkeys, who typically reconcile less often and less easily than the stump-tails, learned from them how to reconcile readily and just as often as that species does. De Waal summarizes the results of this fascinating experiment by exclaiming that, "[l]ike chemists altering the properties of a solution, we had infused a group of monkeys of one species with the 'social culture' of another."[9]

Human cultures are, of course, much more elaborate and complicated than the primate cultures that De Waal and other primatologists analyze. They are conscious, intentional, symbolic, linguistic, and technological to a degree that no animal cultures appear to be. The point being made here, however, is that they are not entirely different either. We cannot assume, as is often done, that what makes humans unique among creatures of the earth is their possession of culture. The difference between humans and other social species in this regard is one of degree, not of kind, showing that it makes more sense to regard highly developed human cultures as a gradual outgrowth of natural processes than it does to view them as something wholly human and nonnatural. Here we have an example of nature actualizing at the human level, through biological evolution, potentialities resident within it that are evident in other life-forms as well.

A sixth and final way in which humans can be shown to be a part of nature, and not apart from it, is the conscious, subjective, inward character of their lives. Humans do not just function mindlessly or mechanically in the world. They experience pleasure and pain. They know anxiety and sorrow as well as anticipation and joy. They have wishes and desires, likes and dislikes. They can be lonely and bored. They have purposes and make choices. Humans experience their lives from within; they are consciously aware of their world.

In all of the ways mentioned above, the lives of humans resemble those of many other types of natural beings. These beings also have interior, conscious, firsthand perspectives on their environments and the sensations, feelings, dispositions, expectations, outlooks, and goals belonging to these perspectives. Conscious awareness no doubt varies in quality and degree from species to species, and it is, in all probability, most sophisticated and refined in humans among the creatures of this earth. It also is essential though to recognize that consciousness is amply present elsewhere in nature, not just in humans, and that it can be understood as a natural, progressive outgrowth of an evolutionary process that has produced subjective awareness in numerous other organisms, most notably in vertebrates with neural systems whose complexity of organization approaches the neural system of humans.

The claim that species other than the human species possess consciousness is a controversial one that requires some defense. Since the time of René Descartes in the seventeenth century, there has been a strong tendency in the West to deny consciousness to creatures other than human beings and to regard their possession of consciousness as the trait that most sharply distinguishes humans from other creatures and sets them apart from nature. Descartes regarded animals and other organisms as mere machines with no subjectivity or interior consciousness. According to him, only humans have the soul or "thinking substance" (*res cogitans*) that makes consciousness possible. The bodies of humans have no capability of consciousness in themselves; in fact, their bodies, like the bodies of animals, are nothing more than machines that are somehow directed and controlled by their minds or separate mental substances. Their minds, in turn, are somehow influenced and affected by their bodies. Descartes was never able to give any convincing explanation of how two completely different types of substance, physical and mental, could have any interractions with one another, but his insistence that only humans have conscious lives has exerted a strong influence on the thought of the West and continues to do so today.

There are at least three reasons for the persistence of this outlook, which I regard as untenable because it runs contrary to the evidence we have at hand. We can label these reasons religious, scientific, and moral. None of them can stand up to critical scrutiny, as we shall see, and there are convincing reasons in support of the view that consciousness is not restricted to humans but is relatively commonplace in nature. If both of these assertions hold true, then consciousness per se is not a phenomenon that radically separates humans from other species but is rather one more piece of confirming evidence for their intimate connection to nature.

The religious reason for thinking that humans alone are conscious is the long-standing belief in the West that only humans have immortal souls that will persist in being after the death of their bodies, and that they will either be rewarded or punished in the afterlife for their behavior in this life. Of all of the creatures of the earth, human souls alone have the capability of going to Heaven or Hell and living forever in one of those domains. Moreover, the earth is thought to exist primarily, if not exclusively, for the sake of human beings. It is their testing place or vale of soul making, not their real home. Their real home is in Heaven with God. If they fail to attain that home, they will languish forever in the fires of Hell.

Since the earth was created by God as the theater of human redemption, that is, of the saga of human history that will culminate in God's final judgment of every human soul, nothing in it other than human beings has any lasting significance or importance. Everything on earth is transitory or fleeting, except the human soul. This world is a mere stage prop or background for what happens ultimately to human beings. Since animals have no significant part in the saga of redemption, it is assumed that they have no immortal souls, and because it is the soul alone that makes consciousness possible in this view, it follows that animals have no consciousness or interior awareness.

The denial of consciousness to animals has accorded well with the worldview of traditional Christian culture in the West, but that worldview is no longer unquestioned or dominant in the way that it was in the Middle Ages, the Renaissance, or the early Modern period. This observation is particularly true after the advent of Darwin's theory of natural selection in the middle of the nineteenth century, with its forthright inclusion of the origins of humans and their mental life in evolutionary history, so this religious reason no longer carries the conviction it once had. It is not a convincing reason in today's world for denying consciousness to animals or other natural beings.

A second reason that helps explain why the view has been so persistent that animals have no consciousness is scientific. By *scientific* I mean that this view grows out of assumptions among many scientists about how animals and other organisms are to be studied scientifically and what the conclusions of such a program of study, thus understood, imply. These scientists assume that the scientific study of animals must be completely objective. It must focus solely on the overt behaviors of animals. They further assume that, since no interior life of animals can be observed with the objective techniques of scientific research, no consideration can or should be given to the possibility of such an interior life. In their view, it would be flagrantly unscientific to speculate about the possibility of animal consciousness, because scientists can have no direct empirical access to such consciousness. A further assumption strongly held by these scientists is that scientific study alone can give us reliable information about, or understanding of, animals.

In sum, this second line of reasoning alleges that (1) because animal consciousness cannot be made a subject of scientific study, with its exclusive focus on objective behavior or what can be directly experienced, and because (2) it would be unscientific to speculate or theorize about the possibility of animal consciousness, and because (3) scientific study is the only dependable way to draw conclusions about the nature of animals or any other biological organisms, it follows that (4) consciousness must be deemed *nonexistent* in organisms other than humans. All of the premises of this line of reasoning, however, can be questioned.

The first two conveniently overlook the fact of widespread theorizing in scientific reasoning and the routine recourse among scientists to theoretical entities or processes as modes of explanation (e.g., elementary particles, quarks, superstrings, gravitational fields, black holes, the Big Bang). Scientists are not restricted in their findings to what can be directly observed. They draw inferences from what can be observed to what cannot be observed and make frequent use of the latter as an essential part of their explanatory reasoning. In fact, many scientific theories blend high levels of speculative theorizing with empirical observations; such theories are not restricted to what can be directly observed. Observations gain significance in light of the theories, and the theories have their empirical grounding in the observations. The two necessarily go together.

No sophisticated science can exist that simply gathers empirical evidence without the guidance of theoretical hypotheses, hypotheses that frequently posit theoretical entities or processes not accessible to direct observation. If the admission of an interior life for animals helps explain or make better sense of important aspects of animal behavior, then there is no in-principle scientific reason for not including it as part of a theoretical explanation for such behavior.[10] At the very least, scientists should keep an open mind about the possibility of animal consciousness. The notion that scientists do not or should not speculate beyond what can be directly observed is naive and wrong-headed. It does no justice to the history of science or the actual practices of scientists.

We already have had occasion to criticize premise 3 in the above line of reasoning. We did so in chapter 3, where we characterized the natural sciences as selectively abstract. If the argument presented there for this characterization is sound, as I believe it to be, then the natural sciences are not the only way to gain understanding about the nature and activities of animals or other organisms. Farmers or ranchers who work frequently with animals but who are not laboratory scientists may be in a better position to understand some aspects of animal nature and animal behavior than those scientists. Nonscientific pet owners, with their intimate and empathetic interactions with certain animals, may have insights into their pets that scientists, with their more detached analyses and artificially constructed laboratory experiments, may lack. For all their wealth of information and explanatory detail, the natural sciences tell only part of the complex story of animals, not the whole story. Even if animal consciousness could be shown convincingly to lie beyond the pale of scientific investigation, that conclusion in itself would not entail that animals are not conscious. Thus the second general reason for denying consciousness to animals fails.

The final reason fails as well, as I shall now proceed to show. I have labled this reason a moral one. In his book *The Unheeded Cry*, animal ethicist Bernard Rollin argues that one reason there has been a strong tendency in Western thought to dismiss the idea that animals are conscious is that, once we admit that they are conscious, we have to begin a complicated process of thinking about how to regard animals morally, a process that might well require a revolution in our attitude toward and treatment of animals. Our reluctance to undergo such a revolution or to admit the need for it has, according to Rollin, been a principal reason for our not wanting to recognize consciousness in animals.[11]

It is far more convenient to think that animals do not experience suffering, pain, anxiety, fatigue, loneliness, boredom, or despair, for example, than it is is to think that they do, for if they do, we should be much more hesitant to inflict these things upon them than we often are. Ways in which we typically treat them, such as in factory farming, laboratory experimentation, medical research, rodeos, or training, might have to be reconsidered and basically revised. We might even have to reconsider, from a moral perspective, our widespread practice of killing animals for food, whether by slaughterhouses or by hunting or fishing. We shy away from the possible need for such radical reconsideration and changes in our treatment of animals. It threatens to open up a hornet's nest of problems with which we would rather not have to deal.

Thus we deny consciousness to animals. If they are mere machines or automata, then we can pretty much treat them in any way we like and need have no moral reservations about doing so. A flagrant example of the potential evil in this attitude is contained in Nicholas Fontaine's *Memoires*, published in 1738, in which he reports on a physiological laboratory he visited where followers of Descartes' philosophy were experimenting on dogs.

> They administered beatings to dogs with perfect indifference, and made fun of those who pitied the creatures as if they felt pain. They said the animals were clocks; that the cries they emitted when struck were only the noise of a little spring that had been touched, but that the whole body was without feeling. They nailed poor animals up on boards by their four paws to vivisect them and see the circulation of the blood which was a great subject of conversation.[12]

This moral reason for denying consciousness to animals goes a long way toward *explaining* why we do so, but it hardly serves as a *justification* for doing so. It is an evasion of the issue not a conscientious wrestling with it; hence it fails to offer any convincing reason for believing that animals lack consciousness.

If we grant that none of the above three reasons for denying consciousness to animals carries weight, are there any convincing positive reasons for asserting that at least some animals or natural beings other than humans are conscious? This topic is a large one, and we do not have space to do justice to it here, but I do want to contend briefly for the view that other beings in nature are conscious, and that we ought to regard humans' possession of consciousness as one important thing they have in common with other creatures in the natural world.

The first argument is based on animal behavior. Many animals give every behavioral indication of pain and pleasure, anticipation and desire, hope and disappointment, joy and sorrow, anger and love, and the like—indications that would lead us effortlessly to attribute these experiences to human beings. Why do we not then attribute them to animals as well? Do not commonsense and ordinary language lead us to do so? "Spot was disappointed that he could not go on the trip with the children, and we heard him howling his displeasure when we left" is just one of many such assertions we commonly make about our pets. Another is, "Grover cried out in pain when he stepped on the thorn." Others are, "You could see the hunger in Lady's eyes as she gazed at the beef bone she hoped to get," or "Toots had a lot of fun today chasing and jumping for her Frisbee," or "Jocko got mad when Bowser tried to take his toy away from him." Are we just being anthropomorphic when we make such assertions, or are we justifiably inferring from the behavioral indications of animals that they have feelings, emotions, and conceptions similar to our own?

I think the latter, because there is no compelling reason not to make the same or at least similar inferences from animal behaviors as we do from our own, even if animals do not have the linguistic capacity to explain to us what, if anything, they are experiencing firsthand. The warrant for acknowledging consciousness in animals becomes especially evident when we are inclined, for whatever reason, to inflict upon an animal what would be *painful experiences* for us. Is it not best to give the animal the benefit of the doubt and to assume that when the animal yelps, winces, withdraws, writhes, or gives some other indication of possible pain experience that it is indeed having that experience? Is not common sense our best guide in such situations, both epistemologically and morally? That common sense is our best guide would seem especially the case when we take the trouble to peel away the gauze of ideological bias, such as that implicit in the religious, scientific, and moral attitudes discussed above, that might blind us to what would appear to be widespread empirical evidence for animal consciousness.

A second reason for acknowledging consciousness in animals is the intriguing observation by Rollin that at least some animals must have something similar to concepts, and the consciousness of concepts, in order to survive. They must have concepts, he argues, because without them they could not organize and synthesize their experiences. Their access to the world is via sense organs that are similar to our own but that could provide only isolated fragments of experience were there not some manner in which those fragments are organized into persistent, meaningful experiences. "After all," says Rollin, "an organism with no power of generalization and abstraction, which could experience only particulars, could neither learn nor survive."[13] He acknowledges that it is an open question as to how these concepts or abilities to pick out common features of the world are symbolized, but he remarks that "it is plausible to suggest that animals have some mental tokens or images which serve in this capacity."[14]

Rollin goes on to show that an animal must have something similar to a conceptualization of the continuity of its own self, as distinguished from the continuity of objects in the world, even though we do not know what form this sense of self takes. Animals know what happens to them and what does not, and they know this over sequences of time. Moreover, they are capable of learning from such experiences. Their ability to protect themselves testifies to a continuity of self-awareness that is correlative with an awareness of the continuous features of the world, and to their comprehension of the all-important distinction between themselves and the surrounding world.[15] It is true that we do not know the details of this animal awareness of self and world, or to what extent it might vary from species to species. Nor do we fully understand the ways in which it might, in all of its variations, compare and contrast with our own consciousness. It seems entirely appropriate, however, to attribute some such consciousness to animals as well as to ourselves, especially to those animals with sense organs, neural systems, and brains similar to our own.

Speaking of similarities of neural systems and brains, there is a third line of argument for consciousness in animals that Rollin also discusses, based on the likenesses of pain receptors and pain blockers in the brains of humans and animals. We can take note of it by concluding our consideration of some positive arguments in support of the claim that humans share with many animals the trait of conscious awareness, and that this sharing provides another kind of confirmation of the close relations of humans to nature.

Rollin indicates that pain and pleasure centers such as those found in humans have been reported in the brains of birds, animals, and fish, and that the neurophysiological systems responsible for pain behavior are similar in all vertebrates. He also notes that anaesthetics and analgesics control what looks like pain in all vertebrates and some invertebrates. Finally, he observes that the feedback mechanisms for controlling and diminishing pain in vertebrates (e.g., endogenous opiates such as serotonin, endorphins and enkephalins, and substance P.) are commonly found in nonhuman vertebrates and other kinds of organisms as well as in humans.[16] If animals do not directly experience pain as we do, it is difficult to understand why these endogenous opiates would be needed, or why anaesthetics and analgesics would work on animals and other organisms as well as they do.

The most parsimonious explanation would seem to be the correct one: animals are conscious and are aware of pain, just as we are. Keeping in mind one of the three reasons for denying consciousness to animals considered earlier, namely, that objective techniques of scientific investigation must exclude serious consideration of subjectivity in animals, it is instructively ironic that purely objective, wholly scientific investigations of the physiology of brain tissues, structures, and functionings can be seen, via this third positive argument, to give powerful evidence of subjectivity in animals as well as in humans.

In this first section I have presented six basic arguments in support of the proposition that humans have an intimate relationship to nature and crucial commonalities with other natural beings, which show that humans themselves are natural beings in the full sense of that term, not beings who exist outside of or over against nature, or who somehow transcend the constraints and capacities of nature. To recapitulate the lines of argument, they are based on (1) the embodiment of humans; (2) their evolutionary origins; (3) the central role played by DNA in the development and coordination of the myriad specialized cells in their bodies; (4) the social nature and behavior they share with many other organisms, with due notice of implications of this trait for the emergence of moral thought and practice among humans; (5) their having culture, at least as minimally defined, in common with other animals; and (6) their possession of subjective awareness or consciousness, a characteristic that seems in various, and probably in all cases more attenuated forms, to be relatively widespread among other creatures of nature.

Now that these commonalities have been noted and humans have been clearly identified as natural beings, we are in a position to consider some conspicuous traits that are distinctive to humans as a species. These traits do not place humans outside of nature, and I shall argue that they are all differences of degree, not of kind, as far as their relations to traits of other creatures in nature are concerned. They are highly significant differences, however, and they give expression to potentialities in nature that come most fully to light on earth in human life and human history.

THE DISTINCTIVENESS OF HUMAN BEINGS

The first and perhaps most obvious thing that demarcates humans from other beings in nature is their possession and use of language. More than any other trait, this linguistic ability in both its spoken and written forms facilitates and explains certain other characteristics, soon to be indicated, that also are notably distinctive to the human species. The term *distinctive* is not meant to signify absolute difference in kind, nor would we expect it to imply that, since the emphasis throughout this book is on the continuity of humans and nature. It does signify though a *remarkable difference in degree*. It is important that we do as much justice as we can to what is distinctive about humans, just as we want to take fully into account what is common to them and other creatures of the natural world. Neither should be allowed to eclipse or minimize the importance of the other.

There are anticipations of human language in the animal kingdom and approximations to some of its features. Animals communicate with one another by sounds and gestures, for example, and some animals, such as chimpanzees, have been taught to convey some of their needs and wants to their trainers through the use of American sign language, colored tiles, or computer consoles. The significance of experiments with animal communication, which have been going on for decades, is still widely debated among primatologists, psychologists, linguists, philosophers, and others. A recent book, *Apes, Language and the Human Mind*, written by Sue Savage-Rumbaugh, a well-known ape researcher, Talbot J. Taylor, a linguist, and Stuart G. Shanker, a philosopher and psychologist, touts the ability of apes to learn and regularly use language, including at least some rudimentary forms of grammar.[17] De Waal and Rachels, however, insist that there is nothing in animal communications, as seen so far, that gives any indication of their having anything approaching the syntactical complexity

101

of human languages. Moreover, Rachels seems to favor the view that much, if not all, of what might have looked like linguistic or proto-linguistic communication between animals and humans is in fact the result of unconscious cuing by the trainers. He flatly asserts that "there is still no animal who can converse with humans in any meaningful sense."[18]

Rollin, on the other hand, observes that "[p]rimates have scored 75 to 85 on standard IQ tests, have put signs together in novel ways to express new ideas, have shown the ability to lie, have taught signing systems to others, and so on." He regards these data as "too impressive to ignore" and rejects the "cuing" explanation of apparent animal communication with humans as unconvincing and unduly influenced by ideological assumptions. He goes on to insist that even if the animal communications "fall short of true (human) language, they certainly reflect mentation."[19]

Mentation and language, however, are different things; the first does not unarguably presuppose the second. Whatever we may think about the results of important, ongoing experiments in animal communication, they seem by implication, at least to date, to give a more convincing indication of the considerable *dissimilarities* between animal communication and human language than of overwhelming similarities between them. This observation holds true even if we conclude, as I would, that the patent dissimilarities are ones only of signficant degree rather than of absolute difference in kind. The continuity with other species remains, but the human species has developed to an outstanding extent a capability to communicate by language and to utilize language as an instrument of thought.

This extraordinary linguistic ability, in both its spoken and written forms, goes a long way toward accounting for other distinctive traits of humans, traits that make them stand out from all other life-forms on this planet. These traits are human beings' reasoning ability, their purposive freedom, their capacity for creating sophisticated cultures, and their technological proficiency. The four traits are, along with human language itself, the most salient ones distinguishing humans from other earthly species. Let us take a brief look at each one in turn.

The *reasoning ability* of human beings is largely made possible by their capacity for language. Whitehead states, "Apart from language, the retention of thought, the easy recall of thought, the interweaving of thought into higher complexity, the communication of thought, are all gravely limited." He concludes that "the mentality of mankind and the language of mankind created each other."[20] Language enables humans to communicate with great subtlety and precision, conveying to one another their ideas and imaginings as well as their innermost experiences and feelings. It also can facilitate the resolution of conflicts or the articulation of common goals between or among human beings, though we should not forget that uses of language can sometimes cause grave misunderstandings or raise expressions of hostility to new levels of vividness, thus impeding cooperation and commonality of purpose.[21] In any event, oral and written language, especially the latter, allows for the preservation of communicative exchanges (as well as of individual reveries, to be discussed below) for reference at other times and enlarges the possible audiences for these exchanges, even across cultures and down through generations. Thus one human being can build upon the experiences and reflections of others, with a possible expansion of awareness, perspective, and understanding, and groups of humans can benefit over time from the insights and accomplishments as well as from the mistakes and failings of predecessor groups, as recorded in oral traditions and written languages.

Much more than complex and detailed communications from person to person or group to group are made possible by language. Language also creates or expands the capacity for sustained thought on the part of each individual person. With the aid of written language, for example, one can carry out long processes of reasoning without having to keep everything in one's head, and one can come back again and again, after the refreshment of rest, to reflect upon and revise one's remembered or transcribed thoughts of an earlier time when these thoughts are enshrined in language. Hence, as Whitehead puts it, language is not only "converse with another, . . . it is converse with oneself," and "an articulated memory is the gift of language, considered as an expression from oneself in the past to oneself in the present."[22]

This converse with others and with oneself that is so essential to the growth of reason is made possible by a central feature of human languages, namely, their generality and abstractness. Language probably began its development in contexts of particular needs, wants, necessities, and dangers, and its uses were perhaps mostly confined to those immediate contexts. "I'm cold," "I'm hungry," "This plant is edible," "This water is safe," "The gazelles are grazing yonder," "The center pole of the lodge goes here," "There's a lion," "Here come our enemies," and so on were characteristic locutions. The key terms were implicitly general, but usages of them tended at first to be particular. However, over millennia, a high level of abstraction from immediate environments was achieved in the development and exploitation of language, and humans were able to use their languages to explore increasingly more general concepts and complex interrelations of these concepts. Thus they could examine conceptual and formal relations independently of any concrete content.

Not only did the thought processes of humans become much more speedy and efficient as a result, they also gained greatly in penetration and depth. New discoveries could be made through thought-experiments alone, and these conceptual discoveries often could be profitably applied to concrete situations. With the aid of linguistic abstractions and their associations, humans could roam in thought across reaches of space, time, and possibility that far outstripped their immediate sensate experiences. In this way, they acquired the ability to think speculatively and hypothetically, and that ability has given rise to many of the distinctive accomplishments of humans over the ages.

Humans also have been able to abet the increasingly general, more conceptual capacities of their developing natural languages with the creation of artificial languages such as logic and mathematics, in which abstraction from particular content or circumstance, as well as from some of the limitations of natural languages themselves, is achieved to an extremely high degree. These artificial languages have helped humans to become aware of the purely structural and formal relations already implicit in their natural languages, to explore the often surprisingly fruitful uses and applications of this extremely abstract kind of reasoning, and thus to expand their thinking in that direction.

Another quality of natural languages, however, is their concreteness of imagery rather than their abstractness, the extent to which certain words, phrases, or sentences can be discovered to have, or be made to have, multiple overtones of meaning and suggestiveness. Herein lies a principal key to the peculiar powers of literary arts such as poetry, drama, the short story, and the novel. Human beings have not only discovered in their languages potentialities of abstract cerebration but also have found in them resources of metaphor, allegory, symbolism, and story with which to probe and give expression to depths of wonder, perplexity, yearning, grief, anxiety, remorse, sorrow, joy, humor, hope, and the like, and to provide penetrating insights into general features of the human condition and the human experience of the world. Here, linguistic allusion, association, and imagery have a vital role to play, evoking levels of understanding and awareness that more abstract modes of expression are not competent to convey.[23] The crucial role of suggestive metaphors, analogies, and models in more abstract modes of reasoning also should not be overlooked, including reasoning in the realm of the natural sciences.[24]

Can we also call this literary, evocative, or suggestive use of language a type of *reasoning*? I do not see why we should refuse to do so. This use of language, so characteristic of human beings and their history, assists us in understanding and learning to deal with essential aspects of our experience of the world and in that way makes us more knowledgeable and aware. Not only purely conceptual relations, then, but more figurative and imaginative associations as well can be brought to light and put into play by language, and both kinds of relations have made fundamental contributions to the distinctive character and style of human thought and life.[25]

A second distinctive trait of human beings that is greatly facilitated by their possession and use of language is *purposive freedom.* As we have already seen, language provides for ease of communication, fosters constructive imagination, makes possible the articulation and retention of general concepts, beliefs, and theories, and contributes substantially to the development, preservation, and transmission of cultural contexts. In these and other ways it helps open up ranges of relevant alternatives to immediate experiences, thus enabling humans to envision, deliberate over, and choose among those alternatives. Language not only permits humans to think more clearly about what John Dewey calls possible "ends-in-view," it also empowers them to consider and weigh carefully the relative merits of alternative ends prior to their choosing and acting. Thus, as Dewey explains, an end-in-view functions as "an aim, purpose, a prediction usable as a plan in shaping the course of events." It is a projection of "possible consequences."[26] With such purposes, aims, and predictions in sight, as articulated by language and held in that way in thought, humans are able to exercise their freedom with a high level of awareness, foresight, and effectiveness.

James Gustafson insists that animals "cannot think about their ends and the means of fulfilling them in the way that human beings can."[27] He thus implies that animals do not exercise freedom in the way that humans do, and this admitted fact is largely due to the central role that language plays in human thought and experience. However, I want to gloss his statement—which by itself might be taken to mean that animals have no freedom—with the reminder that there is abundant evidence from their behaviors that at least some animals are capable of purposive action and choices among alternatives, though not *to the extent* or *over the range of envisioned alternatives* that humans are.

Support for such claims about differences between human and animal freedom is all around us as we take note of the radical transformations, both for good and for ill, that humans have produced throughout this planet by their inventions, projects, and choices. One only has to fly over a country such as the United States to witness the imprint of the human hand that lies over the whole landscape. Forests are removed, fields are cultivated and irrigated, dams and canals are constructed, rivers are rerouted, roads are laid out, cities are built, and mountains are mined—as far as the eye can see. "[A]ll biologists know," says Tzvetan Todorov, that "the human species is distinguished by its flexibility, by its capacity to adapt to new circumstances. We are the species that is not content to follow its instincts. We are capable of invention and change."[28] This extraordinary capability gives eloquent testimony to the purposive freedom of human beings.

I argued in chapter 2 for the view that free acts of human beings cannot be entirely accounted for in efficient causal terms. These acts occur within a causal context, and such contexts are necessary for their occurrence, but the causal factors are not sufficient to explain them. Thus humans have the capacity to choose among alternatives within a causal context, that is, different choices are possible for them even though the efficient causes remain the same. So it is this non-compatibilist, "could-have-done-otherwise" conception of purposive freedom that I have in mind here.[29] I do not claim that humans alone have such freedom. I only want to observe that they have it to a remarkably high degree, and that the extent of their purposive freedom is one of their distinctive traits.

The combination of reasoning ability and purposive freedom, both greatly assisted by language, also is tied closely to the technological proficiency of human beings, a trait implicit in the comment above about their pervasive impacts upon the face of the earth. I shall discuss it in more detail in a moment, but first let us consider the human capacity for the *creation of sophisticated cultures*, a third distinctively human trait that language helps make possible.

In one of his books, Holmes Rolston III states that "nature transcends itself in culture," and in another he contends that "culture is a contrast class to nature," including biological nature.[30] Instead of saying that nature transcends itself in culture, I contend that it expresses part of its potentiality in culture. Hence, culture is not so much a contrast class to nature as one of the myriad ways in which nature manifests its latent powers. In other words, culture is natural; culture and nature should not be opposed to one another. The production of cultures is one of the things nature does through its creatures, and culture can be found not just among humans but among some other animals as well, as I have previously argued. Although language plays a fundamental role, as Rolston rightly observes, in "the development, transmission, and criticism" of *human* cultures,[31] it is not a necessary part of the definition of culture as such. The two defining characteristics of culture that I identified earlier in this chapter do not involve or imply a central role for language, and I argued there that, by this definition, culture is not unique to humans but is present elsewhere in nature.

These caveats having been entered, however, it seems to be the case that the cultures of human beings are much more advanced, complicated, and sophisticated than the other types of culture to be found elsewhere on this earth. Furthermore, they are distinctive in that they are transmitted largely through language. Whitehead notes the intimate connection between human culture (he calls it civilization) and the human capacity for rational thought, which, as we saw earlier, he connects closely to the generalizing and abstracting powers of language.

> The hermit thrush and the nightingale can produce sound of the utmost beauty. But they are not civilized beings. They lack ideas of adequate gener-

ality respecting their own actions and the world around them. Without doubt the higher animals entertain notions, hopes, and fears. And yet they lack civilization by reason of the deficient generality of their mental functionings.[32]

With the aid of language, as Brian Swimme recounts, humans have been able to supplement their evolutionary development, based primarily upon the shaping of their genetic architecture, with a cultural evolution tied mainly to their symbolic constructions.[33] Through their creation and development of these symbolic constructions, the further evolution of human beings—now a cultural and not just a biological evolution—has come to be subject to a significant degree to their conscious planning and purposive freedom.

Thus the capacities of humans for language, reasoning, and purposive freedom go a long way toward accounting for the production of their sophisticated cultures, and these cultures, in their turn, have provided context, stimulus, nurture, and material for the continuing enlargement of human capacities for reasoning, language, and freedom. Each of these traits aids and abets the others, and each is enhanced by the others. It is entirely correct to say, as Whitehead does, that the higher animals "lack civilization" or to affirm, with Kenneth Bock, that "man differs from other animals in being civilized,"[34] as long as we mean by *civilization* or *civilized* the manifestation of complex, advanced cultures in which language and linguistically guided reasoning and freedom have played and continue to play a dominant role. In this sense of the term, civilization is distinctive to human beings, at least on this planet.

It is important though for us to understand that civilization is a type or subset of culture, not the whole meaning of culture, and civilizations as well as cultures in general should be viewed as expressions of nature and aspects of nature, not as something set in opposition to nature. Human beings and their cultures and civilizations are squarely within the natural order, not outside it or over against it. They depend critically upon the nature of which they are a part, and the rest of nature is deeply affected by their actions or inactions.

This fact has profound moral implications. It means that our occupational niche or ecological task as human beings relates fundamentally to our character as custodians of advanced cultures or civilizations. Our niche or task can be regarded as that of building and sustaining cultures that are in balance and harmony with nature and that enhance nature's well-being. Our cultures and their productions and activities should not be threats to the rest of nature's creatures, as they have so often been in the past but our distinctive way of making intelligent, empathetic, ongoing contributions so that they flourish as much as we do. It has been a dangerous, destructive delusion of our history that we have frequently seen ourselves as transcending nature in our cultures and civlizations—as entering into another order of being that is somehow sheltered or shielded from the natural world—and thus as being set free from our dependence upon that world or from any significant responsibilities toward it. In the third section of this chapter we will discuss in more detail the responsibilities of humans toward the rest of nature that stem from their character as natural beings and from their special traits as one species of natural being.

Before we leave the topic of their production of sophisticated cultures as one of the salient traits of human beings, we should note more explicitly one feature of human cultures that helps explain their distinctiveness and, in that way, the distinctiveness of humans themselves. That feature is the *teaching* of cultural traditions. De Waal thinks that the active teaching of cultures (as opposed to the transmission of instinctive behaviors or modifications of behavioral patterns caused simply by example, as in the case of the rhesus monkeys mentioned earlier) is probably unique to humans.[35] Rolston agrees, asserting that

> [w]hat is missing in the primates is precisely what makes a human cumulative transmissible culture possible. The central idea is that acquired knowledge and behavior are learned and transmitted from person to person, by one generation teaching another, ideas passing from mind to mind, in large part through the medium of language, with such knowledge and behavior resulting in a greatly rebuilt, or cultured environment.[36]

Drawing on Daniel C. Dennett's *The Intentional Stance*, Rolston distinguishes between three orders of intentionality. First-order intentionality, the intent to change the behavior of other animals, is clearly present, he says, in vervet monkeys and other animals. Second-order intentionality is intent to change the mind of another, that is, to teach by passing ideas from mind to mind. Third-order intentionality is knowledge that another (e.g., a teacher) is seeking to change one's mind. Neither second-order nor third-order intentionality is conspicuously present in animals other than humans, Rolston contends, and this absence is largely due to the meagerness of linguistic facility in those animals.[37] I think that the observations of De Waal and Rolston are correct.

Animals have only minimal ability, in other words, to communicate states of mind to one another or to relay and reflect upon the kinds of complex ideas, beliefs, and attitudes that are involved in the transmission of sophisticated cultural traditions. This is mostly because of their lack of language. The ability to teach cultural traditions across generations that language makes possible allows for the continual growth, development, and criticism of cultures over large stretches of time. This ability explains how cultures can become increasingly more complex and sophisticated as new generations of human beings are taught the cultural traditions and learn to work within those traditions to modify and expand them.

The teachability of human cultures, especially through the medium of language, is therefore a principal feature of and key to the crucial bearing that the cultural heritages of humans have upon what is distinctive in human thought and practice, as compared to the functionings of other organisms on earth.

The last distinctive trait of humans to be indicated and discussed here is their *technological proficiency*. Examples of human technological invention and achievement are rampant in human history and include such things as written language; agriculture; the organization and governance of towns, cities, nations, and other institutions; fire; the wheel; the hatchet, hammer, chisel, and saw; the domestication of animals; the selective breeding of animals and plants; the stirrup; the blowgun, sling, spear, bow and arrow, and cannon; money; printing; irrigation; the water pump; the barometer and thermometer; the steam engine; the telegraph and telephone; electric lights and electric motors; advances in medical research and treatment; the automobile; the airplane; dynamite; atomic energy and the atomic bomb; the computer; the transistor; space vehicles; robots; and the Internet. Nothing in the animal kingdom compares to the sheer diversity and pervasive effects upon the earth of human technology, nor with the extent to which that technology has been guided by purposive intelligence and freedom. The bower bird builds an intricate nest, honey bees construct hives, beavers locate and build their dams, squirrels store their nuts for the winter, apes use sticks to access termites, and so on. All of these practices, however, tend to be repeated from generation to generation without modification or change; they are guided more by instinct than by flexible, innovative intelligence and freedom; and they have had limited impacts upon the earth as a whole. The difference between animals and humans is again only one of degree, but it is one of an extremely important degree.

Human language, reasoning ability, purposive freedom, and cultures have all contributed greatly to and, in turn, been fundamentally affected by the technological accomplishments of human beings. Language makes high levels of reasoning possible, and high levels of theoretical reasoning have led to many practical technological inventions. The first and second scientific revolutions of the past 300 to 400 years were possible only because of the subtle interweaving of theoretical and practical intelligence. New theories have led to new instruments, for example, and instruments have been used to test theories as well as to suggest novel theories. Technologically guided thought and experimentation have gone hand-in-hand. Technology has also vastly extended the range of human freedom, whether for good or ill, and it has had decisive effects on the content and direction of cultures. The present ecological crisis serves as an urgent reminder of the far-reaching consequences of human technology throughout the world.

One result of human technology is the production of artifacts. An artifact is something that humans make, and, as is seen in the closely related term *artificial*, artifacts often are contrasted with things that are natural (i.e., produced by nature without the intervention or aid of human beings). I contend though that human technology and its artifacts are natural, because humans are natural beings, and when they invent and use technology they are expressing potentialities of nature that come to be realized in their activities as natural beings. Yet it would seem that there is some point to the contrast between natural and artificial. This distinction is useful and has important meaning. How can we keep the insight that human technology is natural, a fruit of nature acting through human beings, and at the same time preserve at least some significant distinction between the natural and the artificial? In his book *Philosophy of Technology*, Frederick Ferré comes to our aid by identifying two senses of the term *nature*. The first is "the collective term for *all that exists apart from the artificial.*" The second "includes within its scope *all that exists in the evolving universe of space and time.*"[38] We are focusing on the second sense throughout this book, but there are contexts where the first sense is certainly appropriate and useful.

We should view this first sense, however, as calling attention to a contrast between *the human* and *the nonhuman* aspects of nature, not to a contrast between human beings and nature as such. For humans and their accomplishments, including their technology and artifacts, are as much a part of nature and of the evolutionary history of all living beings in nature as are the presence and activities of other natural beings. As Stephen David Ross declares, "Artifice is no less 'natural' than nature," and "[t]o criticize technology for its artificiality is to bifurcate nature, denying that its powers and possibilities include both technology and art."[39] In making these statements, Ross has something like Ferré's second sense of the term *nature* in mind, and it is this more fundamental, more metaphysical sense of the term that I want to keep at the forefront of our attention. Ferré's second meaning of *nature* attests to the metaphysical ultimacy of nature and thus to the central theme of part 2 of this book.

We have identified five traits of humans that, at least in their relative complexity and scope, are distinctive to human beings: language, reasoning ability, purposive freedom, creation of sophisticated cultures, and technological proficiency. These traits help demarcate the human from the nonhuman aspects of nature, but they should not be taken to imply that humans transcend or stand outside of the natural order itself. In identifying and discussing these distinctive features of human life, we should not forget for a moment that there are other impressive and distinctive features that animals may have that humans lack. Our hearing is far less acute, for example, than bats'. We do not have the keen vision of eagles. Our sense of smell is greatly inferior to wolves'. We do not run as fast or swim as gracefully as many creatures do. We cannot fly unaided by technology. We cannot breathe underwater without some kind of apparatus. We cannot navigate through the skies over long distances in the way that some birds and butterflies can without consulting our maps and instruments.

Yes, we are distinctive, but so is every species of natural being, and some more notably than others. That we belong in the latter group should not blind us to the fact that we are deeply kin to all creatures of nature; we are dependent upon nature and belong to it no less than they. We need those other creatures just as they need us, for we are all part of the same biological history and the same web of life on earth. The miracle of human life, like all forms of life, is manifestation of the unfathomable, inexhaustible mystery of nature. Nature's marvelous creations, both living and nonliving, lie in panoplied splendor all around us; nature is the source and sustenance of our as well as their existence. Nature sustains us together, as parts of one vast, intricately ordered system, not in isolation from one another. In this fact lies the key to our responsibility toward the rest of nature, a responsibility that flows from our commonalities with it as well as from our distinctive gifts.

THE HUMAN RESPONSIBILITY TOWARD THE REST OF NATURE

As humans, our many commonalities and connections to the rest of nature forcefully remind us that we are indeed an integral part of the system of nature on this planet. We reside on this earth as one species of organisms, the current total number of such separate species numbering well over 1 million, if not many times that. The earth is our household, just as it is the household of all of the ecologically entwined creatures of this planet. The etymology of *ecological*, from the Greek word *oikos*, meaning *household*, points to our being at home here, to our being members of a vast, diverse, interdependent family of natural beings. We are not aliens or sojourners, as was often assumed in the past, but belong wholly to this world. We can rightfully claim it as our natural home. The living earth as our household accepts us as one of its own, but it also imposes significant duties and responsibilities on us, just as any household does.

Lest we overestimate our importance in this household, or assume that we hold inviolable sway at the top of some sort of hierarchy of status and privilege within it, Wilson gives us a sobering piece of evidence showing how critically dependent we are upon the flourishing of certain others of earth's creatures, the seemingly humble and unimportant, though strikingly prolific, insects. "So important are insects and other land-dwelling arthropods," Wilson writes, "that if all were to disappear, humanity probably *could not last more than a few months.*"

Most other creatures, such as reptiles, amphibians, and birds, would then also become extinct, as would most species of plants, especially the flowering plants dependent upon insects for their pollination. The earth would soon return to its state in early Paleozoic times, with perhaps a few small trees and bushes but with almost no animal life.[40] No such comparable catastrophe would occur if humans themselves were to become extinct.

We are not exalted lords, then, but mere citizens of the earth—if I can be permitted to shift the metaphor from household or family to community—and two of our principal duties toward the earth and its creatures are to cultivate and practice the virtues of helpfulness and humility. In seeking our own good as a species, we must of necessity concern ourselves with the good of others in the wider community of all of the earth's beings. The good of one species is the good of all, and the suffering or degradation of one species may well threaten the suffering or degradation of all. The earth's species are linked in complex relations that require mutual cooperation and support if any or all are to survive. For the most part, this cooperation and support are built into the economy of nature and function more or less automatically, but at the human level, they are subject to reflection and choice. This reflection and choice become increasingly critical and far-reaching in their effects upon the earth as human technology continues to develop.

David Oates notes that taking seriously the radical interdependence of all biological beings, including ourselves, requires that we give up the hallowed assumptions and ideals of rugged individualism, unbridled technological "progress," and unrestricted competition that have been so rampant in the modern era. He surmises that the "ecological picture of interconnectedness and harmony" may "prove to be ... one of the most enduring products of the twentieth century."[41] We can hope, for our own sake as well as for numerous other organisms critically affected by our actions (or inactions), that he is right, and that this ecological picture will become emblazoned on our souls.

We are probably the most distinctive, and certainly in many ways the most powerful, of all of the earth's species. As those to whom so much has been given in the way of distinctiveness and power, much is also required. We bear a heavy burden of responsibility toward the rest of nature. Our particular gifts as a species can be used for good or ill. They can either be used to bless the earth as we learn how to live in harmony with its other creatures and contribute as fully as we can from our special strengths to their well-being, or these gifts can be misused to wreak havoc through the widespread destruction of other species and the devastation of delicate ecosystems. Sadly, the latter process is well underway, and its deplorable effects are spreading at an exponential rate in our time.

Our reason gives us the capacity to reflect critically upon the aims and outcomes of our actions. Our purposive freedom enables us to choose among alternative aims and outcomes, selecting and acting upon those that are best not only for us but for other creatures as well, and best not only in the short run but in the long run for the whole community of species. Our technological prowess provides a powerful means for the realization of our envisioned ends. We thus have a capacity for cultural evolution that complements our biological evolution, and our cultural evolution is, to a significant extent, subject to our rational planning and free decisions. How our cultural evolution proceeds has, in its turn, fundamental implications for the well-being of all of earth's creatures, so human cultural evolution and biological evolution are conjoined. The second has produced the earth's creatures over eons, and the first can either assist and preserve the myriad creatures of the earth or bring about widespread destruction among them—and in an astonishingly brief span of time.

The human factor in the system of nature on the earth is thus of critical importance, at least for the foreseeable future. The rest of nature will no doubt survive our devastations and rebuild itself over time, if we choose to ignore our responsibility to our fellow beings and plow ahead in a myopic, selfish, and imbicilic manner. We may, however, not be here to participate in that rebuilding, and innumerable species born of the patient workings of evolutionary process over hundreds of thousands of years may by that time have become extinct, and the special grace and flavor that they impart to the earth will have been lost forever.

Our duty is clear. We should do everything in our power to prevent such an outcome. We should be meliorists, not destructors, working to make things better rather than allowing things to become steadily worse. We should try in every way that we can to be a blessing to the earth, not a curse. We have eyes to see, we possess wills with which to choose, and we have or can devise the technological means with which to act for the good. To be a member of the earth's household and a citizen of the earth's community of creatures—and to be the distinctive type of members and citizens we are as human beings—is not just a privilege but a gloriously demanding and challenging responsibility. Our greatness as a species consists not in what we can take from the earth but in what we are capable of giving to it.

We are talking about a responsibility and outlook here that are not just prudential and ethical but profoundly spiritual and religious. Not only our practices but our vision of ourselves and of our place within the world must undergo fundamental alteration. Our worldview must be thoroughly ecological, and we must come instinctively to regard and feel ourselves as ecological beings. We must learn to *reverence and hold in awe the sacredness of the earth as our beloved community and household* rather than view it merely as the backdrop or setting for self-contained, self-regarding human enterprises. Deeply rooted religious sensibilities and commitment are required.

I shall argue in part 3 that nature itself, especially in this ecologically perilous time, is the most appropriate focus of our religious commitment and concern. We should no longer direct our religious energies toward a putative God who exists outside of nature and does not depend upon it, and we should no longer think of ourselves as sharing this airy transcendence in our own essential being. The religious ultimate is within the world or, more correctly, is the world, not something outside of it, and we are through and through creatures of nature, not of some other allegedly more wondrous realm. Our duty and responsibility lie here, and nowhere else. We can no more step outside of nature and escape our absolute dependence upon it and grave responsibility toward it than we can step out of our skins. As we shall see, there is much to be learned, contemplated, and acted upon religiously in this realization.

Part 2 of *A Religion of Nature* has been a defense of the metaphysical ultimacy of nature. Nothing lies behind or beyond nature; nothing is more fundamental than nature; and nothing is required to explain the existence of nature. Nature is given, and all else is to be explained and understood in terms of it. I have argued that nature, in its character of *natura naturans* or unceasing creative energy, is the most fundamental given or metaphysically ultimate aspect of itself, meaning that nature is to be seen as an ongoing process, and not merely as a static form. From this conception of nature as metaphysically ultimate, then, we turn in part 3 to nature as religiously ultimate, as both eliciting and deserving our utmost dedication, loyalty, and faith.

Part 3

A Religion of Nature

6

The Nature of Religion
and a Religion of Nature

Those who contemplate the beauty of the earth find reserves of
strength that will endure as long as life lasts. There is symbolic as
well as actual beauty in the migration of birds, the ebb and flow of
the tides, the folded bud ready for the spring. There is something
infinitely healing in the repeated refrains of nature—the assurance
of dawn comes after night and spring after the winter.
—Rachel Carson, *The Sense of Wonder*

Can nature, as characterized in the preceding chapters, be an appropriate focus
of religious commitment and concern? We in the West do not usually think of
nature in this way, given our strong tendency to connect religion to God or the
gods. Even if we extend our understanding of religion beyond the Western
world to the traditions of the East, nature does not come immediately to mind
as having religious significance in and of itself. Usually it is seen to point
beyond itself to a deeper, more transcendent reality in which it is grounded or
from which it is derived. Moreover, despite considerable discussion these days
of the urgent need for environmental *ethics* and the continuing development of
new *theologies* where the natural environment is given a much more central
place than it was allotted in earlier theological thought, there has as yet been
little consideration of the possibility or desirability of developing religious outlooks that focus on *nature itself.* The principal task of this chapter, therefore, is
to argue for recognition of nature as among the significant claimants for religious aspiration or devotion, alongside more familiar claimants such as God, the
gods, Brahman, or Tao.

What constitutes religious commitment and concern? We need to reflect on the character and function of religion before addressing the issue of whether or to what extent nature can be considered a suitable candidate for religious faith. Accordingly, this chapter is divided into two sections. The first offers a brief analysis of the nature of religion, while the second draws on this analysis in order to exhibit the feasibility of a religion of nature.

It is one thing to show that nature can be *an* appropriate focus of religious commitment, which is what the present chapter aspires to do, but it is quite another to argue that nature is the *most* appropriate object of religious faith. In the next chapter I respond to some major objections to a religion of nature and indicate why these objections do not hold. In the last chapter of this book I offer further reasons in support of a religion of nature. The case for the metaphysical ultimacy of nature developed in part 2 provides important background for arguments bearing on the religious ultimacy of nature in part 3.

THE RELIGIOUS PERSPECTIVE

What does it mean to be religious? How does religion function in human life and thought? I addressed this question in *Interpretive Theories of Religion*, most specifically in chapter 7 of that work, "A New Theory of Religion."[1] There I asserted that the function of any basic object of religious concern[2]— Yahweh, Allah, the Triune God, Zeus and the panoply of gods ruled by him, Tao, Brahman, and so on—can be characterized by six "role-functional" categories and their interrelations. I shall make use of that analysis here. The discussion in this section may seem rather abstract, but abstractness is unavoidable in a theory of religion that purports to describe the role of religious objects in general. The necessity for abstractness or of a high degree of generality becomes especially evident when we remember the great diversity in the religions of the world. In the second section of this chapter, our reflections shall become more specific and concrete as we apply the theory of religion to nature in order to assess the appropriateness of nature as a candidate for religious devotion.

The role-functional categories are Uniqueness, Primacy, Pervasiveness, Rightness, Permanence, and Hiddenness. Each is intended to identify an aspect of the distinctively religious function performed, or role played, by religious objects in the life of the religious person and in the cosmos as the religious person views it. Hence, each of the six categories has a personal and a cosmic side, and all six, along with their patterns of interrelatedness, interpret the nature of religion by portraying the putative common function of religious objects. It is important to note that these categories designate central aspects of the *function* of religious objects, not the *attributes* of such objects. Attributes of religious objects vary greatly from religious system to religious system, but, according to the theory of religion now under discussion, their function or role remains the same. This shared function demarcates them as objects of religious concern.

The category of Uniqueness indicates that the religious object, on its personal side, has a singular, unparalleled place in the life of an individual. It is not like ordinary interests or preoccupations; it is extraordinary, highly special, in a class by itself. On the cosmic side, the religious object is unique in that it contrasts with everything else; it is held in awe as something radically different or set apart.[3]

The category of Primacy calls attention to the fact that the religious object is the most important, most commanding object of interest for the religious person. It is not only more important than this or that particular interest, it is more important than all other interests taken together. It is not just one concern among many others but the *ultimate* concern of that person. On the cosmic side, the object of religion is conceived of as taking precedence over everything else in the universe, as the root principle, power, or being on which everything else depends or from which all else is derived. Thus the religious object is not only marked off from everything else, it also is ranked above all else. It has these roles both in the life of the religious person and in the world as conceived of by the religious person.[4]

The category of Pervasiveness alerts us to the function of the religious object as relating, or being expected to relate, at the deepest levels to every aspect of a person's life, and as bringing the diverse elements of that life into unity. The religious object is the most significant integrating force in personal existence, the common point of orientation and commitment around which feeling, thought, and volition finally turn. On the cosmic side, the religious object is seen as suffusing or underlying the world as a whole and as integrating it from within. The religious object thus permeates and orders personal existence and is seen by the religious person as permeating and ordering the cosmos. It provides a unified conception of self and world and establishes a bond between the deepest levels of the self and what is believed to be the core of reality.

The fourth category, Rightness, makes explicit the valuative function of the religious object. It defines the goal of human existence, laying out a path of spiritual progress toward that goal.[5] It also gives assurance of power or means to attain the goal and to persevere in the face of the perils and temptations that threaten its attainment. At the same time, the religious object serves as standard or critic, assessing each human life for the extent to which it fulfills or falls short of the purposes and values characterizing ideal human existence. It functions as the most profound healing, transforming, saving force in the life of the religious person and does so in the context of the strict requirements of its envisioned aim for human life. Thus it is redemptive in the two fundamental senses of that term: *assurance* and *demand*. In its cosmic aspect, the category of Rightness points to a goodness or fitness that the religious person regards as lying at the heart of the world. It means that human beings are not simply left to their own resources but reside in a universe that, due to the cosmic Rightness (as well as Primacy) of the religious object, is in its depths responsive—not indifferent or inimical—to their yearnings and strivings for the triumph of the salvific ideal[6] in themselves and in their world. Trust in this aspect of the category of Rightness is a significant ground of religious hope.

The category of Permanence denotes a fifth basic function of religious objects. On the personal level, the religious object provides a definitive way of coming to terms with the changeable, precarious character of temporal existence. Life in time contains threats, frustrations, and enigmas such as the fading into the ever more distant past of cherished experiences and accomplishments; regrettable mishaps or misdeeds locked in an unalterable past; a future with contingencies of fate beyond prediction or control; anxiety about future goals we fear may not be attained; the malaise of emptiness and boredom, where there seems to be far too much time rather than not enough; the inevitable alteration or dissolution over time of familiar surroundings, relationships, and institutions; the declining health of aging loved ones and friends or their loss to death; one's own steadily advancing age, with the physical and mental changes it brings; and the prospect of one's own impending death. The religious object offers guidance and strength for coping with these and other problems of temporal existence, and in that way it decisively affects the lives of religious persons. On the cosmic level, the religious object is regarded as something within or behind the cosmos that is immune to the threats and ravages of time. It is not a mere mortal thing like everything else in human experience, coming into being and passing away, but something unborn and indestructible, enduring forever or even existing outside of time altogether. It is thus either *everlasting* or *timeless*. In either case, it is a major source of security and equanimity in confronting the menaces of temporal life.

The last role-functional category, Hiddenness, brings to mind the overpowering sense of mystery and awe experienced by religious persons as they contemplate the religious object. This object is beyond speech or characterization; it lies in depths of awareness and feeling that cannot be fathomed by ordinary ways of thinking. It can only be spoken of elliptically, with symbols, metaphors, analogies, and stories that point feebly beyond themselves to levels of experience so intimate and profound as to finally reduce the religious person to reverential silence. One function of disciplined meditation in religious traditions is to still the anxious turbulence of the mind as it seeks in vain to comprehend modes of religious awareness that elude conceptual clarity or verbal expression. The importance of rituals for religious persons and religious communities can be at least partly understood as ways of acting out, rather than inquiring into or endeavoring futilely to describe, the stupifying mystery that surrounds the religious object on its personal side. Hiddenness as a cosmic function points to the religious object as the most mysterious of all realities, impervious to full exploration because it is the secret wellspring of all that is, the primordial source of existence, meaning, and value for the cosmos as a whole. To claim ability adequately to characterize it or understand it would be to betray one's failure to grasp the staggering enormity of its depth and range.

NATURE AS AN APPROPRIATE FOCUS OF RELIGIOUS CONCERN

Now that we have some sense of what it means for an object of interest to function as an object of *religious* interest, we are in a position to raise the important question of whether nature by itself can function in this way. I will address this question by considering each of the role-functional categories in turn and asking if nature can play the role or perform the function named by that category, in both its personal and its cosmic aspects. My thesis is that it can, for all six of the categories, and hence that nature can be an appropriate focus of religious concern. Let us first consider applications of the categories of the theory of religion to nature in its cosmic aspect; we can then assess their applications to nature as an object of religious concern on its personal side.

A case for the cosmic or metaphysical *uniqueness* of nature has already been made in chapter 2. There is only one nature, and everything else contrasts with it. Moreover, nature is not simply the sum total of particular things but the dynamic system of complex relations among them. One might object that I have also, in that chapter, argued for a succession of systems of nature, made possible by nature in its character of *natura naturans*. Are there not many such systems unfolding through time and not just one? How then can the present system of nature be unique? My answer is that the concept of nature should not be restricted to nature in its present form. Nature is to be viewed as a blend of stability and change, pattern and process. It is this blend that is unique, the trajectory of a nature appearing in set forms that may endure for enormous periods of time but that will also eventually give way to new forms on account of the restless workings of novelty and chance. Nature as I conceive it, then, is a combination of relative permanence and ongoing change, and it is this volatile, processive pattern of relations among particulars—itself continuing to give rise to new particulars, new types of particulars, and new sorts of relations—that is unique.

The cosmic *primacy* of nature is another term for its metaphysical ultimacy. The chief burden of part 2 was to argue for that ultimacy. Such ultimacy or primacy means that nature is aboriginal and self-sustaining. Nature is the last word in explaining the existence and character of particular things, and it does not require anything beyond itself in order to exist. The cosmic *pervasiveness* of nature is implicit in the idea that everything that exists is an expression of the potencies of nature. Nature is everywhere, encompassing, sustaining, and interrelating all things, human as well as nonhuman. What the Psalmist said of Yahweh can thus be asserted of nature:

> Whither shall I go from thy Spirit, or whither shall I flee from thy presence? If I ascend up into heaven, thou art there; if I make my bed in hell, behold, thou art there. If I take the wings of the morning and dwell in the utttermost parts of the sea; even there shall thy hand lead me, and thy right hand shall hold me.[7]

We must eliminate from this passage its references to a personal being, of course, and substitute "its" and "it" for "thy" and "thou," for I do not mean to endorse any sort of personalistic theism in relation to nature, including pantheism or panentheism. With this important qualification, however, the passage's emphasis on pervasive presence, guidance, and support can be heartily affirmed when we substitute nature for Yahweh. There are implications here for the personal side of religion as well; I shall return to them later.

We can relate the cosmic *rightness* of nature to Wendell Berry's characterization of "faith" as "our life's instinctive leap toward its origin, the motion by which we acknowledge the order and harmony to which we belong."[8] Religious faith in nature is this confident, grateful commitment to it as the universal system of order and harmony from which we and our species arise, of which we are an integral part, and upon which we absolutely depend. When Rachel Carson, in the quotation used as the epigraph to this chapter, speaks of the "assurance," "strength," and "healing" that come from contemplation of "the beauty of the earth" and "repeated refrains of nature," such as "the migration of birds, the ebb and flow of the tides, the folded bud ready for the spring," she is making implicit reference not merely to admirable *aesthetic* qualities in nature but to something of profound *religious* significance as well. She is giving testimony to her own perception of sacred grandeur and rightness in the regular processes of nature and to her lifelong experience of their power to rejuvenate and save.

Carson's testimony to a religiously sustaining rightness or fitness of nature—what I earlier called the *assurance* aspect of a religious object's redemptive function—is echoed throughout the history of humankind. Farmers and hunters have exulted from ancient times to the present about their rootage in the land, just as fisherfolk and sailors have sung of their love of the sea. Much of the passion of patriotism and nationalism arises from the feeling of attachment to a particular place on the earth, often called "fatherland" or "motherland"—this place to which I belong, my home, my beloved country. Religious traditions such as Taoism and Shintoism abound with references to the sacred mysteries of nature. Even those religions that insist upon a power greater than nature itself, on which nature depends, have made regular use in their texts of aspects of nature as pointers to the transcendent, the sacred, or the divine. The Psalms of the Hebrew Bible and the parables of Jesus in the New Testament are familiar cases in point that could easily be matched in this regard by the literature of other religious traditions. The cultures and customs of nonliterate societies are replete with references to numinous powers of the natural order, powers that must be treated with proper respect and awe. The language of poets of all places and times is shot through with images and symbols taken from nature, evoking feelings of mystical oneness with nature.

In daily life, too, reverence for nature often plays an important role. A walk in the woods or along the beach brings refreshment and rest to the soul. The crisp coolness of the morning air with the song of birds in the background makes one glad to be alive. A person in the final hours of life earnestly requests to be taken outside to experience for one last time the precious glories of the natural world. As I write these words, I gaze out my back window at a broad bayou in northwest Florida, strangely warmed and deeply moved by the sight of least terns wheeling in the cloud-strewn sky, porpoises surfacing for a gulp of air, and pelicans soaring easily over the surface of the sea with scarcely a flap of their huge wings. All of this is magic, miracle, wonder. I am part of it, and it is part of me. Here are rightness, fitness, and goodness.

My father also senses what I am trying to communicate, as we sit in rickety lawn chairs by his sea wall and watch brown pelicans fishing on the bayou. Each pelican is accompanied by at least one seagull, who lands near it when it makes its sudden, plummeting dives into the water. The gulls apparently hope to pick up morsels of the fish the pelicans are catching. One gull is even so bold as to land on the back of a particularly large pelican. The pelican seems not to notice and continues to float and watch for fish under the surface, with the other bird perched on its back, occasionally flapping its wings for balance. My father exclaims with delight in his voice, "That big old pelican is a fine, friendly, patient fellow. He doesn't even complain if the seagull wants to take a ride!"

The statement itself is made in jest and is unabashedly anthropomorphic, but I sense within it something that we at that moment share, a feeling of kinship with nature at the deepest levels of consciousness, in our very bones.

Is there not much in nature though that is dangerous and destructive as well? Are there not floods and cyclones, pestilences and diseases, droughts and famines, volcanic eruptions and avalanches? Is nature not rife with cruel predations? Are not many of its creatures, human and nonhuman, born with sad deformities or devastated by tragic accidents? And is not nature flagrantly wasteful with, and finally indifferent to, all of its progeny? How then can we speak of rightness, fitness, or goodness?

I reserve discussion of these important questions for the chapter to follow, where they can be taken up with the carefulness and detail they deserve, but I do want to make two comments in passing. First, the problem of moral ambiguity in its object of faith can hardly be fatal to a religion of nature's being considered a claimant to religious commitment, because it affects most, if not all, of the religions of the world, and their claim to being religions is generally not on that account questioned. Remember that in this chapter we are not discussing the issue of how a religion of nature compares to other religions, or how successfully its claims to truth can be defended. We are only concerned with the more limited issue of the plausibility of its designation as a religion.

Second, terms such as *rightness*, *fitness*, and *goodness* are themselves fraught with vagueness and ambiguity. They cry out for careful definitions, in the contexts of their use. Elisabet Sahtouris wisely observes that many of nature's alleged "imperfections" are the key to its creativity, to its being the admirably dynamic, resourceful system that it is. "Nature is orderly without being perfect," she writes. It is

> a live, self-creating process forever making order from chaos, forever free to do something new—to reorganize itself when necessary, even if only to stay the same, to create new forms when old ones no longer work. Perfection would be the end of evolution, the end of freedom, the end of creativity . . . nature is far less than perfect for a very good reason—for the same reason that nature is far more than mechanism![9]

Thus an assumed ideal of static, machine-like perfection, with no element of hazard or uncertainty for the present constitution of nature or any of its creatures, must be seriously questioned before we presume to apply it unthinkingly to the natural world. We should not confuse the cosmic rightness of nature now under discussion with inappropriate, unexamined conceptions of what the term *rightness* must be taken to mean. We shall return to this topic in the next chapter.

The cosmic *permanence* of nature as a religious object can be seen in its character of *natura naturans*, the dynamic power that continues forever to generate and underlie (even if eventually also to undermine and destroy) successive world systems. According to the view of nature set forth in this book, nature in some form or another always has existed and always will exist. In that sense, it is clearly everlasting, without beginning or end.

As for the cosmic *hiddenness* of nature, let me suggest several ways in which it is evident. First of all, it is exemplified by nature's sheer givenness. According to the concept of nature laid out earlier, we cannot account for the fact of nature's existence or creative ongoingness. We can only explain particular aspects of the universe in terms of their relations to one another. The existence of nature itself must remain utterly inexplicable. "Why do some things exist rather than nothing?" is a question that admits of no answer. Nature is not the work of some more fundamental principle, being, or power. It is itself ultimate, and as such, it is the ultimate mystery.

Second, there is profuse ground for wonder in discoveries of the workings of nature. For example, since the double helix character of the DNA molecule was figured out, chiefly through the labors of Francis Crick and James Watson in 1953, we have gained an increasing awareness of marvelously intricate, closely coordinated structures within the cells of biological organisms. The more our knowledge of these structures grows, the greater our amazement that such complexity of composition and function should be so commonplace on earth. Even as we continue to expand our understanding of nature's operations—from distant stars to living beings to electrons and atomic nuclei—we are filled with feelings of awe that these finely correlated processes are there to be investigated and comprehended. It also is found frequently to be the case that as old questions are answered, new ones emerge to take their place. The relation between the growth of understanding and the sense of mystery thus turns out to be direct rather than inverse.

In the third place, our conceptions of nature, as we have already seen, are a blend of our experiences and conceptual models. We cannot talk meaningfully of nature in itself, only of nature as experienced and conceived. Experienced or experienceable nature is the final test of our conceptual schemes, and our conceptual schemes give form and significance to our experience. No such scheme or combination of them, however, can begin to exhaust the complexity and richness of our experience of nature, which includes our deepest feelings of relation to it. There is always an abundance left over that the schemes fail to capture or elucidate. This penumbra or fringe of mystery not only surrounds our schemes, it suffuses them, leaving us in awe of what we can only hope to partially understand.

Fourth, we are creatures of nature, and we are privileged to have the experience of ourselves from within, yet there is much about ourselves that we do not comprehend. The relation of our minds to our bodies, of consciousness to the structures and functionings of our brains and other aspects of our physical makeup, is a mystery for which we have no convincing solutions, despite our most ingenious efforts. We can understand that certain physical events have mental correlates, and vice versa, but it is one thing to describe the physical pathways of the experience of pain, for example, and quite another to understand precisely how these physical events can give rise to an actual, firsthand experience of pain. How such physical processes also can give rise to an awareness of self, or to technology, language, the arts, religion, science, and other aspects of human cultures, is even more baffling. This realization does not require that we opt for some kind of mind-body dualism, but it does mean an admission of a significant gap in our understanding that we seem to have no conceptual resources sufficient to bridge. Somehow, a part of nature has become conscious of itself in creatures such as us, but precisely why or how it is capable of such conscious awareness we do not know. Perhaps we shall never know.

Fifth, mystery lurks in the relations of chance and causality, and in the relations of the two of these to purposive freedom. As was noted earlier, chance and freedom are by definition phenomena for which complete causal explanations cannot be given. They are phenomena of a different order than the order of cause and effect; they occur within causal contexts but cannot be entirely explained by those contexts. Yet nature exhibits, at least in the account of it presented here, an intricate interweaving of causality and chance, and it has somehow produced beings like us with purposive freedom. The mystery of the precise characters and relations of these three salient features of nature—causality, chance, and freedom—is something we have no present ability to clearly understand. It is an important part of the hiddenness of nature.

This fifth mystery of nature is closely related to the third one, for without purposive freedom there could be no development of conceptual schemes to guide our experiences of nature and no recognition of the failure of these schemes to take full measure of the complexity of our experiences. Freedom to ask probing questions and to compare and assess answers to these questions in light of the available evidence, as we saw in an earlier chapter, is essential to the meaning of theoretical inquiry. Furthermore, without purposive freedom, there could be no inquiry into cause and effect relations or their connections to chance and freedom, and a significant aspect of the mystery of consciousness is the mystery of freedom. So there are connections between the fifth and the fourth mysteries of nature as well. These five mysteries, and others that could have been mentioned as well, amply confirm the cosmic hiddenness of nature, considered as a religious object.

Let us now turn our attention to the question of how nature might function as a religious object in accordance with the personal aspect of the six categories of the theory of religion. Nature plays a *unique* role in the lives of persons when it functions for them as something sacred and set apart, a singular object of piety and reverence. A suggestion of what this means for proponents of a religion of nature is conveyed by sea captain Joshua Slocum, when he tells of sailing over the Great Bahama Banks and observing "on the white marl bottom" of the "crystal sea" "many curious living things, among them the conch in its house of exquisite tints and polished surface, the star-fish with radiated dome of curious construction, and many more denizens of the place, the names of which I could not tell, resting on the soft white bed under the sea." When he later gave some of the natural specimens he had collected on his voyage to a friend, she exclaimed, "[A]ll these curious and beautiful things are His handiwork. Who can look at such things without the heart being lifted up in adoration?"[10] If we substitute "nature's" for "His" in the friend's statement and reflect on the captain's own wondering admiration for the diversity and beauty of curious creatures on the bed of the sea, we can get some inkling of the singular piety and reverence for nature to which I allude. For some, like the captain and his friend, awe and veneration evoked by the splendors of nature are compelling evidence for a transcendent creator, and it is this religious object that is for them singular and set apart, playing a unique role in their lives. For proponents of a religion of nature, there is nothing more sacred, wonderful, and distinctive than nature itself, nature nurtured and sustained by its own immanent powers.

Nature is *primary* on the personal level for individuals when it is more important to them than anything else, the ultimate loyalty to which all of their other loyalties are subordinate. The "primary law of the universe" for such persons, in the words of Thomas Berry, is "that every component member of the universe should be integral with every other member," and "the primary norm of reality and of value is the universe community itself in its various forms of expression, especially as realized on the planet Earth."[11] In this religious vision, conscientious care for all of nature, not just those parts of it immediately useful for human habitation, takes precedence over all other concerns. The highest duty is to understand and take responsibility for an appropriately sharing and contributing role of humans within the diverse community of all of nature's creatures.

Commitment to nature is personally *pervasive* when it deeply affects every aspect of the outlook and practice of persons, so suffusing and ordering their other concerns as to give unitary focus and direction to their lives. In this manner, nature as a religious object fundamentally shapes their conceptions of themselves and of their relations to the world. Advocates of a religion of nature see themselves, first and foremost, as natural beings, close kindred of all other natural beings of earth. They acknowledge their special gifts of consciousness, culture, and freedom but also recognize that with these special gifts must come special obligations. An awareness of these obligations, which extend not merely to human societies but to the much broader societies of earth's creatures, and a continuing sense of gratitude for the privilege of being present members of the ongoing community of living beings that has populated the earth since ancient days permeate the thoughts and experiences of those who adhere to a religion of nature.

Our talk of obligation and duty in connection to the personal primacy and pervasiveness of nature as a religious object leads readily into nature's role of *rightness* in the lives of those devoted to a religion of nature. This talk relates especially to the *demand* aspect of redemptive rightness that we made mention of earlier. Religious faith in nature requires much of human beings in the way of work for maintenance of the health, diversity, beauty, and integrity of biological communities on earth. As part of this charge, it requires dedication to the well-being of human beings and their communities, as one important class of biological communities on earth and one that can only exist in close interdependence with the others, so human ethics and ecological ethics are encompassed in the demand aspect of a religion of nature. From its perspective, the first should really be seen as a subset of the second. I shall have more to say about these matters in the next chapter.

As for the *assurance* aspect of the redemptive power of nature, we have already found it necessary to indicate some of its meaning in our discussion of the cosmic rightness of nature. Since I also deal with the topic of assurance at greater length in the next chapter, which is devoted in part to defending the application of the category of Rightness to nature in response to arguments that it falls far short of the category, we need not pursue the subject any further here. Enough has already been said about the rightness of nature, in both its personal and cosmic senses, to exhibit in this important respect nature's suitability to be at least a live *candidate* for religious concern.

What can be said about the *permanence* of nature as a religious object on the personal level? To see ourselves as creatures of nature is to see ourselves as immersed in time and change. Like all else in this world, we come into being and pass away. Yet nature itself, in some form or another, endures forever. What it is at the present moment is the accumulated effect of all of its past moments, just as its future will be constituted by what is done with that past by each successive present. We are part of nature's ongoingness and can make our own contributions to it. Most of us are able to do so by our genes when we sexually reproduce, and all of us have the opportunity to contribute to the ongoingness of nature by our choices and actions. Our influence, for good or ill, lives on in the experiences and memories of relatives, friends, colleagues, and others with whom we come into contact or affect in some way. Each of us leaves his or her mark on the face of the earth by drawing upon its resources wisely or unwisely; our institutions do so as well.

In the perspective of a religion of nature, no promise is held forth of living forever in personal form. We are finite beings, and our lives shall someday come to an end, just as they came into being at a particular time. It is likely that our species will someday cease to exist as well, but there is life to be lived here and now, sorrows and disappointments to be borne, goals to be achieved, and joys to be experienced. Through it all there is a quiet contentment and gratitude for the gift of being alive, even if for only a limited span of time. The measure of a human life, for a religion of nature, is not its duration but its donation—what it contributes to the world from whence it came and to which it shall return.

"You shall be as gods," rang the ancient temptation. A religion of nature helps us to see through the temptation's hubristic lure by allowing us confidently to affirm what we are—one species of life among others, with the awesome privilege of being conscious of ourselves and the world around us, of our immense debt to the fecundity and shelter of the earth, of our freedom to act for the good of our own species and for that of all other living beings. We are not immune to the ravages of time, but it is far better to live in time than not to live at all. Our future death and our susceptibility to dangers as well as opportunities of an uncertain future are part of the price we pay for the gift of life. Our disappointments and sorrows, also the results of a life in time, can be healed by its flow as memories of them fade and new, more reassuring experiences come to take their place.

But what of our evil deeds locked in an unalterable past? Is there any such thing as forgiveness in a religion of nature? We can find forgiveness among those we have wronged, as they amazingly continue to accept us despite our felt unacceptability. This is part of the mystery of human love, and we can experience something similar to it with animals we have wronged as well. The pet dog at whom we yelled in a fit of temper, because of some minor inconvenience he caused, comes to our side later wagging his tail, with no resentment or grudge. In a religion of nature, we also can learn to face toward the future rather than the past, to amend for past misdeeds by future deeds rather than wallow in guilt over what cannot be undone. There also is the healing power of nature itself, experienced through the continuing contemplation of its ever-lasting sublimity and wonder. An awareness that so much of life is a gift can also help make us aware that even though forgiveness is not the sort of thing that can be merited or earned, it can be gratefully accepted. Grace in many guises abounds throughout life in time.

The *hiddenness* of nature as a religious object on the personal side lies in our awareness of it as the secret source of all that is, including ourselves and all of our human achievements. Its ultimate depth and mystery are felt to be inexhaustible, no matter how much about it we might come to understand or claim to understand. The wellspring of each new life, from the tiniest unicellular organism to a human being, is nature, and that is its most wondrous mystery. No science, philosophy, or art can obliterate this mystery. Even our best efforts at understanding ourselves and the nature from whence we come are tiny shafts of light projected into an infinite night.

The central task of this chapter has been to demonstrate the suitability of nature as an object of religious faith. To the extent that I have been able to give a credible account of the character of religious faith and to show, by use of the personal and cosmic sides of the six categories of the theory of religion presented here, that nature can qualify as a significant claimant for such faith, the purpose of the chapter has been realized. If, however, we now grant that nature qualifies as a possible object of religious faith, we still need to ask: How *well* does it qualify? How successfully or convincingly can the case for a religion of nature be made? The task of the last two chapters of this book is to respond to this question. In the next chapter, I consider several serious objections to a religion of nature, showing how it can be defended against these objections. In the final chapter, I present additional reasons in support of the religious ultimacy of nature.

7

Objections to a Religion of Nature

Imagine a being like nature, wasteful beyond measure, indifferent beyond measure, without purposes and consideration, without mercy and justice, fertile and desolate and uncertain at the same time; imagine indifference itself as a power—how could you live according to this indifference?
—Friedrich Nietzsche, *Beyond Good and Evil*

In this chapter I respond to six objections to a religion of nature. The first three I call *moral* objections. They allege a wanton wastefulness, unrelenting cruelty, and widespread indifference of nature and argue on these grounds that nature cannot qualify as *a* desirable, to say nothing of being the *most* desirable, focus of religious concern. The fourth and fifth objections I call *metaphysical*. The fourth maintains that since nature, as it has been conceived in the previous chapters of this book, has no personality, intentionality, or conscious awareness (i.e., it is said to contain no God, gods, or animating spirits to whom worship and prayers can be addressed or with whom one can enter into personal, I-Thou relations), then it cannot provide effective religious solace, support, guidance, or meaning. The fifth objection contends that nature cannot, with justification, be regarded as metaphysically ultimate, because it is merely contingent or lacks necessary being. Hence, it cannot have what in the previous chapter we saw to be an essential function of objects of religious concern, namely, cosmic primacy. The final objection is *practical*. It argues that since there are no existing organizations, traditions, rituals, symbols, or practices associated with a religion of nature, as here conceived, such a proposed outlook cannot nurture and sustain a robust religious life in the way that already available religious traditions and institutions can. These are formidable objections. An effective defense of a religion of nature depends to a large extent on how plausible and convincing the responses to them can be. Let us consider each of these six objections in turn under the categories indicated above.

MORAL OBJECTIONS

1. *The alleged wastefulness of nature.* The first objection is that nature is unfit to be an object of religious concern because of its rampant wastefulness. Nature, so the charge runs, carelessly and routinely squanders life-forms, species, and ecosystems. The female chinook salmon lays about 5,000 eggs. Approximately 4,000 of these will hatch, and about 400 of those that hatch will survive predators and other hazards to reach the ocean. A paltry *four* from that number will likely live to return to the parent stream for spawning.[1] Lung worms fatally infect herds of bighorn sheep, and plague decimates prairie dogs. A numbat lays waste a whole community of termites with a few swipes of its claws. Spruce and pine forests are attacked by beetles that burrow under the bark of trees, eventually killing them. Flood, fire, and lava ravage delicately interdependent systems of plants and animals built up over centuries.

About 98 percent of all biological species evolved since the onset of life on earth has now become extinct because of natural causes, and yet nature continues to churn out new ones, almost all of these also headed for the dumping ground of eventual extinction. As Stephen Jay Gould comments, biological evolution is "a massively chancy and basically destructive process," one that "must lead to a lot of dead ends, as does any branching mechanism in our largely random world."[2]

Insects constitute about three-fourths of the total number of species of life on the earth. Pondering the staggering variety of insect species, Annie Dillard is struck with the image of a nature that is "above all, profligate."

> Extravagance! This is what the sign of the insects says. No form is too grue-some, no behavior too grotesque. If you're dealing with organic compounds, then let them combine. If it works, if it quickens, set it clacking in the grass; there's always room for one more.[3]

Because each new species of clacking, voracious insects must eat to survive, its advent requires that some already established form or forms of life become its prey and perhaps even become extinct by losing out to the competitive pressure imposed by the new form of life.

In the eyes of nature, then, it would seem that nothing is singular or precious; nothing—individual species nor ecosystem—can claim the right to be cherished or preserved. Devastation, superfluity, and disregard are everywhere. Nature's ways are those of the prodigal, recklessly dissipating the wealth entrusted to its care. There is little here to be honored or admired and certainly nothing worthy of religious veneration.

This picture of an improvident, rash, and wasteful nature can be criticized, however, in a number of ways. The critical responses I shall present in this section are more or less standard and make sense as far as they go, and they are needed correctives or counterbalances to the first objection. But I shall push my responses to a deeper level as the chapter proceeds, so these responses should not be regarded as final or complete. There is some air of superficiality or insensitivity about them, or at least some of them, that I hope to correct toward the end of the next section.

First, it is a matter of perspective what counts as waste and what counts as gain. Waste for the young salmon and termites is gain for the hungry merganser or numbat. Second, despite the severe depletion of living beings by natural processes in the case of the chinook salmon, enough survive to continue the species from year to year, and a balance of predator and prey is maintained. Third, predation and disease may help weed out the less fit in a population or select for more adaptable mutants, thus ensuring the continuing viability of a species's gene pool. Fourth, the devastation of one ecosystem may pave the way for the development of another.

Fifth, the irrepressible fecundity of nature does not need to be seen as mere wasteful superfluity but can be viewed as creative upthrust and ongoing experimentation, working by a continuous process of trial and error to produce the panoplied history of biological evolution. Sixth, the extinction of some species, such as those of the ancient dinosaurs, can make room for the thriving or emergence of others, such as the various species of mammals (including us). Seventh, species may endure for millions of years, despite their eventually becoming extinct. They need not endure forever to be of significance and value. And eighth and most important, little in the nonhuman part of nature is really wasted, because almost everything is recycled. For example, certain animals and insects feed on dung and carrion, and plants make use of these materials as fertilizer. Birds and other creatures employ the hollows of dead trees for their homes, downed trees make spaces of light that allow other plants to grow, and decaying, fallen trees are returned to the soil. Streams and rivers flow into the sea, and the water of the sea is evaporated into clouds that bring back moisture to the land. The human part of nature is sometimes flagrantly wasteful, but not the nonhuman part.

One of the prices of this recycling, of course, is the suffering and death of sentient creatures. Is it not too high a price? Does not the profusion of pain and death in nature—by routine behaviors that sometimes seem unbearably gruesome—radically disqualify it as a fit object of religious concern, making it an emblem of evil rather than good, of rampant cruelty rather than redemptive rightness? Let us next consider some arguments against the feasibility of a religion of nature that focus on nature's alleged cruelty to see how they can be countered.

2. *The alleged cruelty of nature.* A "Far Side" cartoon by Gary Larson has a portly, robed, sandled, bespeckled, and bald-pated but otherwise flowingly hirsute God standing before an array of newly created animals who face him in male and female pairs. He says, "Hmmmmm . . . not bad, not bad at all. . . . Well, now I guess I'd better make some things to eat you guys."[4] There is, of course, no God in the religion of nature now under discussion, but the implication of pervasive cruelty in nature remains a fundamental indictment against any claim to its religious ultimacy.

Life in nature, as Dillard puts it, appears to be "a universal chomp."[5] What is any insect or animal after all but dinner on the hoof for other insects or animals—a handy packet of much-needed protein? The lion fells the fleeing gazelle, tearing into its neck with powerful jaws. The blue fox preys on the arctic hare, and the arctic skua conveys a steady diet of insects and lemmings to the eager beaks of its young. The stalking heron lifts a thrashing fish from a lake and proceeds to swallow it whole. The scorpion dispatches a toad with a thrust of its poison-tipped tail.

Even plants may sometimes be victors, and not mere victims, in the universal system of kill or be killed. The Neem tree of India and Burma, for example, defends itself against insect pests with a substance (azadirachtin) that resembles a molting hormone in the gypsy moth caterpillar. Having ingested the substance by feeding on the tree, the caterpillar fails to produce enough of its molting hormone to metamorphose; hence, it dies.[6]

Grisly acts of cannibalism, though relatively rare in all of nature, do regularly occur in some species. To cite a well-known example, the female preying mantis not infrequently chomps off the head of the male who mates with her. His decapitated trunk, in the meantime, may continue its mating pulsations atop her body as she turns her head back and calmly consumes it.[7] Richard Dawkins notes another example of routine cannibalism in the behavior of blackheaded gulls. They nest in large colonies, with the nests close together. When a neighbor's back is turned or when it is off fishing to bring back food for its young, an adult gull may grab one of the neighbor's newly hatched chicks and swallow it. The adult "thereby obtains a good nutritious meal," Dawkins wryly observes, "without having to go to the trouble of catching a fish, and without having to leave its own nest unprotected."[8] At every level of the blandly named "food chain," organism preys upon organism in a macabre, unceasing dance of death. What could be religiously exemplary, inspiring, or healing about such a ghastly spectacle?

My initial responses to the second objection to a religion of nature are similar in character to those I made to the first objection, in that they take us some way toward an understanding of how nature can be an appropriate focus of religious commitment despite the presence in it of so much predation, pain, suffering, and death. These critical responses, like those of the first section, are needed correctives to the points made by the objection, but neither set of responses is adequate by itself. Both need to be taken to deeper levels, a task that will be undertaken toward the end of this section. Readers should keep this proviso in mind as they contemplate the responses.

The first thing to be said in response to this second objection to the religious ultimacy of nature is that the charge of cruelty seems inappropriate, a category mistake. Nature is not a conscious being, acting with deliberation and intent, as the term *cruelty* seems strongly to imply, nor do most of its creatures act with anything like a conscious aim to be cruel, what lawyers call "malice aforethought." Perhaps with this objection we have a residue of conventional theism being brought tacitly into the discussion. A critical feature of the religion of nature under discussion here is that nature itself is simply given, the stubborn, unavoidable way things are. It is not the creation of a conscious being or beings, not the outcome of choice, purpose, or design. Hence there is no one to accuse or blame for its being what it is. Purposive beings (e.g., humans) have emerged within nature, but we should avoid attributing purpose or purposiveness to nature as such. To complain of cruelty in nature seems to overlook this crucial idea and to fall back into a different, more traditional way of thinking.

It might be argued that the *effects* are cruel, even though those effects may not be intended, but to speak of cruel effects seems strange if no cruel intentions are involved. Would we want to speak of the cruel effects of a rock slide, tornado, or flood? Such use of the term *cruel* is careless and misleading. It would be more accurate to speak of the *destructive* effects of such natural phenomena. A similar point holds true for attribution of cruelty to nature or to creatures who do not intend to act cruelly.

Second, the charge of rampant cruelty in nature betrays an anthropomorphic way of thinking, an unconscious reading of fully developed human qualities and sentiments into other creatures of nature. We have already alluded to this anthropomorphic tendency in our first response by criticizing the charge's implication that organisms such as the heron, scorpion, or preying mantis are performing consciously intended cruel acts in the manner of those human beings who may rightly be said to act cruelly. Elisabet Sahtouris warns us against the temptation of anthropomorphic interpretation of animal suffering when she takes account of "evidence that bodies which have evolved the capacity to feel pain as a trouble signal know when they can no longer protect themselves and turn off their pain system so they will not suffer needlessly."[9] It would seem far better for a weak or inept animal to die a mercifully quick death from predation than for it to perish slowly from starvation through inability to fend for itself, as would often otherwise be the case, so we should not uncritically assimilate the sufferings of nature into our human frame of reference. This observation states an important truth, even though, as we saw in chapter 5, we also should be careful not simply to dismiss the suffering of animals as nonexistent or as *totally* unlike our own suffering. We also noted in chapter 4 that pain, suffering, and death in nature are genuine *disvalues* and are to be regarded with utmost seriousness as such.

Third, the charge of pervasive cruelty in nature tends to ignore the fact that routine deaths, far from being gratuitous or unnecessary, are essential to the operation of the whole system of nature. Death is not only a means to nutrition, to allowing one group to feed on another, it also is a means to population control that benefits the members of an ecosystem over long periods of time. And it is an efficient way of recycling finite resources of nature. In addition, we need to remember that, as Holmes Rolston III and Paul Colinvaux have indicated, while suffering by death and predation are inevitable, given the kind of system that nature is, ecological balance keeps them to a minimum, and there is much peaceful, noncompetitive coexistence among living beings in their ecological niches.[10] Thus we should not exaggerate the extent of suffering or preying on sentient life in nature. Furthermore, without death, there would have been no such thing as biological evolution on earth, and no humans to ponder the religious significance of nature. In fact, no biological organisms of any kind would now exist here, for any populations of them, expanding without limit, would long since have exceeded the planet's carrying capacity.

However, I do not wish to be interpreted as a Stoic or a Dr. Pangloss about the natural order. There is a sense in which things in nature work together for much good, for example, the good of sublimely ordered ecosystems, existent on earth and probably elsewhere in the universe as well, in which incredible varieties of interdependent life-forms emerge and flourish. However, we also must take full cognizance of the fact that things work together in nature to produce much suffering and pain.

Rolston is right to insist that nature is "pro-life,"[11] but it also is pro-death. And as a character in one of Susan Howatch's novels observes, "Despite all the volumes written by learned men on the meaning of life the reality is very simple: all things die except life; despite death life gets handed on."[12] Hence, while death in nature is indeed for the sake of life, we must take due notice of the fact that life is handed on by suffering and death. This fact does not make nature itself literally cruel for reasons already indicated, but it does bar the way to a glib "big-picture" response to the charge of cruelty in nature.

The unity of nature is not one that simply swallows up its parts, rendering their sufferings insignificant and unreal, mere passing phases of the all-important, completely salutary functioning of the whole. I reject such "through-and-through" unity, as William James calls it, and opt for an axiological version of what he calls "concatenated unity."[13] A concatenated unity, according to James, is the sort of unity we find in the experienced world. It combines elements of order and disorder, causality and chance, internal and external relations, and intelligibility and inexplicability. A through-and-through unity, in contrast, exhibits only the first in each of these pairs. It is the kind of world envisioned by rationalists such as Benedict Spinoza and F. H. Bradley. I am adding to James' analysis elements of good and evil, life and death, and enjoyment and suffering.

In this concatenated unity view of nature is an irreducible dialectic of parts and whole, meaning that while we need to see the parts in relation to the whole, we also need to see the whole in relation to the parts. Neither is to be subsumed under the other. Therefore, goods of the whole that are achieved through the sufferings and deaths of the parts are attenuated and qualified by those sufferings and deaths, just as the sufferings and deaths can gain some positive meaning from the goods of the whole they make possible. Moreover, evolutionary processes do not always do what is best for all concerned, nor do they always act in the most efficient manner. The goodness of nature, in other words, is a qualified, restricted, partial, ambiguous goodness. It is interwoven with elements of irremediable pain and loss that have to be recognized and taken fully into account. For the reasons given, it is a mistake to regard nature as cruel, but it also is a mistake to be oblivious to the suffering, pain, and death that are constituent, ineliminable parts of the system of nature.

Having said all of this, however, we must admit that the amount of predation, pain, suffering, and death in nature is deeply disturbing. Is the system that makes it all necessary really a good system, even on balance? Here is an example of what I have in mind. I once lived on a lake. I was standing on the back porch of my house, looking out at the shore of the lake through my binoculars. There were some Canadian geese there, and, as it was late in the spring, there were some yellow goslings swimming in the water with their parents. Everything was pretty routine, and after watching for awhile, I started to lower my binoculars. Suddenly, from the right, a coyote began to run toward the water at high speed. In an instant, it grabbed four goslings right out of the shallow water, turned around, and began running back toward the trees and bushes on the shore with eight tiny black legs dangling from his mouth. I felt revulsion and horror, even though I knew that the coyote was probably taking the babies back to its den to be consumed by its own newly born young. Scenes similar to this one are repeated all over the world every day. We should not pretend that the eating of one species by another, or cannabilization within a particular species, is an intrinsic good. *It is an intrinsic wrong or evil.*[14] I use the term *evil* advisedly, recognizing that it is likely to mislead the Western reader into too dualistic or dichotomous an understanding of the distinction between good and evil.[15] In my account, good and evil interfuse in nature and constitute its axiological ambiguity. Some kinds of intrinsic evil are a necessary means to intrinsic goods—that is the way nature works, but recognizing this fact does not diminish the intrinsic evils or convert them into intrinsic goods. Despite its tendency to mislead, I think the term *evil* is the right one, because it captures the heinous, deplorable, inexplicable, ineliminable character of pain, suffering, and death among sentient creatures.

The system of nature that makes these wide-scale intrinsic evils necessary is *to that extent* an evil system. It is not totally evil, but the point I am making here is that it also is not totally good. Whatever positive *instrumental* value such sufferings and deaths may have, they are *intrinsically* evil. We should never forget this fact, nor should we in any way minimize or downplay it. The nature that is the focus of a religion of nature has a radical ambiguity, as far as considerations of good and evil are concerned. It is partly good but also partly evil. It contains rampant disvalues as well as rampant values. None of the responses I have made to the first two objections to a religion of nature should be allowed to blur this essential truth. They tell part of the story of nature but not the whole story. They help correct the one-sidedness of the objections but do not succeed in dismissing or resolving them entirely. Both the objections and the responses contain truth, but not even when taken together do they encompass all of the truth.

Hence, a religion of nature contains elements of irreducible mystery, stupor, revulsion, and terror within it, just as traditional theistic religion does. *There is no adequate explanation or resolution for the large amount of intrinsic evil in the world*, whether we are talking about the human or the nonhuman part of the world. Thus we cannot base our moral outlook on the whole of nature, only on some parts of it, just as traditional theists cannot base their moral views on every act of God reported in parts of the Bible. The God who commanded Saul to utterly destroy the Amalekites and fight against them until they were consumed and who vowed forever to blot out the remembrance of their name (I Samuel 15:18, Exodus 17:14, Deuteronomy 25:19) is a genocidal God. He is clearly not in that respect a fit exemplar of the moral life, nor do practicing Jews or Christians generally regard him as such. Similarly, a vision of nature that sees it as *wholly* good, serene, comforting, supportive, beautiful, and untroubling is false at its core. Much in nature is to be revered, and it is a fit object of religious devotion, but we should not suppose that the widespread intrinsic evils made necessary by the ways in which the present system of nature works are nonexistent, are completely compensated for, can be entirely justified, or can be fully explained. There is something stupifyingly mysterious and inexplicable about all forms of evil—however, whenever, and wherever they occur.

3. *Nature's alleged indifference to human beings.* Even if we grant that nature is neither flagrantly wasteful nor pervasively cruel, and even if we see it as a complex blend of values and disvalues, good and evil, it still seems to be completely indifferent to the torments and pains, strivings and ideals of human beings. In his essay, "Nature," John Stuart Mill recounts the ways in which people are regularly terrified, diseased, deprived, maimed, bereaved, or slaughtered by natural processes. He then attributes to nature "the most supercilious disregard both of mercy and of justice," and "the most callous indifference" to human well-being.[16] Pondering his father's painful death from intestinal cancer, a character in James Gould Cozzens' novel *By Love Possessed* reflects that "to justify to men these ways of nature, no tongue or pen ever successfully asserted anything—that was impossible. As of course, nature's inhumanity to man passed even man's to man."[17] Gerald Birney Smith draws a similar conclusion when he says, "[i]f we take the facts as we find them, we are compelled to recognize that the cosmic process seems to be largely indifferent to moral values."[18] Nature's apparent utter obliviousness to the deepest needs and concerns of human beings then would seem to radically disqualify it from being a proper focus of their religious hope and commitment.

The first thing to notice about this third objection to a religion of nature is that it treats nature as though it were something entirely separate from or external to human life. This approach seems to assume radical dualisms of mind and body, humanity and nature and to ignore the serious conceptual problems posed by such dualisms. In so doing, it also paints a distorted picture of nature as lived, as directly experienced by human beings, and it fails to take into account the pivotal contributions of evolutionary and ecological biology to an understanding of the place of human beings in nature. I shall not comment further on the notorious difficulties plaguing metaphysical dualisms, since they are generally well known, at least among philosophers.[19] I also have talked earlier in this book and elsewhere about the critical importance of conceiving nature as concretely lived, noting the centrality of this idea in John Dewey's philosophy of nature and showing how it bridges yawning rifts between humans and nature argued for or assumed in philosophies of the modern period.[20] I focus now on the bearing that the closely related sciences of evolution and ecology have on the notion that nature is something alien and external to human beings.

As we have noted in previous chapters, the biological sciences in our time do not portray human beings as being radically separated from nature but integrally related to it. According to the theory of evolution, humans are natural organisms and have evolved by the same processes and principles that gave rise to other organisms. They are participants in a history of origination and development common to all living beings on earth. Ecological science, for its part, provides ever-increasing evidence of the most subtle, intimate connections and reciprocities among organisms, including human beings, and between every organism and its natural environment.

David Oates beautifully describes this intricacy of relatedness in both time and space:

> The trick of seeing things separately—say, an individual tree abstracted from its forest and climate—is as artificial and misleading as looking at a river without reference to the region it drains. Neither trees nor rivers exist in isolation. In the dimension of time, a tree's biological history connects it to perhaps millions of other individuals. And in the dimensions of space, a tree both affects and is affected by hordes of other creatures, from the microscopic life in its roots to the birds and animals in its branches, from the squirrel that buried its original seed, to the plants which for some reason left a place for it to grow, to the termites and beetles and saprophytes that will consume it when it dies. An "individual" tree, in this tradition of ecology, is in some significant ways less meaningful than the tree seen as an embedded aspect of a history and an ecosystem.[21]

What holds true for trees also holds true for human beings. Sahtouris gives just one small indication of this fact when she notes that every molecule of air we "breathe, with the exception of trace amounts of inert gases such as argon and krypton, has actually been recently produced inside the cells of other living creatures."[22]

Nature, then, is not something outside of us or set against us; it suffuses and sustains us in countless ways, through every moment of our lives. As Bruce Wilshire puts the matter, each human self "is a field being, involved in some way in the cycles of the self-regenerating, interdependent universe."[23] To the extent that the third objection to a religion of nature assumes otherwise, it seems to fly in the face of much important evidence.

A second thing to notice about this objection is that it is curiously one-sided. It depicts nature as a capricious, always menacing power that gives scant solace or support to human life, and it can find no relations—other than purely destructive ones—between nature, on the one hand, and the meanings and values embedded in human cultures and human consciousness, on the other hand. An example is the stark contrast that Bertrand Russell draws between the cultural creations of human beings and the "trampling march" of natural forces, "blind to good and evil, reckless of destruction," that portend the doom of these creations after human history has had its "little day."[24] However, while we do experience aspects of nature as frighteningly unpredictable and destructive, the objection neglects to note that most of the time we experience nature as providing ample nurture and support for our lives and being so predictable and reliable in its ongoing processes—including our bodies'—as to be taken for granted.

My heart has beat its regular cadence for nearly seventy years, for example, and I have rarely paid attention to its pulsations. Were they to cease for only a few moments, I would no longer be alive, yet they do not cease, and life-giving blood flows throughout my body, maintaining my existence and my ability to write these words. Not everyone enjoys good health, and this sad truth should not be dismissed or overlooked, but the fact that so many do means that nature cannot adequately be portrayed as *only* indifferent, inimical, or destructive.[25] It has a supportive side as well as a destructive side, and the former side is amply evidenced in all of the life-forms of the earth. This supportive side is apparent in the long history of human life and its cultural creations that nature has made possible.

We would be mistaken if we thought that nature contributed nothing to the meanings and values enshrined in human cultures, or to the pervasive importance of the pursuit of values in individual human experience. Rolston rightly asks, "How do we humans come to be charged up with values if there was and is nothing in nature charging us up so?"[26] Our penchant for envisioning and striving for the attainment of values—moral, aesthetic, and religious; our possession of intelligence, consciousness, and freedom; our ability to fashion languages and diverse, ever-developing cultures—all of these things are nature's gifts to us. Here is no bland indifference to things human but moving testimony to nature's boundless creativity and continuing support.

Still, this support is not consciously intended. Nature is not itself personal, conscious, or purposive, nor—in the perspective of this book—is it the product of deliberation or design on the part of a conscious deity or group of deities. Thus to speak of nature as being indifferent is perhaps to commit, or at least to flirt with, the same category mistake that we earlier associated with speaking of it as cruel. However, if we mean by *indifferent* lacking any evidence of ongoing support, sustenance, or empowerment, nature clearly is not utterly indifferent to the accomplishments, values, and prospects of human beings.

My third response to the objection to a religion of nature now under discussion is to note again how nature can have redemptive significance for human beings and thus to counter in another way the notion that it has or can have no positive bearing on their existential concerns. I discussed the topic of the redemptive significance of nature in the previous chapter, but I now want to say a bit more about it here. Let us look briefly at how the two aspects of assurance and demand that were associated with the idea of religious redemption in chapter 6 can be related to a religion of nature.

A religion of nature can provide the fulfilling confidence that comes from the conviction of having found the meaning and end of our lives. For the religion of nature, we are natural beings through and through. We belong to the cosmos, and it to us. We are comfortably at home, as we saw in chapter 5. Principles and laws of nature that apply to other organisms apply to us. Distinctive though we are as a species, we are not aliens on the earth but one of its numerous offspring, generally sheltered and sustained—although sometimes threatened and harmed—by its immanent powers. Like all natural beings, we are vulnerable, and we come into being and pass away. We can, however, have a keen sense of privilege to be here as creatures with knowledge and awareness, capable of contemplating nature's imposing majesty, its awesome beauty, its restless creativity, its incredible diversity—and its complex interdependencies that encompass us and our cultural activities.

Oates testifies to the redemptive effect of such awareness when he tells of how, after at first feeling assaulted and victimized by a terrifying lightning storm on a high peak, he somehow broke through to a deeper comprehension that nature was not an indifferent power standing against him but a sustaining presence of which he was an intimate part. "I was connected. I can scarcely convey what a deliverance this news was to me. I was not some alien being wandering a dead world, but a living part of the living earth. I belonged here." In this new mood of "curious calm," as he describes it, he was able to see lightning storms as appropriate expressions of the "realness" of the mountains, of their being "simply themselves."[27] His exposure to such fearsome power, he saw, was no different from that of other earthly creatures, and he no longer yearned for the human situation to be otherwise.

The price exacted by the sense of belonging, in other words, is that of being able to come to terms with the laws of our natural home, and with our susceptibility as finite beings to the operations of those laws. The privilege of belonging is to be able to say with restful assurance of our relation to nature what the *Upanishads* affirm of Brahman: "That thou art!" A religion of nature can thus abundantly satisfy what Oates characterizes as "one of the most powerful of human longings: the desire to be rooted in nature."[28] In this way, it can rejuvenate, inspire, and redeem.

Don Cupitt warns us, however, against putatively religious visions that lack seriousness and depth because they make no demands on us.[29] If a religion of nature is to qualify as being *redemptive* in the complete sense of that term, it must call for more than a mere passive celebration of our rootedness in nature. With the recognition of our connectedness and belongingness comes the recognition of accompanying serious responsibilities. Only by understanding the demands that our relations to nature impose upon us can we begin to become attuned to the natural order and experience a religion of nature's transformative powers.

Let me sketch some of the outlines of this dimension of demand. First and most obvious is the demand that we strive to be ecologically responsible. We must abandon the delusion that nonliving and living parts of nature are there simply to be utilized by us, in any way that we see fit. We must exhibit by our actions, both individually and collectively, a reverence for ecosystems, species, and particular life-forms. We must control our human population and learn to keep our technologies in balance with nature. We must recycle and conserve. We must restore those parts of the earth that our agricultural and industrial practices have ravaged. We must find ways to cease disrupting and destroying our natural home and to build harmonious relations with all of its creatures. We must set aside and preserve wild places for their own sakes and to remind ourselves of the abiding significance and value of that nature of which we are part. The meaning of ecological responsibility has been much discussed in our time, and I need not belabor its details here. I want only to emphasize its fundamental place in a religion of nature.

Second, we would do well to try to emulate some aspects of nature in our political systems and in our relations with one another. Given the axiological ambiguity of nature stressed earlier, we should not assume that acknowledging the ultimacy of nature requires that we try to imitate all of nature's ways in a slavish, unthinking fashion. The mistake of Social Darwinism in the late 1800s and the early 1900s was to think that the nonhuman part of nature, in all of its aspects, must furnish norms for human conduct, but the nonhuman part of nature can forcibly bring home to us certain crucial moral demands.

Here are two examples. On the one hand, the teeming diversity of ecological systems projects an ideal of striving for human societies in which differences such as those of cultural background, individual temperament, and personal freedom are cherished, supported, and allowed to flourish. The tight networks of interdependency and interrelatedness in ecosystems, on the other hand, suggest the critical moral demands of shared responsibility and mutual respect, of learning to live together despite our differences, and of seeking high levels of dynamism and progress in society through encouraging creative interactions of its diverse constituencies.

However, the demands of a religion of nature do not stem exclusively from nonhuman nature. That notion is not what the ultimacy of nature means, at least not in the religious outlook being described here. We need to remind ourselves again that in the perspective of a religion of nature, human beings, with their cultures and patterns of social existence—impressively distinct as these are compared to other aspects of nature—are an integral part of nature and manifest its inherent potentialities. The moral demands of our human social existence, as enshrined in our various moral traditions and reflected in our ongoing struggles to build more just societies, have an integrity and importance that cannot simply be reduced to established practices in the rest of nature. Nevertheless, these moral demands are to be viewed as a central component of the redemptive significance of a religion of nature, because all human activities are seen as being in and of nature, not external to it or set over against it.[30]

A basic point to keep in mind here is that human morality cannot be derived directly from the nonhuman part of nature, although there are suggestions and implications in this aspect of nature for developing an adequate human morality. In any event, I do not think of morality as being directly derivable from one's religious outlook, whatever the character of that outlook. Morality has a separate, autonomous character, and we must address and seek to resolve moral questions on their own terms. We have to work out a morality appropriate to our lives as human beings, and no other part of nature can automatically do this for us. However, it is nature that has evolved us with the incentive, capacity, and resources (e.g., language, culture, consciousness, freedom) to think and act morally, and in this fundamental sense our moral intuitions, moral systems, and the moral underpinnings and aspirations of our hearts and cultures are gifts of nature. Our moral intuitions as humans also are a basis on which we can critically examine what aspects of the nonhuman parts of nature are to be most significant for us, not only morally but also religiously. Our religious outlook can thus be deeply informed and guided by our moral insight and awareness, just as our moral lives can be given inspiration, context, scope, and direction by our vision of nature and of our place within nature.

For a religion of nature, the moral demands incumbent upon human life cannot be restricted to human communities or human social interactions. This fact brings us back to the theme of our ecological obligations. What H. Richard Niebuhr writes from his own perspective of Christian theism is especially appropriate for a religion of nature: "[O]ur life . . . takes place within a society whose boundaries cannot be drawn in space, or time, or extent of interaction, short of a whole in which we live and move and have our being."[31] For a religion of nature, that whole is nature itself, and the full range of responsibility and demand adumbrated in Niebuhr's statement constitutes a crucial part of the redemptive significance of this religious vision. This significance, in its two dimensions of assurance and demand, helps lay to rest the misguided notion that nature must be regarded as being wholly indifferent to human activities and concerns.

METAPHYSICAL OBJECTIONS

4. *The absence of personality, intentionality, or conscious awareness in nature.* We can imagine a person saying at this point, thus raising the first *metaphysical* objection to a religion of nature identified at the beginning of this chapter, something like the following: "All that you have said so far about nature evoking a modicum of religious sensibility and concern may be true enough as far as it goes. But nature by itself, without some kind of personal spiritual presence lying behind or within it, a presence that has purposefully created it and/or lovingly guides it and sustains it in being, cannot begin to compare in religious power, value, or allure with those religions, such as Judaism, Christianity, and Islam, where such a presence is assumed to exist and is the focus of religious faith.

"What is most wanted in the religious life," our imagined objector continues, "is responsive *personality,* a cosmic Self (or at least a community of cosmic selves) who deeply cares for us and for what happens to us, who is responsive to our prayers and desperate yearnings and needs, who loves us and seeks actively to redeem us. We cannot find fulfillment in some faceless, impersonal system of nature that is itself unaffected by and oblivious to whether as individual human beings we live in hope or despair, joy or anguish, enrichment or emptiness—or, indeed, whether any particular one of us lives at all. In a religion of nature there is no God with conscious mercy and grace, no cosmic personality with whom we can commune and to whose steadfast purposes we can turn for guidance and assurance, no personal being who works tirelessly for goodness and fights against evil, no outstretched everlasting arms to which we can look for encouragement and rest. In comparison with religions where divine personality, intention, and awareness are believed to lie at the heart of things and to give meaning to our lives in the world, a religion of nature pales into relative insignificance."

This objection is an important one; it correctly notes that, in the metaphysics of nature presented in part 2 of this book, no creating, underlying, or suffusing God, gods, or animating spirits are present in nature or beyond nature, nor are such beings required to explain the existence of nature. The metaphysics of part 2 is neither theistic, pantheistic, polytheistic, nor animistic in character.

For this metaphysics, nature itself has no purpose; it is not the outcome of conscious design, nor is it guided by the purposive will of a personal being or beings. The metaphysics in whose name the objector calls into question the adequacy of a religion of nature is one in which personality and purpose are not just outcomes of evolutionary processes within nature but the heart and soul of reality itself. Thus we have the clash of two markedly different metaphysical outlooks. I do not intend in this section to offer any further philosophical elaboration or defense of my metaphysics of nature as such, but I do want to defend it against the charge that its vision of nature is hopelessly inadequate or inferior when brought into a religious perspective.

A good place to begin this defense is to note the fact that *wanting* something to be a certain way is by no means an argument for its *being* that way. The adequacy of a religious vision is crucially dependent upon the truth of its central assumptions and assertions. We might grant that there is much that might be desirable in a vision of nature as undergirded by conscious purpose and design, but what is the evidence for this vision? None of the arguments that I have encountered so far convince me that there is a central, controlling being or combination of conscious beings that gave rise to this vast universe and continues to sustain and direct it.[32] I also do not find convincing those arguments that purport to show that there is some kind of conscious spirit or spirits suffusing the cosmos that ensoul it, guide it, and continually lure it toward goodness. There are lures to goodness in the world, and I shall discuss some of these in the next chapter, but I do not think that these lures are *consciously* intended or directed. To show that they are is a daunting task, and in my judgment it is not one that has been carried out successfully, at least to date. In fact, there are some significant advantages in not thinking about ourselves or the world along the lines of traditional Western religious beliefs, and I shall present and discuss these as this chapter and the next unfold.

I remain open to new evidence, and I respect the views of those who think differently than I do. I simply state that the evidence so far adduced in support of believing in God, gods, or animating spirits claimed to explain or be at the heart of nature is not convincing to me. Many thinkers of my time also remain unconvinced. The point of this first response to the fourth objection to a religion of nature then is that it is *the truth, not the desirability*, of claims about personality, intentionality, or conscious awareness underlying, informing, or accounting for nature that is at stake. These are two separate issues that should not be confused. I am arguing that the focus should be on the question of truth. If we conclude, as I have, that the truth of these claims has not been adequately shown, then that finding may mean that we must look elsewhere for religious sustenance and direction.

It does little good for people of our day to pine nostalgically for the metaphysics of an earlier time if they no longer find that metaphysics philosophically convincing, religiously meaningful, or in accordance with central parts of their worldviews. To continue to adhere or pretend to adhere to ways of thinking that people in all honesty no longer find tenable is hardly a route to authenticity in their religious lives. If they are to continue to love the traditional God or gods—or variants of them—religiously, they must do so with their whole hearts, souls, *minds*, and strengths. When such traditional religious ultimates no longer command the assent of their minds, then something fundamental in their makeup has been left out, meaning that the putative ultimates fail to satisfy the function of *pervasiveness* at the personal level. They would also not be convinced intellectually of the *primacy* of such alleged ultimates, insofar as their respective views of the world are concerned. These statements convey the stubborn truth of the case, no matter how hauntingly attractive or desirable the traditional ultimates or some aspects of the systems of thought that turn on them may continue to be. My first response to the fourth objection to a religion of nature then is that longing for something to be convincing or true does not make it so.

My second response is that there is a great advantage in nature's not having a traditional divine consciousness and intentionality behind it. The advantage is that there is no Job-like predicament in a religion of nature. Nature and its concatenated ambiguities are not the outcome of purpose or design. Sufferings, pains, and losses need not be ultimately traced—as in the Book of Job—to the inscrutable personal will of an all-perfect, all-powerful God who has created the universe and everything in it, and who continues to preside over its fate. Hence, we have no need in a religion of nature to try to construct some kind of theodicy intended to explain why a God of absolute power and perfect goodness should have created or wanted a world in which so much suffering and sorrow exist.

In the first section of this chapter, I defended nature against three moral objections, and in doing so I offered a version of what might, with some tongue in cheek, be called *physidicy*, a coined word suggesting the "justice" (Greek: *dikē*)—that is, the religious value and significance—of nature (Greek: *physis*) in the face of such serious moral objections. This physidicy, however, does not have to contend with the idea that a conscious, purposeful, knowing, and loving being created nature in its present state. The task of physidicy is thus in that important respect much simpler to carry out than is the task of traditional theodicy, and this relative simplicity is one of the distinct advantages of a religion of nature, compared to traditional theological views. Traditional theology founders on the problem of evil in a way that a religion of nature does not. An existential problem of evil, that is, how to cope with evil in daily life, remains in a religion of nature, as it does in all religious outlooks. But there is in it no conceptual problem comparable to the intractable conundrum posed by belief in an all-knowing, all-loving, all-powerful God and trying to make that belief consistent with the presence of so much suffering and evil in the world. The best that the God of Job could do with that problem was to say to Job, "I am God, and you are a mere mortal. There is no way in which you could possibly understand why I have created the world in the way that I have, or why I rule over it in the way that I do. So be quiet, quit objecting, and worship me!"[33] Such "put-your-mind-in-neutral" advice does not seem conducive to a fully integrated, wholehearted religious life. It threatens to make religious faith arbitrary and irrational by reducing it to unthinking acquiescence and blind credulity.

A third response to this fourth objection notes that while there is no purpose *of* nature in a religion of nature, there is purpose *in* nature. For example, human beings are conscious, purposive, reflective beings, and they can find plenty to live for and be responsible for within the immanent domains of their own lives, their circles of families and friends, their workplaces, their communities, and their natural surroundings. An externally imposed purpose or set of purposes would have no meaning anyway, unless these purposes could be confirmed as being valuable and important in each person's own experience and thought.

It is enough that the cosmos has produced beings capable of living purposive lives and of evaluating and criticizing possible reasons for choice. In beings such as we are, products of the creativity of biological evolution, a portion of the earth has reached a relatively high level of self-consciousness and, with that, an ability to deliberate and choose freely among alternatives. We humans can find purpose, challenge, and direction in this purely immanental process of deliberation and choice by seeking to discover and act upon the possibilities for personal and social development—intellectual, moral, aesthetic, spiritual, and so on—that are available to us in the conditions of our lives, and by coming to understand and accept the responsibilities we have to one another and to our natural environments.

A fourth response to the objection to a religion of nature now under discussion calls attention to the fact that there are a number of religious traditions or religious outlooks that do not endorse the idea of distinct personality or consciously entertained purposes, responses, and decisions in their religious ultimates. Thus a religion of nature is hardly alone in this respect, nor is it necessarily deficient for this reason.

Pantheistic or panentheistic deities, for example, tend to be impersonal. Benedict de Spinoza's pantheistic conception of God, laid out in his *Ethics in the Geometrical Order*,[34] identifies God with nature and pointedly denies personality to God. There are no "I-Thou" relations with God in Spinoza's scheme, nor does his deity create the world, have conscious awareness, make decisions, or respond to prayers. The pantheistic tradition of Advaita Vedanta in Hinduism, to cite another example, claims that the deepest understanding (or, more accurately, the deepest level of experience) of Brahman as its religious ultimate requires that we deny to it any specific qualities, including those associated with consciousness and personality. To conceive of Brahman as a separate personal being is to be in the grip of *maya*, a Sanskrit word that can be translated in this context as "misperception" or "misunderstanding." Such a conception is not altogether false, because it has some approximation to truth and some existential value, but it does not express the highest truth.

Protestant theologian Sallie MacFague's recent defense of a version of pan*en*theism, in her book *The Body of God*, presents a view of deity that she herself readily admits is "amorphous" in contrast to the traditional theistic view. She claims that this amorphous character is a "great asset" of her model of God, because it avoids the strongly anthropocentric tendencies of the traditional view and promotes "cosmocentrism" instead.[35] MacFague seems to want to be deliberately vague about how such a God, conceived as containing the world as its "body" but also as being much more than the world, can be engaged in personal terms or provide specific guidance and direction for human life. In fact, she explicitly denies mind or will to God, does not wish to speak of God as self or soul, and prefers to refer to God as "it."[36] For her, God is not person but *spirit*, "permeating, suffusing, and energizing the innermost being of each and every entity in creation in ways unknown and unknowable in our human, personal categories."[37] MacFague argues that her model of God more closely accords with contemporary scientific accounts of the origin and nature of the universe, and that it is especially consonant with Darwin's theory of evolution and with the ecological understanding of the relations of human beings to nature.

Finally, neither Theravada Buddhism nor Taoism, to cite two other profound and long-lasting religious traditions in addition to Advaita Vedanta, endorses a conception of the religious ultimate as a separate personal being. Taoism is a kind of mystical pantheism rather than personalistic theism, and Theravada Buddhism has no God or gods of any kind at the center of its religious outlook. Thus it is by no means obvious that only a religion claiming a personal God (or class of gods) as its religious ultimate is capable of providing adequate inspiration, empowerment, or meaning for religious life.

Nor does it go without saying that alleged values of traditional theism in particular, such as those posited in the fourth objection, outweigh the well-known, widely discussed intellectual problems that this position poses. Three standard examples of such problems are the notorious and seemingly insoluable problem of evil already alluded to, the problem of why a transcendent, disembodied, timeless, self-sufficient being would have wanted to create this world in the first place, and the problem of how a being so conceived can relate meaningfully to the world. The last problem focuses on the dualism of God and the world implied by traditional theism. So radically different are God and the world said to be, so stark the claimed contrast between divine infinitude and the finitude of the world, that it is not at all clear what basis there would be for the two to have any kind of reciprocal relations with one another.

It therefore should not be assumed out of hand that positive arguments for a personal religious ultimate are or are generally going to be more persuasive—either religiously or metaphysically—than those that can be presented for nonpersonal conceptions of it. I believe, for example, that the case for a religion of nature is both existentially and intellectually more compelling, all things considered, than arguments known to me purporting to show that the universe as a whole is the creation of a conscious divine being or beings, or that it is undergirded by such a being or beings. Clearly, the existence of nature itself is not debatable in the way that the existence of God, gods, or the animating spirits of the world has been. I return to this point in the next section.

A fifth line of critical response to the fourth objection to a religion of nature is that it seems anthropomorphic, presumptuous, and hubristic in its assumption that something closely resembling human personality must lie at the core of the universe. Moreover, it tends to set up an ideal of existence, especially human existence, that goes against the grain of our character as natural beings. In making a personal being or beings the ultimate principle of things, the objection tacitly elevates humans to a place of prominence within the universe as a whole, thus endorsing a hierarchical view of nature with us at the pinnacle of the hierarchy. We are the most important thing in the universe other than the religious ultimate, the objection seems to imply, because we so closely resemble that ultimate, and it so closely resembles us.

We are, however, just one offshoot of the immensity of nature, a nature that manifests its incalculable potentialities in myriad ways. Biological evolution here on earth, for example, is multidirectional not unidirectional. It is not the story of "the ascent of man" but of a dense bush with many branches leading out in different directions. It is not directed toward us, nor does it culminate in us. Nature is a web of interdependencies, not a hierarchy leading upward and finding its apex in human beings. Why, then, should it be so readily assumed that a being or beings like us must be at the heart of nature?

This assumption seems arrogant and ill advised. It lacks appropriate humility in the face of the diversity, immensity, and mystery of nature. It seems to be pre-Copernican, pre-Darwinian, pre-galactic, and pre-ecological. It makes something similar to us the spider in the web rather than sees our form of being as only a tiny part of the web. Perhaps there is no spider after all, no personal source and sustainer of nature resembling us, but only the web of nature, continually generating its multiple forms of being, including us. Something akin to this picture of nature is what I am arguing for in this book.

The fourth objection to a religion of nature, to the extent that it is tied to the traditional theistic view, also suggests that the ideal form of existence is one of being transcendent and disembodied, of being free from the laws and constraints that bind nature's creatures, of ruling over nature from without. Not only are these ideas traditionally associated with God, but they also have been traditionally associated with humans, conceived of as being created in the image of God. The traditional conception of God thus tends to perpetuate a view of humans as well. Their souls are immaterial and immortal. Humans were created to have dominion over nature. Nature is the mere temporary stage setting for the events of their history and relations with God. Nearly all of the focus then is on humans, not upon nature itself, and the role of nature is to subserve the needs of human beings.

This view of the ideal form of existence is part of the "great chain of being" tradition in metaphysics and theology, with God at the top of the chain and humans only slightly below, "a little lower than the angels." It stands in stark contrast to the ecological vision of nature here on earth, where the place of humans is not one of dominance over a system of nature that they somehow stand outside of but rather one of radical dependence on a nature of which they are an integral part. Here the ideal form of existence is being privileged to be a part of the web of nature and a full participant in its processes, not being independent of that web and lording over it from without. Far from being religiously or metaphysically desirable then, the notion of a radically transcendent God as having no need of nature and presiding over it from the outside, and of humans resembling God in their essential nature, perpetuates an ideal of existence that makes humans something other than natural beings and places the emphasis not on mutual dependence with and responsibility toward other creatures of nature but on exploitation and self-sufficiency. Perhaps the traditional picture of God and the disembodied, dominating, non-ecological picture of humans go hand in hand. I venture to suggest that the traditional idea of God may really be—at least in some important respects—an uninformed, outmoded, and presumptuous image of the place of humans in the universe magnified and projected onto the heavens. At the very least, this possibility should give us pause before we rush to the judgment that metaphysical and religious ultimacy must be accorded to a conscious being or beings similar to ourselves.

But what about prayer? How can we conceive of a vital religious life if there is no conscious, purposeful being with whom we can commune and communicate in prayer, and to whom we can give worship, thanks, and praise in prayer? My sixth and final response to the fourth objection to a religion of nature considers this part of the objection. It is true that prayers of petition seem inappropriate in a religion of nature, given that there is no conscious being or beings to whom such prayers can be addressed. It also is true though that the notion of prayers of petition presents serious problems in religions where conscious personality is the assumed religious ultimate. Do such prayers remind God or the gods of something he or they have forgotten to do and need to be reminded to do by human prayers? Do the prayers somehow persuade God or the gods to do something he or they would otherwise not be inclined to do? An affirmative answer to such questions seems to bespeak a rather low, unworthy, and implausible conception of the religious ultimate.

I was talking to a person who believes in God about an airplane crash that occurred a few years ago in the Florida Everglades, one in which a large number of people were killed. She had seen an account on television of one of the men who were searching for the instrument box from the plane that might disclose why it had crashed, and thus help to prevent future airplane crashes. This man had prayed to God that the group searching for the box might find it, and it was he who eventually did find it. My friend said something like, "See, this event shows that God does answer prayers." But did God really have to be persuaded or reminded to help in the search? Could someone else's prayers earlier on for a safe journey have persuaded God to prevent the plane from crashing? Is the operation of God's love and care in specific instances really contingent upon whether or not someone happens to pray for it?

My point is that the inappropriateness of petitionary prayer in a religion of nature is made less problematic or troubling when we reflect critically on how difficult it is to find plausible explanations of how this kind of prayer is supposed to work in religions having a powerful and caring God or gods as their focal point of concern. Instead of petitioning God or the gods for specific things, should humans not give thanks that God or the gods are knowledgeable and loving and simply express in their prayers their intent to align themselves with the good purposes of the deity or deities?

If so, then the contrast between a religion of nature and religions with personal religious ultimates is greatly mitigated, for in a religion of nature it also is possible to express gratitude, trust, and personal resolve in meditations upon nature. One does not have to believe in a God or gods to be grateful for being alive or to strive to be a trustworthy citizen of the community of the earth, and it is entirely appropriate to have rituals or ceremonies in which one articulates this spirit of gratitude and striving. While *worship* in the proper sense of the term is probably only appropriate for religions with a personal ultimate, one can certainly meditate on nature and on one's place in nature in a thankful, praising, aspiring spirit, giving recognition to its greatness and grandeur and resolving to live responsibly as one of its creatures.

Similarly, one can confess and repent of one's sins and failures and resolve to ask for forgiveness from one's fellow creatures whom one has wronged, so something akin to prayers of thankfulness, praise, confession, repentence, and endeavoring to live a more worthy life are appropriate in a religion of nature, even if prayers of petition, worship, and requests for forgiveness from nature itself are not. These appropriate kinds of meditational prayers, both alone and in company with others, can help give to the lives of those persons who adhere to a religion of nature an ever-deepening spiritual quality, a sensitivity and willingness to work for the needs of others (including those others of the nonhuman part of nature who are affected by our human actions or inactions), and an intensity of commitment.

5. *The claim that nature is contingent and thus cannot be metaphysically or religiously ultimate.* The fifth objection to a religion of nature insists that nature does not qualify as a focus of religious commitment, or at least not as the most appropriate focus, because nature is dependent upon something more fundamental than itself. It thus lacks cosmic or metaphysical primacy, and we ought to devote our religious lives to that which is truly primary or ultimate, namely, the ground of nature—that which is required to explain the origin of nature and/or its continued existence. Only that which exists necessarily and not merely contingently, so the objection goes, is worthy of religious faith and commitment, and every aspect of nature, as well as nature itself, is contingent. All things in nature come into being and pass away, each and every thing is dependent upon something else for its existence, and we cannot explain the origin or persistence in being of the system of nature as a whole unless we postulate a necessary being that has brought it into existence or continues to sustain its existence moment by moment and day by day.

Where did nature come from? Why do some things exist rather than nothing? Why do these particular things exist rather than some other things? According to the objection, these questions expose the contingency of nature and point toward the need for a more ultimate source or explanation for it, but do the questions really lead to that conclusion? My response to this objection questions this assumption, if it is meant to imply the existence of some kind of necessary being other than nature itself. We can question the assumption in the first place by noting that all of the questions apply as much to God as they do to nature. Where did God come from? Why does God exist rather than no God at all? Why this particular God rather than some other God? Explaining nature by appeal to a putative necessary being beyond or behind nature simply pushes the explanation back a step, a step where the same questions must again be raised.

In the second place, all explanations, if they are truly that, must terminate at some point. An infinite regress of explanations does not qualify as an explanation. The logic of explanation requires that something must be accepted as given, on the basis of which something else can be explained, and there is no compelling reason not to conclude that the given is nature itself. I noted in chapter 1 Bertrand Russell's point that we do not need to explain nature because it is the given. We explain one thing in terms of another within the context of nature, but we need not think that we must provide an explanation for nature. The two sorts of explanation are quite different, and it is important that we not confuse them or think of them as amounting to the same thing, nor should we think that the first sort of explanation leads necessarily to or requires the second. The need for the second is not nearly so straightforward, logical, or clear as the obvious and continuing need for the first. Something has to be accepted as given, and nature itself can be regarded as that something. I agree with Russell's reasoning.

In the third place, we can even conceive of nature as existing necessarily, as long as we identify nature with *natura naturans* rather than *natura naturata*. For as I indicated in chapter 2, I share the view of Alfred North Whitehead and others that, because of the relentless workings of novelty, there is an endless succession of cosmic epochs in which one particular sort of universe gives way, over eons, to another sort, each universe having its own constituents, principles, and laws. Thus nature as we presently experience it (*natura naturata*) is admittedly contingent, in the sense of coming into being and eventually ceasing to be, but that which exists necessarily and thus never will cease to do so is the creative power (*natura naturans*) underlying and producing all of the systems of nature that ever have been or ever will be.

Nature in its most fundamental character, as I view it, is a dynamic, ever-changing process, not a static state. Its dynamism is always operative within and upon existing structures, so each new universe or phase of development within an existing one is a transformation of older forms rather than an utterly new beginning. Change is the name of the game, but there is no such thing as change without structures in and in relation to which change takes place. Thus nature conceived as *natura naturans* does exist necessarily and does have cosmic ultimacy, and this means that it can qualify for religious primacy. There is no need to appeal to some other putative given such as God, the gods, or animating spirits to account for nature's origin or continuing existence.

In the fourth place, nature as the proposed metaphysical and religious ultimate (or given) has the advantage of being something that is open to scientific investigation and understanding. It is something perceivable and all around us, not some mysterious presence, being, or beings of an entirely different order than nature itself. Nature as a dynamic, ever-changing system is the subject matter of the natural sciences and something that can readily be admitted to exist by everyone. Unlike the alleged existence of God, gods, or animating spirits of nature, the existence of nature itself is beyond debate. Nature is thus, I submit, a more plausible candidate for the given to which all explanations must ultimately appeal than is the reputedly personal but notoriously vague and elusive being (or beings) from which nature often is said to derive or by which it is said to be informed and sustained. Such a being or beings do not really explain much, because they are far more mysterious and their existence is far more questionable than is the character or existence of nature itself. It is true that we do not know nature through and through, and that in all likelihood we never will, but it makes eminent good sense to surmise, as did Julien Offray de la Mettrie in the eighteenth century, that "causes hidden in her breast might have produced everything."[38]

6. *The practical objection.* The final objection is a practical one. Even if we grant that the preceding five objections can be met and that a convincing case can otherwise be made for a religion of nature, a fundamental obstacle to its feasibility remains and stubbornly stares us in the face. There are no practicing communities, no institutional structures, no duly constituted cadre of leaders, no body of traditional beliefs, no rituals or ceremonies, no revered founders or scriptures, no stories, myths, and symbols, and so on that are explicitly devoted to a religion of nature. The absence of these essential components of vital religion means that a religion of nature must be a purely private affair, probably forever restricted to a tiny number of isolated individuals, with no guidance and support of an established, flourishing community of like-minded persons. Making an *intellectual* case for a religion of nature and showing how it could realistically be put into *practice* by significant numbers of people are two entirely different things. Difficult as the first task may be, the difficulty does not begin to compare with the second one. It is not at all clear how a religion of nature could be a practical option for most persons in the way that established religious institutions and their historic traditions continue to be. As I noted in chapter 1, there are no churches

of nature in our neighborhoods, nor will we find a listing for them in the *Yellow Pages* of our telephone books.

I regard this objection as a highly significant one, and I have no ready or detailed answer to it. In fact, I think that providing even the respectable beginnings of a detailed answer would require another book at least as long as this one, and I may not be the best person to write such a book. My skills, such as they are, are mainly those of a contemplative philosopher and religious thinker, not those of an active, effective organizer of new institutions, but I do think that an essential step, and probably the first step, in the establishment of new institutions and traditions, religious or otherwise, is the articulation of a convincing and empowering vision.

I am trying in this book to contribute toward the envisioning of a religion of nature. Others may and no doubt will develop aspects of this vision differently and more profoundly than I present it here. I am glad to join with them in this momentous and ongoing task. Still others may show us how to put the vision of a religion of nature into practice on an institutional scale, that is, how to begin creating communities of persons dedicated to helping one another to think through, express, and live up to its ideals, and to rearing their children in its newly developing traditions. I invite and welcome their contributions as well.

We also need to remind ourselves that there are established religious traditions, such as Taoism, Shintoism, and Native American religions, that are close in many ways to a religion of nature, and most of the great religions—past or present—have underlying motifs of fascination and awe directed at nature as the context within which the powers of the sacred or divine operate and manifest themselves. Thus the institutionalization of a religion of nature does not have to take place in a vacuum. There is already a fertile field of potential materials—ideas, values, precepts, stories, myths, symbols, rituals, and the like—in existing religious traditions from which a religion of nature can draw in developing beliefs, evocations, objectives, and practices appropriate to itself. No new religion has ever begun from scratch; all new ones have been transformations of one or more older ones. An emerging Judaism probably worked with ingredients of Egyptian and Canaanite religion and, later, with Persian Zoroastrianism; Christianity was born in the womb of Judaism; Islam borrowed from Judaism and Christianity; Buddhism was a critical reaction to Hinduism but also was deeply influenced by it; and so on.

So even though I regard this sixth objection as serious, I do not see it as a fatal objection to a religion of nature. The work I do here toward the articulation and defense of a religion of nature is only the barest beginning, an invitation to further thought and discussion among persons with intimations, inclinations, and strivings similar to my own. It also is an invitation to those with organizational and administrative skills far greater than my own to consider how we might begin to build communities and institutions that find ways to conceptualize, express, and practice a reverence for and devotion to nature that we in the West have formerly reserved for God.[39]

8

The Religious Ultimacy of Nature

Oh Nature! from thee are all things, in thee all things subsist, and
to thee all tend.

—Marcus Aurelius, *Meditations*

In this final chapter we consider a further set of reasons for according religious
ultimacy to nature. These reasons take the form of showing why and in what
respects nature can be regarded as the principal source of good for all of its
creatures, including human beings. I submit that this claim remains resound-
ingly true, even when we take into account the moral ambiguity, that is, the
admixture of values and disvalues, goods and evils of nature, described in chapters 4 and 7. Nature is a source of good in at least four major ways. First, as
natura naturans it has produced the beauty and sublimity of the present physical
universe, including the extraordinary splendor of our homeland the earth. This
splendor has inspiring, healing, and humbling powers for the human spirit. Second, through the workings of biological evolution, nature is the source of life
on earth in all of its diverse and interdependent forms (and, in all probability,
of myriad forms of life elsewhere in the universe as well). It also sustains these
evolved species and individuals in the face of threats and dangers, and it restores
ecosystems and life-forms when they have been devastated. Third, nature is the
ultimate source of the good of human life itself, and of all the specific goods of
human history, civilization, and experience. Finally, nature has evolved humans
in such a way as to implant in them a yearning for the preservation of established goodness and for the attainment of ever-increasing goodness in themselves and in the rest of the world. This persistent lure to goodness in the
human breast is a fourth way in which nature subserves the good.

NATURE AS BEAUTIFUL AND SUBLIME

Beauty and sublimity abound in nature. These goods are inspirations to poets, musicians, and painters, as well as to philosophers and scientists, and they have enthralled and ennobled the human spirit since the dawn of human history. There are things of enduring beauty in nature and things of ephemeral, fleeting beauty. Snow-capped peaks and wave-swept crags are examples of the former, and fiery sunsets and fragile blossoms are familiar examples of the latter. Astounding beauty also exists in the unfathomable depths of a starry night, the damp stillness of a forest after a rain, the frothy turbulence of a tumbling stream, and the elaborate structures of an animal or insect body. My favorite personal example of abounding beauty in nature is the male mallard duck. Its iridescent green head is precisely banded by a line of white around its neck. Its bill is yellow, and its legs and feet are a vivid orange. It has a blue speculum and a white bar along the leading and trailing edges of its wings. Its black undertail contrasts with the whiteness of its tail, and it has a chestnut breast that contrasts with the greyness of its sides. The mallard drake is an incredibly lovely creature, and yet it is commonplace in lakes, marshes, and waterways. The sight of it delights the eye, awakens joy in the heart, and brings to mind the wonder and goodness of the nature that produced it.

The pervasive beauty of nature appeals to our better instincts and inspires reverence, awe, and respect. It lifts us out of our narrow selves and stretches our horizons of appreciation and concern. It reminds us of the privilege of being alive and of being consciously aware of ourselves and the marvelous world in which we live. A person who savors the beauty of particular aspects of nature finds impulse to love and cherish all of nature, from its infinite reaches to its finest details, from its galaxies, suns, and planets to its insects, microbes, and atoms. The love for nature kindled by experience of its beauty can have moral as well as aesthetic import, as William Barrett observes in a discussion of Immanuel Kant's aesthetic theory.

> The beautiful scene in nature is not only captivating to our senses, but also uplifting. It resonates with spiritual overtones that awaken our moral sentiment. Here the aesthetic and the moral are allied.[1]

Love for nature's haunting beauty also can have abiding religious significance, awakening in us feelings of wonder, gratitude, and devotion that center on nature as the source and ground of our being.

The sublimity of nature is its sometimes terrifying—if not horrifying—and always daunting power and vastness. The raging violence of earthquakes, floods, and forest fires is an expression of nature as sublime, as is the staggering vastness of outer space and of earth's oceans, mountain ranges, and deserts. David Oates' description of being subject to a frightening lightning storm in the high mountains, which we noted in chapter 7, recounts his own transformative encounter with nature as sublime. Such experiences remind us of how relatively small and insignificant we are in the whole scheme of things, thus providing much-needed lessons in humility and perspective. Like experiences of natural beauty, they evoke in us feelings of reverence and awe, but they do so by showing how absolutely dependent we and other creatures are upon nature's predictable, reliable functionings.

Nineteenth-century theologian Friedrich Schleiermacher characterizes this feeling of absolute dependence as the distinctively religious feeling. For him, as a Christian, this feeling is aroused by and centers on God.[2] In a religion of nature, the sublimity of nature is the source and focus of this feeling. Experience of nature as sublime, with the awareness of utter reliance on its regular processes that this experience brings home to us, also points to nature itself as qualifying for Henry Nelson Wieman's functional definition of God: "that Something upon which human life is most dependent for its security, welfare, and increasing abundance."[3] The sublime and the religious are therefore closely conjoined, meaning that we should not restrict the significance of the sublime to the category of the aesthetic. The sublimity of nature has the power not only to deepen our sensitivity and awareness but also to enrich and transform our lives. The experience of it, like the experience of nature's beauty, is thus a fundamental source of goodness in human life, and the beauty and sublimity of nature are goods in themselves, testifying to the wonder and majesty of the world.

NATURE AS SOURCE, SUSTAINER, AND RESTORER OF LIFE

The second way in which nature can be seen as the principal source of good for all of its creatures is its production of innumerable forms of life throughout the history of biological evolution on earth, its maintenance of each of those distinctive life-forms through time, and its restoration of life after its destruction. Two significant values of nature that we indicated in chapter 4 were the presence of life itself and the diversity of the kinds of life exhibited on earth, a radically interdependent diversity in which various creatures within ecosystems contribute to one another's sustenance and well-being, and in which each type of creature plays an important role in the functioning of the ecosystem as a whole. This diversity has been produced by biological evolution and will, by all indications, continue to be produced by it, as older forms of life become extinct and new ones emerge. The human species is part of the incredible variety of creatures brought forth by the evolutionary process, and we indicated in chapter 5 some of humanity's important commonalities with other creatures of earth as well as some of its distinctive characteristics.

Is the proliferation of diverse forms of life restricted to earth? The odds seem overwhelmingly against this being the case. Given the vastness and complexity of the universe as we now know it, something like biological evolution on earth must be at work in numerous places elsewhere, generating on other planets orbiting around other suns forms of life that we cannot even begin to imagine. The powers of nature are astonishingly fecund, and they have given rise over millions of years to the good of life and the good of its diverse forms. These powers also exhibit another value of nature identified in chapter 4, that of nature's ongoing creativity.

Not only has nature produced life in its astounding variety, however, thus manifesting its inexhaustible energy and creativity, it also continues to sustain the forms of life to which it has given rise. Particular forms of life may not endure forever, but they do typically endure for long periods of time. Extant life-forms are hardy and resilient. They stubbornly find ways to survive, even in the face of changing environmental conditions and threats to their existence posed by the struggles of other organisms to endure. The fact that they have survived and continue to do so testifies to their fitness for survival and to the efficient roles that they have been empowered to carve out for themselves in ecosystems. In the previous chapter we talked about the extraordinary power of nature to sustain the complex functionings of our human bodies, a power so regular and routine as to lead us usually to take it for granted. The surviving and thriving of creatures throughout the earth made possible by nature's sustaining power are other indications of how nature functions as the principal source of good for its creatures.

Of course, species do not always survive and thrive. Sometimes their continuing existence is seriously jeopardized, if not extinguished, by natural disasters or by the disastrous effects of some human actions or inactions, but nature has remarkable restorative powers and in this way also shows itself to be the principal source of good for its creatures. A striking example of these restorative powers is the events following the eruption of Mount St. Helens in the Cascade Range in the state of Washington. I draw upon an article in the May 2000 issue of *National Geographic* for a description of the eruption and processes of natural restoration that quickly ensued.[4] On March 27, 1980, this beautiful, conical-shaped mountain began a series of eruptions, and on May 18 the furious explosions produced a colossal landslide, the largest in recorded history, that took 1,300 feet off its crown and destroyed some 230 square miles of territory surrounding the mountain. A fan of devastation reached as far as fifteen miles from the volcano, wreaking havoc upon plants, animals, and their ecosystems.

However, by spring 2000 wildflowers were blooming, willow and alder trees had come back, shrubs and other trees had taken root, new populations of large and small animals were developing, insects and birds had returned, and fresh grasses had begun to grow over the desolate landscape. The astounding creative resilience of nature began to stubbornly and speedily assert itself here, just as it did through eons of geological and biological change throughout the history of the earth. Nature's powers of renewal, so graphically illustrated in the short span of twenty years at the Mount St. Helens' eruption site, are another manifestation of its character as a fundamental source of good. Nature not only creates and sustains, it also heals and restores. To scenes of widespread destruction and devastation it brings newness of life. Its relentless powers of re-creation can inspire profound feelings of gratitude and awe.

Nature is healing and restorative on a smaller scale as well. Our human bodies have remarkable powers of recuperation after illness, as do the bodies of other organisms. The medical arts are largely devoted to finding ways to remove obstacles to the body's own inherent healing powers, ways to allow the body *to heal itself*. Nature also gives to most human beings the ability to survive terrible tragedies and the inner resources to go on living despite searing sorrow, disappointment, and pain. Somehow, most of us find the courage to live despite the threats and setbacks to our self-affirmation inherent in our character as finite, fragile, vulnerable creatures who must live in a precarious world.

There are exceptions to this generalization, of course, and we should not fail to acknowledge them. Some persons—at least in part because of biological, psychological, socioeconomic, familial, or other factors beyond their control—never have, or at some point in their lives lose, the spirit of confident self-affirmation. Such persons may experience deep, all-consuming despair, and their feelings of hopelessness and futility may finally lead them to put their sufferings to an end by an act of suicide. But courageous self-affirmation in the face of frustration, uncertainty, and danger, where it does exists (and by all available evidence it seems to exist on a wide scale among human beings), is a gift of nature, something instinctual and deep-rooted in us. It is what enables us to survive as a species. Something similar to it is found in other creatures. A resilience and resourcefulness are present in living organisms that enable them to persist in living and wanting to live in the face of adversity, and in the case of humans, there is a demonstrated ability to find hope and renewal in the midst of pain, tragedy, or loss.[5] This fact is further evidence of the restorative powers of nature.

Sometimes, for humans, this natural process of healing, reorientation, and reinvigoration is greatly aided by simply being in the presence of nature, becoming acutely aware of clouds drifting across the blue vault of the sky, the caroling of birds, the scurrying of small animals, the crash of sea waves, the freshness of the morning dew, the rustle of wind in tall trees, or the quiet majesty of distant stars. There is a mood of serenity at such times, a feeling of rightness, a sense of belonging, an intimation of kinship with the earth and all of its living creatures. Experiences and times of awareness such as these have the power to restore our souls. Most, if not all, of us have encountered the healing force of nature in periods of pensiveness, sorrow, desperation, or need, and we continue to crave it in the depths of our being.

NATURE AS THE ULTIMATE SOURCE
OF THE GOOD OF HUMAN LIFE

Human life, like all life, is rooted in and gives expression to the creativity of nature. And all of our distinctively human creations, for example, our language, art, technology, science, morality, philosophy, religion, and political and social systems, are made possible by this same creativity of nature that brought us into being as a species. Hence, nature is the ultimate source of the intrinsic good of human life and of all of the goods that human life and human civilization have produced in the past and are capable of producing in the future. Nature has empowered human beings with the distinctively human traits we discussed in chapter 5, and those traits, working in concert with traits common to humans and other species, have produced everything that is special, remarkable, and admirable about the history of the human species on earth. Farms, cities, cathedrals, temples, skyscrapers, literature, painting, music, dance, saints, sages, philosophers, scientists, engineers, economists, administrators, ships, trains, automobiles, airplanes, spaceships, telephones, radio, television, computers, medicines—these and other examples of human creativity all give testimony to the creativity of nature itself. Where they work for good, they reveal a palpable power of goodness in nature.

Could we not by the same reasoning attribute all of the *evils* of human civilizations, all of the wars, crimes, exploitations, bigotry, deceit, cruelty, indifference, and the like to nature as well? Is there not then a power for evil at work in nature? Since everything, according to this book, comes from nature, it is no surprise that we should attribute whatever goodness there is in human life to nature, but must we not then also attribute whatever is evil in human history— *and there is a staggering amount of it by any account*—to nature? If nature is a force for such pervasive evil as well as for good, how can commitment to nature be of any constructive use, interest, or value to us religiously?

My answer to this probing question is that we should seek to align ourselves with and build upon those tendencies in our character as natural beings that have worked and can work for good, and that we should eschew and struggle against those tendencies in us that have worked and can work for evil. As I indicated in the previous chapter, we should not slavishly follow the nonhuman part of nature in all of its aspects but critically distinguish those aspects of its functionings and potentialities that are worthy of our allegiance and work to maximize them in the world. Similarly, we should seek critically to discern and develop in our own makeup those factors and possibilities that can work for good.

As human beings, we have the ability to think and choose, and thus to decide rationally how we shall live and what sorts of contribution we shall aspire to make to one another and to our other fellow creatures on earth. This ability means that we have the power to align ourselves with the forces for good in nature and in our own nature, forces that have produced so much that is undeniably exemplary and excellent in human life and experience. It is these forces that we affirm and these forces to which we are finally committed in a religion of nature.

Nature does not so much give us a blueprint of how to live but the capacity to decide for ourselves, on the basis of our own experience and reflection, what the patterns of our lives shall be. Thus as we have seen before, while there is no purpose of nature, there is the emergence of purpose in nature. As a proponent of a religion of nature, I purposefully affirm such human values as altruism, not egoism; compassion, not hate; helpfulness, not hurtfulness; knowledge, not ignorance; tolerance, not bigotry; benevolence, not indifference. These are some of the constructive values that we need to commit ourselves to as human beings, and to the extent that we do so, we can give expression to the forces for good that lie latent in nature and can reach clarity of manifestation in ourselves as natural beings.

THE YEARNING FOR GOODNESS IN HUMAN BEINGS

There is something in us that aspires toward goodness. This something also is a gift of nature or, to put the matter somewhat differently, a fundamental aspect of our own nature as an evolved species. We crave goodness in ourselves, in others, and in the world that surrounds us. We want to be better than we are, we want the world to be better than it is, and we want to find ways to work for our own and the world's improvement. Each of us is not merely locked up in himself or herself, wholly preoccupied with his or her own interests, desires, and needs. We have instincts and impulses of sympathy and fellow feeling that drive us to identify with the needs of others and to actively seek their good. These instincts give expression to our character as social animals, and they have undoubted survival value in that they can lead to cooperation in common enterprises and joint protection against mutual dangers.

However, more than these factors seems to be involved. We humans have an eros, a striving, a *conatus*, a wistful, irrepressible longing for that which is noble, exemplary, virtuous, healing, integrative, constructive, helpful, and saving, and in our best moments we desire these values, not only for ourselves or for those closest to us but for all peoples and all creatures. We are not satisfied with what *is* but ardently yearn for what *ought* to be. The whole history of human civilizations—especially in their religious, moral, and legal aspects—reflects the workings of this impulse toward goodness and its persistent struggles against those forces, also sadly active within our species, that impel us toward the base, the inhumane, the selfish, the destructive, and the wicked. The moral ambiguities of nature are mirrored in the moral ambiguities of human nature and human history. But the point I am emphasizing here is that nature has implanted in us a powerful impulse toward the creation, maintenance, and furtherance of goodness, showing in yet another way why it can be aptly characterized as the ultimate source of goodness in the world.[6]

Of course, not all persons respond to this impulse in the same way or to the same degree, but those who do respond to it and dedicate themselves to moral excellence and the service of others, including nonhuman others, can accomplish much good. They also can inspire other human beings to do good. Not only are these persons exemplars of the moral life, but their lives also actualize and make evident the aim toward goodness that lies latent in all of us, an aim that stems from our makeup as evolved natural beings. With the proper nurturance, development, habituation, and education, this aim, rooted in nature itself, can be strengthened and made effective, and human beings can become active forces for good, finding creative ways to maximize goodness in the world.

Let me cite a few examples of what I have in mind. In Los Angeles, California, I recently met a high school teacher of mathematics, Kathy Granas, who glowed with love for and dedication to her students. She told me that she was firmly convinced that all students could learn mathematics, no matter what their backgrounds or levels of ability, and that she was committed to finding ways in which each student entrusted to her could learn. She described how she talked at length with each student and worked out strategies for helping that student become competent in mathematical reasoning. She then tailored her teaching to the specific needs of each of her students, working far above and beyond what would normally be expected of her to achieve this goal. She was in Los Angeles because she had won a prestigious national teaching award, and I felt that she richly deserved this award because of all the care and effort she put into her teaching, and because of her evident deep concern for the effective education of every one of her students. She is a source of good in the world, a person who has developed to a high degree her capacity to help others with her particular gifts and skills. Nature has endowed her with an urge toward goodness, and she devotes her life to responding to this urge in her service to others.

My second example is a medical doctor, Margaret van der Kreek, whose work at the hospital of Dr. Albert Schweitzer in Lambaréné, Africa, is described in a book by Norman Cousins published in 1960.[7] "Dr. Margaret," as she was affectionately called at the hospital, had been in Lambaréné for two years when Cousins met and interviewed her. She explained that her father, an artist, and her mother, a poet, had reared her in an atmosphere of kindness and intelligence. Her family had not suffered, even during the Great Depression of the 1930s, and her father sought to help others in whatever ways he could. As she approached maturity, Margaret became aware that her happiness and her family's were not the lot of all people. As a consequence, she felt a strong responsibility to give of herself in service to others, and she decided to serve in the field of medicine. When she read about the famous Dr. Schweitzer and his work in Africa, she was determined to get the best medical and surgical training available and then apply to work at his hospital. After completing her internship, she did apply and was overjoyed to be accepted. When Cousins asked her to explain why she had come, she answered in this way:

> Here at Lambaréné, we do nicely without the frills. We have a purpose and apply ourselves to it. We never have to ask ourselves whether we are really needed. We are never at wit's end for what to do with our time. When our work is over for the day we can sit down and rest or we can make our tea and we talk among ourselves or we can read and we can think. It is very good. Do you find this strange?[8]

Dr. Margaret contrasted her life at the African hospital with life in Europe and America, the latter filled, by her reckoning, with nonessential activity as people strive for things that they do not really need, seek desperately for ways to entertain themselves and pass the time, and struggle unsuccessfully to find satisfaction and meaning in lives devoted primarily to themselves. Here then is another example of a person who has responded positively and fully to the impulse to do good in the world, a person who fills her days giving medical care to persons of another race in a faraway land who come to her in their times of need.

The third example is Millard and Linda Fuller, co-founders of Habitat for Humanity. After attending college and law school in his native Alabama, Fuller became a millionaire at age twenty-nine through a marketing firm started by him and a college friend, but his health, integrity, and marriage were going downhill. After a process of soul searching with his wife, Linda, the two reconciled and decided to sell all of their possessions, give their money to the poor, and begin a new way of life. Eventually they decided to build modest houses on a nonprofit, no-interest basis in order to make houses affordable to low-income families. Prospective home owners invested their own labor into building their houses and the houses of other families in need of housing, and volunteers were enlisted to help with the building. Money for building was placed into a revolving fund so that new houses could be built. This enterprise eventually grew into Habitat for Humanity International, an organization founded in 1976. As of the date of this writing, nearly a half million people now have safe, affordable housing as a result of Habitat's work around the world, and houses continue to be built at a steady rate. Fuller explains his and his wife's commitment to the needs of others by saying, "One of the most beautiful things in the world is to care about someone else. You find the deepest meaning in your own existence when you reach out and touch someone else."[9]

My last example is John Muir, who worked tirelessly throughout much of his life for the preservation of areas of extraordinary natural beauty in the United States. Along with *Century* magazine's associate editor, Robert Underwood Johnson, Muir was able to influence Congress in 1890 to create Yosemite National Park, and he also was personally involved in the creation of Sequoia, Mount Rainier, Petrified Forest, and Grand Canyon national parks. In 1892, Muir and a number of his supporters founded the Sierra Club, and he served as its president until his death in 1914. In 300 articles and ten major books, including *Our National Parks*, published in 1901, Muir inspired his readers and motivated them to action, encouraging them, in his words, to "do something for wildness and make the mountains glad."[10] Muir's intense love of nature, especially of the high country, and the work he did to influence others to respect and preserve natural areas, were his own distinctive ways of actualizing the urge to goodness that nature has implanted within us. His influence lives on in his writings and in the continuing labors of the Sierra Club.

Like Kathy Granas, Margaret van der Kreek, and Millard and Linda Fuller, John Muir found within himself a profound yearning to be of service to others—in his case, primarily the life-forms and ecosystems in the national parks he helped preserve but also the human beings thus enabled to experience those spectacular natural settings in a relatively unspoiled state—and struggled and sacrificed to translate that yearning into a way of life. These five people exemplify a powerful force for good in themselves as natural beings. Nature has similarly endowed all of us; there are an impulse and a potentiality for goodness in each of us that can be brought to fruition and put into practice. Behind this potentiality in us lies an implicit force for goodness in nature itself that we, through our dedication and deeds, can make explicit and effective.[11]

Many other examples in addition to the five I have cited here could be used to call attention to the millions of people throughout the world and in human history whose lives of willing and active service illustrate the presence of an impulse to goodness in human beings. My wife, Pam, and I work regularly one afternoon a week at a Habitat for Humanity thrift store in Loveland, Colorado, which is devoted to providing inexpensive purchases for those in need of them and thus making money to be used for building houses for low-income people. We observe there a constant stream of volunteers who give unreservedly of their time and energy—many far in excess of the little that we manage to do—without praise or reward, simply to serve the needs of others.[12] A similar dedication on the part of volunteers can be observed in the numerous other charitable organizations in the United States and across the world.

There are countless ways in which human beings, the vast number of them quite ordinary and uncelebrated, exhibit a capacity and motivation to look beyond their own personal needs and desires and to do good in the world. They do so, for example, by educating the young, ministering to the sick, providing food and housing for the poor, striving for better working conditions for laborers, struggling for social justice, working to preserve or restore the natural environment, and being gracious, helpful, and kind in their daily dealings with one another. I am not saying that we are all good, or even insisting that we are all fundamentally good. I am saying that we *can* be good and that we *can* be better, and that there is a formidable impulse to goodness in us that can be cultivated. If we are natural beings, as I have contended throughout this book that we are, then our felt urge toward goodness bears witness to a power of goodness in the natural order of which we are a part.[13]

This nature to which we intimately belong—a nature that sustains, renews, and inspires us in countless ways—can command our wholehearted religious commitment. We have no need of God, gods, animating spirits, or other sorts of putative religious objects, nor do we need to pine for another life in another realm beyond the wondrous home we find already in our natural world. Nature itself, when we rightly conceive of it and comprehend our role within it, can provide ample context and support for finding purpose, value, and meaning in our lives.

Notes

CHAPTER 1
FROM GOD TO NATURE: A PERSONAL ODYSSEY

1. Albert Schweitzer, *The Quest of the Historical Jesus: A Critical Study of Its Progress From Reimarus to Wrede*, trans. W. Montgomery (New York: Macmillan, 1950).

2. I refer here to the writings of Swiss theologians Karl Barth and Emil Brunner. They were leaders of the "neo-orthodox" movement in Protestant theology that emerged after World War I and flourished into the 1950s. Both wrote detailed, multi-volume treatises on systematic theology.

3. Alfred North Whitehead, *Process and Reality: Corrected Edition*, ed. David Ray Griffin and Donald W. Sherburne (New York: Free Press, 1978). See especially part 5.

4. William James, *Essays in Radical Empiricism* and *A Pluralistic Universe*, two volumes in one (Gloucester, Mass.: Peter Smith, 1967), vol. 2, pp. 310–11, 318.

5. Richard L. Rubenstein, *After Auschwitz: Radical Theology and Contemporary Judaism* (Indianapolis: Bobbs-Merrill, 1966).

6. Paul Tillich gives a prominent place to these terms in most of his writings, but see especially *The Courage to Be* (New Haven, Conn.: Yale University Press, 1952) and *Systematic Theology*, 3 vols. (Chicago: University of Chicago Press, 1951, 1957, 1963).

7. Tillich, *The Courage to Be*, pp. 186–90.

8. Tillich, *Systematic Theology*, vol. 2, pp. 7–8.

9. This is Benedict de Spinoza's characterization, in his *Ethics*, of the God of popular piety. See Spinoza, *The Chief Works of Benedict de Spinoza,* trans. R.H.M. Elwes, 2 vols. (New York: Dover, 1951), vol. 1, p. 188.

10. Ludwig Feuerbach, *The Essence of Christianity*, trans. George Eliot (New York: Harper Torchbooks, Library of Religion and Culture, 1957).

11. It is available as "The Existence of God—A Debate," in *A Modern Introduction to Philosophy*, 3rd ed., ed. Paul Edwards and Arthur Pap (New York: Free Press, 1973), pp. 473–90. The debate was broadcast in 1948 on the Third Program of the BBC and originally published in *Humanitas* (Manchester).

12. Rudolf Otto, *The Idea of the Holy*, trans. John W. Harvey (New York: Oxford University Press, a Galaxy Book, 1958).

13. Whitehead, *Process and Reality*, p. 351.

14. Religion of nature is one of at least four general categories of religious naturalism. A second is naturalistic theism, which rests belief in God on reflections about experience rather than on special revelations and usually regards God as a wholly immanent being, presence, or power in the universe. Another is religious humanism, where humanity, rather than nature or God, is the principal focus of religious concern. The fourth is the "minimalist" form of religious naturalism set forth by Jerome A. Stone. Here no distinct ontological reality called "God" is affirmed, but Stone argues that we do experience "situationally transcendent" resources and ideals productive of good, and that these can properly be called "divine." See Jerome A. Stone, *The Minimalist Vision of Transcendence: A Naturalist Philosophy of Religion* (Albany: State University of New York Press, 1992), esp. chapter 1.

15. An earlier version of a portion of this chapter was published in *Religious Humanism* 25:3 (summer 1991): 107–16.

CHAPTER 2

CONCEPT OF NATURE

1. Aristotle, *Physics*, Bk. IV, Ch. 5, 212b 14–22.

2. "Nothing is more impressive," Alfred North Whitehead comments, "than the fact that as mathematics [in the seventeenth century] withdrew increasingly into the upper regions of ever greater extremes of abstract thought, it returned back to earth with a corresponding growth of importance for the analysis of concrete fact." See Whitehead, *Science and the Modern World* (New York: Free Press, 1967), p. 32.

3. I owe this point to Milton Munitz. See Munitz, *Cosmic Understanding: Philosophy and Science of the Universe* (Princeton, N.J.: Princeton University Press, 1986), p. 55.

4. The Greek term for nature, *phusis,* has a similar etymological meaning; it derives from the verb *phuein*: "to grow," "to spring up," "to spring forth," "to bring forth," "to produce."

5. Jean-Paul Sartre, *Being and Nothingness: An Essay on Phenomenological Ontology*, trans. Hazel Barnes (New York: Washington Square Press, 1966); *Nausea*, trans. Lloyd Alexander (New York: New Directions, 1964). For a further discussion of this view, as presented by Sartre and others, see my *The Specter of the Absurd: Sources and Criticisms of Modern Nihilism* (Albany: State University of New York Press, 1988), pp. 78–80, 18–27.

6. James Burke, *The Day the Universe Changed* (Boston and Toronto: Little, Brown and Company, 1985), p. 310.

7. I owe this illustration to Ninian Smart. See Smart, *Buddhism and Christianity: Rivals and Allies* (Honolulu: University of Hawaii Press, 1993), p. 53.

8. The examples of mediating hypotheses mentioned here are from the natural sciences, but examples from other fields (e.g., philosophy, the arts, the social sciences) could have been mentioned as well. In chapter 3 I argue that it would be a serious mistake to restrict our overall vision of nature to what can be learned about it from the natural sciences. We need to draw extensively not only on those sciences but on other types of thought and inquiry as well. I also shall argue that we should not rely solely on sensate expe-

riences for empirical tests of models of nature, as important as sensate tests of those models are. Other modes of experience must seriously be taken into account if we are to do justice to the complex ways in which nature and our relations to nature are disclosed to us.

9. John Dewey, *A Common Faith* (New Haven, Conn.: Yale University Press, 1934), p. 85.

10. Ibid., pp. 18–19.

11. A more detailed elucidation and defense of this conception of freedom can be found in Donald Wayne Viney and Donald A. Crosby, "Free Will and Determinism in Process Perspective," *New Ideas in Psychology* 12:2 (July 1994): 129–41. See also my discussion and the diagram in *The Specter of the Absurd*, pp. 344–46.

12. Charles Hartshorne, *The Darkness and the Light* (Albany: State University of New York Press, 1990), p. 35.

13. I reject Hume's doctrine of simple impressions of sensation and reflection, putative elements of experience that have no internal complexity and no essential relatedness to anything else in experience. This doctrine is a philosopher's fantasy; there is nothing in experience to confirm it.

14. Aristotle, *Metaphysics*, Bk. 1, Ch. 6, 987b; Ch. 9, 991a.

15. I am leaving out here the static majesty of Aristotle's "unmoved mover" and its central role in his thought. According to him, the recurrent patterns of change (e.g., the motions of the heavenly bodies or the reproduction of biological species and the life cycles of individuals within those species) that we observe in the universe will never undergo fundamental alteration or evolve into something different, because different types or levels of things in the universe are already responding as fully as they can and in the only way they can to the lure of serene, fixed eternity embodied in the unmoved mover. Their ceaseless, unalterable regularity of functioning is for Aristotle splendid evidence of this response.

16. Alfred North Whitehead, *Process and Reality: Corrected Edition*, ed. David Ray Griffin and Donald W. Sherburne (New York: Free Press, 1978), pp. 21–22.

17. Ibid., p. 225.

18. See the section, "Temporally-Multiple Universes" in George Gale, "Multiple Universes," contained in *Cosmology: Historical, Literary, Philosophical, Religious, and Scientific Perspectives*, ed. Norriss S. Hetherington (New York and London: Garland Publishing, Garland Reference Library of the Humanities, vol. 1634, 1993), pp. 533–45, 540–42. As Gale points out, both Wheeler and Linde hold that, at the instant of maximum collapse of this universe, its entropy will be scrambled and will vanish, allowing completely new worlds to emerge.

CHAPTER 3
SCIENCE AND NATURE

1. See chap. 2, note 18.

2. "One great difference marks off . . . [the] Newtonian world from the world of modern science: in such a machine, time counted for nothing. Processes rolled on their

way in cyclical fashion, completing themselves, like the orbits of the planets, in recurrent definite intervals; but there was no real change. The world had always been such an order, and always would be; of growth, of development, of evolution, the greatest single new conception introduced by the last century, there was not the slightest idea." John Herman Randall Jr., *The Making of the Modern Mind: A Survey of the Intellectual Background of the Present Age*, 50th anniversary ed. (New York: Columbia University Press, 1976), pp. 275–76.

3. The premises and direction of scientific thinking also were changed in fundamental respects in the nineteenth century by Charles Lyell in geology and Charles Darwin and Alfred Russel Wallace in biology.

4. As John Dupré notes, the case is similarly inconclusive or indeterminate with apparent empirical *falsifications* of such theories. Since many auxiliary premises and assumptions are involved in even relatively simple scientific theories and in the empirical testing of such theories, the seeming falsification of a given theory can just as easily be viewed as relating to one or more of these auxiliary factors. This provides an opportunity to attribute the falsification not to the theory that scientists are testing but to one or more of its underlying premises and assumptions. Hence, they are given a kind of license to "seek out any other possible explanation of an apparently anomalous result before rejecting their theories." John Dupré, *The Disorder of Things: Metaphysical Foundations of the Disunity of Science* (Cambridge: Harvard University Press, 1995), p. 231.

5. Dupré, *The Disorder of Things*, p. 229. Dupré makes a convincing case for the stubborn plurality (he also uses the words "disunity" and "disorder") of both science and nature by his concerted attacks on essentialism, determinism, and reductionism, views he shows to be connected in important ways. His discussions are informed by close attention to what scientists actually say and do, in contrast with abstract, idealized interpretations of science making claims about its present or potential unity that are not borne out by the evidence.

6. After reading this novel as well as Tolstoy's *Anna Karenina*, William James exulted, "now I feel as if I knew *perfection* in the representation of human life. Life indeed seems less real than his tale of it. Such infallible veracity! The impression haunts me as nothing literary ever haunted me before." Letter to Theodore Flournoy, August 30, 1896, in *The Selected Letters of William James*, ed. Elizabeth Hardwick (New York: Anchor Books and Doubleday, 1960), p. 161.

7. John Dewey, *Experience and Nature*, 2d ed. (New York: Dover, 1958), p. 25.

8. Ibid.

9. Ibid., p. 24.

10. Harvard biologist E. O. Wilson recently estimated the number of *known* species of organisms at 1.4 million. He also noted that "evolutionary biologists are generally agreed that this estimate is less than a tenth of the number that actually live on earth." See Wilson, *The Diversity of Life* (Cambridge: Belknap Press of Harvard University Press, 1992), pp. 132–33.

11. Thomas Berry, *The Dream of the Earth* (San Francisco: Sierra Club Books, 1988), pp. 91–92.

CHAPTER 4
VALUES IN NATURE

1. I discuss in greater detail this first reason for denial of values to nature in *The Specter of the Absurd: Sources and Criticisms of Modern Nihilism* (Albany: State University of New York Press, 1988), pp. 46–55.

2. For a fuller discussion of these points, see my *The Specter of the Absurd*, pp. 324–25.

3. In his book *Einstein's Moon: Bell's Theorem and the Curious Quest for Quantum Reality* (Chicago: Contemporary Books, 1990), F. David Peat notes that Bell's theorem means that "[i]n the future, *reality* must also be used in a nonlocal sense, suggesting that our concepts of space and time may need to be transcended. The implications of Bell's theorem may well demand an even greater revolution in thought than what had first been expected from relativity and quantum theory" (p. 124).

4. For interesting and persuasive developments of this idea see Israel Scheffler, *Science and Subjectivity* (Indianapolis: Bobbs-Merrill, 1967) and Harold I. Brown, *Perception, Theory and Commitment* (Chicago: University of Chicago Press, 1979).

5. Hilary Putnam makes the excellent point that "talk of testing the system of scientific theory by 'testing predictions' makes sense only when a common world and a common language are already in place. To know that you have tested the same prediction that I have tested I must understand what you say; and that means that issues of interpretation and questions of fact also presuppose and condition one another." Putnam, *Pragmatism* (Oxford: Blackwell, 1995), p. 18.

6. See Charles Sanders Peirce, "The Principles of Phenomenology," in *Philosophical Writings of Peirce*, ed. Justus Buchler (New York: Dover, 1955), pp. 74–97, esp. p. 95; also see "Perceptual Judgments" and "Two Notes: On Motives, On Percepts," in the same volume, pp. 302–5 and pp. 306–9. In "The Essentials of Pragmatism," pp. 251–68 of the volume, Peirce states that "our very percepts are the results of cognitive elaboration," and that "percepts are products of psychical operations" (pp. 256, 268).

7. See Alfred North Whitehead, *Process and Reality: Corrected Edition*, ed. David Ray Griffin and Donald W. Sherburne (New York: Free Press, 1978), pp. 176–83.

8. Jeffrey Stout notes that most disagreements about moral values in our culture take place against a background of "countless [moral] platitudes assented to by almost everybody." Anyone who did not acknowledge these commonly accepted principles "would be recognized in the community at large as morally incompetent." Stout, *Ethics After Babel: The Languages of Morals and Their Discontents* (Boston: Beacon Press, 1988), pp. 43, 214. Many such "platitudes" were the moral basis of the Nuremberg Trials after World War II and are assumed in the Universal Declaration of Human Rights, promulgated by the United Nations.

9. Whitehead, *Process and Reality*, pp. 234, 240–41, 247–49, 253–54.

10. William James, *Pragmatism* and *The Meaning of Truth*, two volumes in one (Cambridge: Harvard University Press, 1975), vol. 1, pp. 42, 34. The italics are in the original.

Putnam notes that the search for coherence by scientists, a concern that James is alluding to in general here, is part of their "aim at a *Weltanschauung*." He thus rejects the claim of some philosophers of science, that all scientists care about is successful predictions by means of their theories. The pursuit of coherence is, he contends, an act of valuation, the acknowledgment and pursuit of a value. Putnam also points out that what counts as coherence, or what may be viewed as a threat to coherence, crucially depends on what is valued by particular scientists. For a significant minority of them, for example, the newer "Many Worlds Interpretation" of quantum mechanics is an appealing alternative to the more standard "Copenhagen Interpretation," dating from the 1930s, while for others, the latter is viewed as being too bizzare to be seriously entertained. Such a judgment, Putnam argues, "is in every sense a value judgment." See Putnam, *Pragmatism*, pp. 15–16.

11. "The Importance of *Not* Knowing a Thing or Two," *Princeton* (summer 1997): 6. *Princeton* is published by the Office of Development Communications of Princeton University. The two Princeton faculty members whose research is referred to in this article are Stephen W. Pacala and Simon A. Levin.

12. Robert T. Pennock, "Naturalism, Creationism and the Meaning of Life: The Case of Phillip Johnson Revisited," *Creation/Evolution* 16:2 (winter 1996): 10–30, 18.

13. Alfred North Whitehead, *Modes of Thought* (New York: Capricorn Books, 1958), pp. 13–14, 114, 12.

14. Charles Sanders Peirce, "The Fixation of Belief," in *Philosophical Writings of Peirce*, ed. Justus Buchler (New York: Dover, 1955), pp. 5–22, 16, the note on this page.

15. Charles Sanders Peirce, "The Concept of God," in *Philosophical Writings of Peirce*, ed. Justus Buchler (New York: Dover, 1955), pp. 375–78, 376.

16. William James, *Essays in Radical Empiricism* and *A Pluralistic Universe*, two volumes in one (Gloucester, Mass.: Peter Smith, 1967), p. 93 of the *Essays*. James labels this amorphous field of experience as "pure experience," and he remarks that another name for it is "feeling or sensation." He also notes that "[i]ts purity is only a relative term, meaning the proportional amount of unverbalized sensation which it still embodies" (*Essays*, p. 94).

17. See John Dewey, *Experience and Nature*, 2d ed. (New York: Dover, 1958), pp. 20–23.

18. John Dewey, "The Construction of Good," excerpted from Dewey's *The Quest for Certainty* (New York: Capricorn Books, 1960), pp. 254–86, in John McDermott, ed., *The Philosophy of John Dewey*, two volumes in one (Chicago: University of Chicago Press, 1981), pp. 575–98, 579–80.

19. Dewey, "The Construction of Good," p. 583.

20. Here I draw on the thought of William James and John Dewey. I briefly indicate their reasons for rejecting the commonly assumed priority of self, or experiencer, to experience in my "Finite Is All Right: Confessions of a Slow Learner," in *Pragmatism, Neo-Pragmatism, and Religion: Conversations With Richard Rorty*, Series on American Liberal Religious Thought, vol. 6, ed. Charley D. Hardwick and Donald A. Crosby (New

York: Peter Lang, 1997), pp. 357–82, 373–74. For a more extended discussion of this aspect of the thought of James, see my essay "Experience As Reality: The Ecological Metaphysics of William James," in *Religious Experience and Ecological Responsibility*, Series on American Religious Thought, vol. 3, ed. Donald A. Crosby and Charley D. Hardwick (New York: Peter Lang, 1996), pp. 67–87, esp. pp. 68–72, 75–76, 83–84.

21. I hold that being, fact, and value exist in relation to the perspectives of animals and plants too, even though they are not capable of the levels of abstract conceptualization that we find in human culture and human thought. I shall say more in a moment about how the relational view that I am advocating can be applied to nonhuman organisms.

22. In the case of organisms not capable of conscious, reflective inquiry, there can still be a nonconscious, largely instinctive experimental probing of the environment for things to be rightly or wrongly valued in the impetus of these organisms toward survival. This is "inquiry" of a sort, although not the intellectual, linguistically guided inquiry of which humans are capable, or the relatively conscious, purposeful investigations into and assessments of value that other highly developed organisms have the ability to carry out.

23. For a more detailed discussion of these points about perspectival knowing, see my *The Specter of the Absurd*, pp. 142–46.

24. Paul Tillich, *The Courage to Be* (New Haven, Conn.: Yale University Press, 1952), p. 78; see also pp. 79, 81.

25. Viktor Frankl reminds us that it is possible to find meaning in extensive suffering. For example, he cites the experiences of prisoners of the Vietnam War who claimed that although their captivity was marked by torture, disease, malnutrition, and solitary confinement, they later looked back upon their time in prison as a beneficial growth experience. Frankl also notes that "even the helpless victim of a hopeless situation, facing a fate he cannot change, may rise above himself, may grow beyond himself, and by so doing change himself. He may turn a personal tragedy into a triumph." Viktor E. Frankl, *Man's Search for Meaning* (New York: Washington Square Press, 1959, postscript, 1984), pp. 170–71. Suffering can have value to the extent that it can deepen the outlook, ennoble the life, and enhance the contributions of a human being, but I am suggesting that there may be *extreme* kinds of irremediable suffering implying that the life afflicted with such suffering would no longer have inherent value. Under these circumstances, a person could be justified in believing that the cessation of his or her life, whatever value it may have had in the past, is now warranted. However, it also is possible that a person in these circumstances might still find his or her life meaningful to the extent that the person is aware of the positive value that the suffering has or could have for himself or herself, or others.

26. In larger evolutionary terms, predation can be seen as a positive value for a biological species, since it helps select for such things as strength, agility, speed, and cunning by taking the lives of animals who lack these traits (since they are less able to escape from predators), keeping them from reproducing, and thus tending to eliminate their particular genes from the gene pool of that species.

27. These statements require the qualification "generally," because there are contexts in which we cannot applaud the flourishing of another organism. We do not rejoice in the lives of organisms that cause smallpox or bubonic plague in humans, for example.

CHAPTER 5
HUMANS AND NATURE

1. Alfred North Whitehead, *Modes of Thought* (New York: Capricorn Books, 1958), pp. 29–30.

2. E. O. Wilson, *The Diversity of Life* (Cambridge: Bellknap Press of Harvard University Press, 1992), p. 216.

3. "Research Mission of the Living Links Center," Yerkes Regional Primate Research Center, Emory University, Atlanta, Georgia, p. 4. Internet address: www.emory.edu/Living_Links.

4. Frans De Waal, *Good Natured: The Origins of Right and Wrong in Humans and Other Animals* (Cambridge: Harvard University Press, 1996), p. 205.

5. Ibid., p. 207.

6. Ibid., p. 209.

7. Ibid., p. 208.

8. Ibid., p. 210.

9. Ibid., p. 180.

10. I do not deny the consciousness of other humans on the ground that their inner conscious lives cannot be directly observed by me. On the contrary, I frequently explain the behaviors of other humans in terms of the assumption that they are conscious and have an inner life similar to my own. There does not seem to be any sound scientific reason for rejecting this routine assumption. Of course, some behaviorist psychologists and eliminative materialist philosophers deny that humans, including themselves, are really conscious or that, if there is any such thing as consciousness, it can be known, but this view is hardly plausible. It is odd, to say the least, to assert, "I think that I do not think," or "I am now aware, on scientific grounds, that I am not aware," or in *trying* to *convince* someone else of the truth of such assertions.

11. Bernard E. Rollin, *The Unheeded Cry: Animal Consciousness, Animal Pain, and Science* (Oxford and New York: Oxford University Press, 1989), p. 164 and *passim*. Moral philosopher James Rachels also makes this point. See his *Created From Animals: The Moral Implications of Darwinism* (Oxford and New York: Oxford University Press, 1990), pp. 129–32.

12. Nicholas Fontaine, *Memoires*, quoted in Rachels, *Created From Animals*, p. 130.

13. Rollin, *The Unheeded Cry*, p. 139.

14. Ibid., p. 140.

15. Ibid.

16. Ibid., pp. 153–54.

17. Sue Savage-Rumbaugh, Stuart G. Shanker, and Talbot J. Taylor, *Apes, Language and the Human Mind* (Oxford and New York: Oxford University Press, 1998).

18. Rachels, *Created From Animals*, p. 139. See also De Waal, *Good Natured*, p. 211.

19. Rollin, *The Unheeded Cry*, p. 247.

20. Whitehead, *Modes of Thought*, pp. 49, 57.

21. David Conner comments to me in a written note regarding this point that "language, and the ability to think by using language, can often make life not better, but worse. Animals who fight with each other usually settle the matter and withdraw. In contrast, their human counterparts often store up a treasury of hasty, hostile words to be repeated later as a way of prolonging and intensifying pain and discord."

22. Whitehead, *Modes of Thought*, p. 46.

23. In chapter 3, the reader will recall, I argued that literary works can have their own distinctive kind of objectivity, and that it is a mistake to view scientific thought alone as providing objective understanding of human beings and the world.

24. Donald Schon, in *The Displacement of Concepts* (London: Tavistok, 1963), exhibits in considerable detail the unavoidability of metaphors in conceptual discovery and in the development of new perspectives on problems. Mary Hesse, in *Models and Analogies in Science* (Notre Dame, Ind.: University of Notre Dame Press, 1970), not only argues for an important role of models and analogies in scientific thinking but also discusses the explanatory function of metaphor in scientific theories in her concluding chapter. Finally, Thomas Kuhn, in the "Postscript" to the second edition of his *The Structure of Scientific Revolutions* (Chicago: University of Chicago Press, 1970), p. 184, comments on the crucial significance, including the heuristic significance, of analogies, models, and metaphors in the reigning "disciplinary matrix" of a given scientific epoch.

25. David Conner, in a personal communication, notes that "language is typically used for purposes other than the conveyance of the clear and distinct ideas of discursive intellect. . . . To my mind it seems likely that we humans very often . . . use language not to communicate high-level abstractions but to share the same kinds of feelings (affection, love, curiosity, approval, hostility, etc.) that animals *simply use other means to convey*."

26. John Dewey, *Experience and Nature*, 2d ed. (New York: Dover, 1958), pp. 101–2.

27. James M. Gustafson, *Ethics from a Theocentric Perspective*, 2 vols. (Chicago: University of Chicago Press, 1981, 1984), vol. 1, p. 270; quoted by Jeffrey Stout, *Ethics After Babel: The Languages of Morals and Their Discontents* (Boston: Beacon Press, 1988), p. 171.

28. Tzvetan Todorov, "The Surrender to Nature," trans. Claire Messud, Review of Edward O. Wilson's *Consilience: The Unity of Knowledge* (New York: Knopf, 1998), in *The New Republic*, April 27, 1998, pp. 29–33; the quotation is on p. 30.

29. The compatibilist view of freedom claims that human freedom and causal determinism are compatible with one another. Agents are "free" as long as they are able to do what they themselves want to do, that is, as long as their acts stem from their own normal states, desires, or motivations, even though these wants, states, desires, or motivations themselves are causally determined.

30. Holmes Rolston III, *Environmental Ethics: Duties to and Values in the Natural World* (Philadelphia: Temple University Press, 1988), p. 184; *Genes, Genesis, and God: Values and Their Origins in Natural and Human History* (Cambridge: Cambridge University Press, 1999), p. 108.

31. Rolston III, *Genes, Genesis, and God*, p. 109.

32. Whitehead, *Modes of Thought*, p. 5.

33. Brian Swimme, "Forward" to Thomas Berry, *The Dream of the Earth* (San Francisco: Sierra Club Books, 1988), p. viii.

34. Kenneth Bock, *Human Nature and History: A Response to Sociobiology* (New York: Columbia University Press, 1980), p. 172.

35. De Waal, *Good Natured*, pp. 211, 254, n. 2.

36. Rolston III, *Genes, Genesis, and God*, p. 111.

37. Rolston III, *Genes, Genesis, and God*, p. 110; Daniel C. Dennett, *The Intentional Stance* (Cambridge: MIT Press, 1987).

38. Frederick Ferré, *Philosophy of Technology* (Englewood Cliffs, N.J.: Prentice Hall, 1988), p. 28, emphasis in original.

39. Stephen David Ross, *Locality and Practical Judgment: Charity and Sacrifice* (New York: Fordham University Press, 1994), pp. 210, 232.

40. Wilson, *The Diversity of Life*, p. 133, emphasis added.

41. David Oates, *Earth Rising: Ecological Belief in an Age of Science* (Corvallis: Oregon State University Press, 1989), pp. 15, 31.

CHAPTER 6
THE NATURE OF RELIGION AND A RELIGION OF NATURE

1. Donald A. Crosby, *Interpretive Theories of Religion* (The Hague, the Netherlands: Mouton, 1981).

2. A basic object of religious concern is the fundamental focus of thought and practice in a particular religious system or outlook, for example, Zeus and the gods in Greek religion or Brahman in Advaita Vedanta Hinduism. For brevity, I refer to such objects of religious concern as *religious objects.*

3. For an illustration of applications of these categories to the religions of the world, and for a discussion of some of their conceptual interrelations and tensions, see my *Interpretive Theories of Religion*, chap. 7.

4. William A. Christian discusses the functions of primacy and uniqueness in religious objects in his *Meaning and Truth in Religion* (Princeton, N.J.: Princeton University Press, 1964), pp. 210–37. He does not, however, draw the kind of distinction that I do between the personal and cosmic aspects of these two categories.

5. The goal may or may not be conceived of as involving a continuing life of the individual beyond the grave. In some religious outlooks, such as traditional Christianity

or Pure Land Buddhism, it does, but in others, such as the Judaism of the biblical period or Zen Buddhism, it does not.

6. This ideal is differently understood, of course, in different religions or religious outlooks. In Theravada Buddhism, for example, it is the cessation of suffering and the attainment of nirvana. The world as envisioned by the Theravada Buddhist at least allows for this possibility and is in that sense hospitable to the salvation of the individual human being. In later Mahayana Buddhism, the concept of the Bodhisattva as a cosmic figure means that there is now something in the world more actively supportive of the hope of salvation for humans and all other sentient beings.

7. Psalm 139:7–10, King James Version.

8. Wendell Berry, "The Obligation of Care," *Sierra* (September/October 1993): 66.

9. Elisabet Sahtouris, *Gaia: The Human Journey From Chaos To Cosmos* (New York: Pocket Books, 1989), p. 191.

10. Joshua Slocum, *Voyage of the Liberdade*, in *Sailing Alone Around the World and Voyage of the Liberdade*, ed. Walter Magnes Teller (New York: Collier Books, 1962), p. 359. Slocum, a perceptive student of nature and especially of the winds, waves, tides, flora, and fauna of the oceans of the earth, was the first person to sail alone around the world.

11. Thomas Berry, *The Dream of the Earth* (San Francisco: Sierra Club Books, 1988), p. 202.

CHAPTER 7
OBJECTIONS TO A RELIGION OF NATURE

1. John H. Storer, *The Web of Life* (New York and Scarborough, Ontario: New American Library, Mentor Book, 1953), p. 94.

2. Stephen Jay Gould, "Eve and Her Tea," *Discover* 13 (July 1992): 32–33.

3. Annie Dillard, *Pilgrim at Tinker Creek* (New York: Bantam Books, 1975), pp. 66–67.

4. The cartoon appeared in the *Denver Post*, March 16, 1990, p. 4E.

5. Dillard, *Pilgrim at Tinker Creek*, p. 171.

6. No author, "Breakthroughs: Pesticide Tea," *Discover* 13 (July 1992): 14.

7. Dillard, *Pilgrim at Tinker Creek*, p. 51.

8. Richard Dawkins, *The Selfish Gene* (New York: Oxford University Press, 1978), p. 5.

9. Elisabet Sahtouris, *Gaia: The Human Journey From Chaos To Cosmos* (New York: Pocket Books, 1989), p. 225.

10. Holmes Rolston III, *Environmental Ethics: Duties to and Values in the Natural World* (Philadelphia: Temple University Press, 1988), pp. 57–62; Paul Colinvaux, *Why Big Fierce Animals Are Rare: An Ecologist's Perspective* (Princeton, N.J.: Princeton University Press, 1979), chap. 13, esp. p. 149.

11. Rolston III, *Environmental Ethics*, p. 221.

12. Susan Howatch, *The Wheel of Fortune* (New York: Fawcett Crest Books, 1985), p. 1157.

13. William James, *Essays in Radical Empiricism* and *A Pluralistic Universe*, two volumes in one (Gloucester, Mass.: Peter Smith, 1967), vol. 1, pp. 107–8.

14. I owe this important point to my wife, Pam. She insists upon it, and after considerable discussion and due reflection, I am convinced that she is right. While the intrinsic evils are generally not consciously intended among creatures of the nonhuman part of nature, for those sentient creatures who suffer and die as a manifestation of them, these evils are indisputably sad and real.

15. My esteemed colleague, James Boyd, one of whose areas of scholarly study and teaching is Eastern religions, ventured this caveat about my use of the term *evil* in a conversation. I appreciate the point and am sensitive to it, but I persist in my use of the term for the reasons given.

16. John Stuart Mill, *Nature and Utility of Religion*, ed. George Nakhnikian (New York: Liberal Arts Press, 1958), pp. 20–21.

17. James Gould Cozzens, *By Love Possessed* (Greenwich, Conn.: Fawcett Publications, a Fawcett Crest Book, 1957), pp. 238–39.

18. Gerald Birney Smith, "Is Theism Essential to Religion?" *The Journal of Religion* 5 (1925): 356–77, quoted in Jerome Stone, *The Minimalist Vision of Transcendence: A Naturalist Philosophy of Religion* (Albany: State University of New York Press, 1992), p. 54.

19. For a discussion of some of these difficulties see my *The Specter of the Absurd: Sources and Criticisms of Modern Nihilism* (Albany: State University of New York Press, 1988), pp. 48–50, 182–83.

20. See my *The Specter of the Absurd*, pp. 317–19; John Dewey, *Experience and Nature*, 2d ed. (New York: Dover, 1958).

21. David Oates, *Earth Rising: Ecological Belief in an Age of Science* (Corvallis: Oregon State University Press, 1989), p. 35.

22. Sahtouris, *Gaia*, p. 66.

23. Bruce Wilshire, *The Moral Collapse of the University: Professionalism, Purity, and Alienation* (Albany: State University of New York Press, 1990), p. 268.

24. Bertrand Russell, *A Free Man's Worship* (New York: Simon and Schuster, 1957), p. 54.

25. William Barrett cites another example of the ways in which nature routinely protects and sustains us and other creatures. We live, he observes, in a "jungle of microbic life" that continually threatens to prey upon parts of our bodies and to gravely endanger our well-being, and yet our marvelously organized bodies generally ward off these threats, protect us, and allow us to thrive. This fact becomes even more impressive to him, says Barrett, when he sees moving pictures of microorganisms showing how cells

and bacilli attack and devour each other with stark violence. See William Barrett, *Death of the Soul: From Descartes to the Computer* (New York: Anchor Books and Doubleday, 1986), p. 27. I gain a similar insight when I look at a medical book and note the huge number of diseases to which the body is susceptible. I marvel that our bodies are able to function so well, at least most of the time, in the face of the innumerable ways in which things could go wrong.

26. Rolston III, *Environmental Ethics*, p. 207.

27. Oates, *Earth Rising*, p. 227.

28. Ibid., p. 57.

29. Don Cupitt, *The Sea of Faith: Christianity in Change* (New York: Cambridge University Press, 1988), p. 249.

30. William Dean, in a verbal critical response to an earlier version of this chapter, has asked, "Why do you not advocate a religion of nature *and* culture, rather than just a religion of nature?" My answer is that nature already includes culture; culture is not something in addition to nature but one expression of its exuberant creativity. I do not deny the crucial importance of culture or cultural values to human existence, but I place culture in the larger context of the ultimacy of nature.

31. H. Richard Niebuhr, *The Responsible Self* (New York: Harper and Row, 1978), p. 285.

32. In the next section I critically discuss the claim that nature cannot be regarded as its own explanation or ground.

33. I heard the philosopher of religion, Keith Yandell, say virtually the same thing in a public debate with another philosopher, Michael Tooley, on the theological problem of evil. Yandell flatly stated that there is no problem of evil with which proponents of traditional theism have to deal, because we humans should not expect to comprehend the purposes or ways of a transcendent God who has created the universe and everything in it. The debate took place at Arapaho Community College, Denver, Colorado, February 25, 2000.

34. Benedict de Spinoza, *The Ethics*, in *The Chief Works of Benedict de Spinoza*, trans. R.H.M. Elwes, 2 vols. (New York: Dover, 1951), vol. 1, pp. 45–271.

35. Sallie MacFague, *The Body of God: An Ecological Theology* (Minneapolis: Fortress Press, 1993), p. 147.

36. Ibid., pp. 144–45.

37. Ibid., p. 147.

38. Julien Offray de la Mettrie, *Man a Machine*, trans. Gertrude G. Bussey and M. W. Calkins (La Salle, Ill.: Open Court Press, 1912), p. 125.

39. Some of the material in this chapter was contained in my essay "The Ultimacy of Nature: An Essay on Physidicy," in the *American Journal of Theology and Philosophy* 14:3 (September 1993): 2–14.

CHAPTER 8
THE RELIGIOUS ULTIMACY OF NATURE

1. William Barrett, *Death of the Soul: From Descartes to the Computer* (New York: Anchor Books and Doubleday, 1986), p. 97.

2. Friedrich Schleiermacher, *The Christian Faith*, various translators, ed. H. R. Macintosh and J. S. Stewart (Edinburgh, U.K: T & T Clark, 1928), p. 12 and *passim*.

3. Henry Nelson Wieman, *Religious Experience and Scientific Method* (New York: Macmillan, 1927), p. 9.

4. Rowe Findley, "Mount St. Helens: Nature on Fast Forward," *National Geographic* 197:5 (May 2000): 106–24.

5. For an insightful discussion and analysis of this remarkable human ability, see Patrick Shade, *Habits of Hope: A Pragmatic Theory* (Nashville: Vanderbilt University Press, 2000).

6. Alfred North Whitehead, in *The Function of Reason* (Boston: Beacon Press, 1958), p. 8, argues that there is an impulse or urge in nature for organisms "(i) to live, (ii) to live well, (iii) to live better," and that the more complex organisms' active, transformative engagements with their environments testify to this impulse or urge. His general argument is similar in some ways to the argument in this chapter, namely, that there are powerful forces working for good in nature, and that the impulse toward goodness that we find in ourselves as natural beings is important evidence of these forces. As intelligent, purposeful, free beings, we are aware of our capacity to interact with our social and natural environments in constructive, ameliorative ways, and there is present within us, though not always fully nurtured or acted upon, a strong aspiration and sense of obligation to do so.

7. Norman Cousins, *Dr. Schweitzer of Lambaréné* (New York: Harper and Brothers, 1960).

8. Ibid., pp. 70–71.

9. For the quotation, see http://www.caring-institute.org/ar/1989AR/fuller; see also http://www.habitat.org/how/millard.html, and Jerome P. Baggett, *Habitat for Humanity: Building Private Homes, Building Public Religion* (Philadelphia: Temple University Press, 2000).

10. See "John Muir: A Brief Biography," http://www.sierraclub.org/john_muir_exhibit, and Gretel Erlich and Lynn Johnson (photographer), *John Muir: Nature's Visionary* (Washington, D.C.: National Geographic Society, 2000).

11. I am, of course, aware that the Fullers and others attribute the impulse of goodness within themselves to God. The Fullers are both staunch Christians, but whatever our view of the ultimate source of this human impulse—for me, nature, for them, God—the examples of altruistic, caring persons that I have cited exhibit the presence of a force for good in human beings that can be cultivated and nurtured in order to do good in the world. William James speaks in *Pragmatism* of "superhuman forces" working for good in the world with which we can align ourselves, and he says that these "pow-

ers exist and are at work to save the world on ideal lines similar to our own." The immanent natural forces working for good that I am discussing in this chapter are, indeed, superhuman, that is, more than merely human, although I deny to them the character of being supernatural, personal, or divine. See James, *Pragmatism: A New Name for Some Old Ways of Thinking*, pp. 143–44, in James, *Pragmatism* and *The Meaning of Truth*, two volumes in one (Cambridge: Harvard University Press, 1975).

12. One example is a couple we met at the Habitat Thrift Store in Loveland, Colorado, who had been traveling to various places in the United States to help with the building of houses and to assist in the Habitat thrift stores. The husband, an electrical contractor, had taken six months off from his work to do this volunteer service, and the wife was home schooling her three children during this time, as well as working along with them in the Habitat program.

13. It is worth noting that the news media tend to emphasize the bad things that people do, precisely because such information is newsworthy and rare. We tend to take for granted and to not notice the supportive, helpful, gracious, and kind things that people do for one another on an everyday basis. The pervasive, commonplace, routine character of such goodness is another important indication of the impulse toward goodness in human beings, which is the focus of the fourth section of this chapter.

Selected Bibliography

Aristotle. *The Basic Works of Aristotle.* Edited by Richard McKeon. New York: Random House, 1941.

Aurelius, Marcus. *Meditations.* Published as *The Golden Book of Marcus Aurelius.* Translated by Meric Casaubon. New York: E. P. Dutton and Co., 1906, Book IV, Section 19, p. 33.

Baggett, Jerome P. *Habitat for Humanity: Building Private Homes, Building Public Religion.* Philadelphia: Temple University Press, 2000.

Barrett, William. *Death of the Soul: From Descartes to the Computer.* New York: Anchor Books and Doubleday, 1986.

Berry, Thomas. *The Dream of the Earth.* San Francisco: Sierra Club Books, 1988.

Bock, Kenneth. *Human Nature and History: A Response to Sociobiology.* New York: Columbia University Press, 1980.

Brown, Harold I. *Perception, Theory and Commitment.* Chicago: University of Chicago Press, 1979.

Buchler, Justus. "Probing the Idea of Nature." In *Metaphysics of Natural Complexes.* 2d, expanded ed. Edited by Kathleen Wallace and Armen Marsoobian, with Robert S. Corrington. Albany: State University of New York Press, 1990, p. 269.

Burke, James. *The Day the Universe Changed.* Boston and Toronto: Little, Brown and Company, 1985.

Carson, Rachel. *The Sense of Wonder.* Photographs by Charles Pratt and others. New York: Harper and Row, 1987, pp. 88–89.

Christian, William A. *Meaning and Truth in Religion.* Princeton, N.J.: Princeton University Press, 1964.

Colinvaux, Paul. *Why Big Fierce Animals Are Rare: An Ecologist's Perspective.* Princeton, N.J.: Princeton University Press, 1979.

Copleston, Frederick, and Bertrand Russell. "The Existence of God—A Debate." In *A Modern Introduction to Philosophy,* 3rd ed., edited by Paul Edwards and Arthur Pap. New York: Free Press, 1973, pp. 473–90.

Cousins, Norman. *Dr. Schweitzer of Lambaréné.* New York: Harper and Brothers, 1960.

Crosby, Donald A. "Experience As Reality: The Ecological Metaphysics of William James." In *Religious Experience and Ecological Responsibility*, Series on American Religious Thought, vol. 3, edited by Donald A. Crosby and Charley D. Hardwick. New York: Peter Lang, 1996, pp. 67–87.

———. "Finite Is All Right: Confessions of a Slow Learner." In *Pragmatism, Neo-Pragmatism, and Religion: Conversations With Richard Rorty*, Series on American Liberal Religious Thought, vol. 6, edited by Charley D. Hardwick and Donald A. Crosby. New York: Peter Lang, 1997, pp. 357–82.

———. *Interpretive Theories of Religion.* The Hague, the Netherlands: Mouton, 1981.

———. *The Specter of the Absurd: Sources and Criticisms of Modern Nihilism.* Albany: State University of New York Press, 1988.

———. "The Ultimacy of Nature: An Essay on Physic's." *American Journal of Theology and Philosophy* 14:3 (September 1993): 2–14.

Cupitt, Don. *The Sea of Faith: Christianity in Change.* New York: Cambridge University Press, 1988.

Dawkins, Richard. *The Selfish Gene.* New York: Oxford University Press, 1978.

Dennett, Daniel C. *The Intentional Stance.* Cambridge: MIT Press, 1987.

De Waal, Frans. *Good Natured: The Origins of Right and Wrong in Humans and Other Animals.* Cambridge: Harvard University Press, 1996.

Dewey, John. *A Common Faith.* New Haven, Conn.: Yale University Press, 1934.

———. *Experience and Nature*, 2d ed. New York: Dover, 1958.

———. *The Philosophy of John Dewey*, two volumes in one. Edited by John McDermott. Chicago: University of Chicago Press, 1981.

———. *The Quest for Certainty.* New York: Capricorn Books, 1960.

Dillard, Annie. *Pilgrim at Tinker Creek.* New York: Bantam Books, 1975.

Dupré, John. *The Disorder of Things: Metaphysical Foundations of the Disunity of Science.* Cambridge: Harvard University Press, 1995.

Eck, Diana L. *Encountering God: A Spiritual Journey from Bozeman to Banares.* Boston: Beacon Press, 1993.

Erlich, Gretel, and Lynn Johnson, photographer. *John Muir: Nature's Visionary.* Washington, D.C.: National Geographic Society, 2000.

Ferré, Frederick. *Philosophy of Technology.* Englewood Cliffs, N.J.: Prentice Hall, 1988.

Feuerbach, Ludwig. *The Essence of Christianity.* Translated by George Eliot. New York: Harper Torchbooks, Library of Religion and Culture, 1957.

Frankl, Viktor E. *Man's Search for Meaning.* New York: Washington Square Press, 1959, postscript, 1984.

Goodenough, Ursula. *The Sacred Depths of Nature.* Oxford and New York: Oxford University Press, 1998.

Gustafson, James M. *Ethics from a Theocentric Perspective.* 2 vols. Chicago: University of Chicago Press, 1981, 1984.

Hartshorne, Charles. *The Darkness and the Light.* Albany: State University of New York Press, 1990.

Hesse, Mary. *Models and Analogies in Science.* Notre Dame, Ind.: University of Notre Dame Press, 1970.

Hetherington, Norriss S., ed. *Cosmology: Historical, Literary, Philosophical, Religious, and Scientific Perspectives.* New York and London: Garland Publishing, Garland Reference Library of the Humanities, vol. 1634, 1993.

James, William. *Essays in Radical Empiricism* and *A Pluralistic Universe,* two volumes in one. Gloucester, Mass.: Peter Smith, 1967. (The epigraph at the beginning of the book is on p. 31 of *A Pluralistic Universe.*)

————. *Pragmatism* and *The Meaning of Truth,* two volumes in one. Cambridge: Harvard University Press, 1975.

————. *The Selected Letters of William James.* Edited by Elizabeth Hardwick. New York: Anchor Books and Doubleday, 1960.

Kohák, Erazim. *The Embers and the Stars: A Philosophical Inquiry into the Moral Sense of Nature.* Chicago: University of Chicago Press, 1984, p. 6.

Kuhn, Thomas. *The Structure of Scientific Revolutions.* Chicago: University of Chicago Press, 1970.

MacFague, Sallie. *The Body of God: An Ecological Theology.* Minneapolis: Fortress Press, 1993.

McDermott, John, ed. *The Philosophy of John Dewey,* two volumes in one. Chicago: University of Chicago Press, 1981.

Mettrie, Julien Offray de la. *Man a Machine.* Translated by Gertrude G. Bussey and M. W. Calkins. La Salle, Ill.: Open Court Press, 1912.

Mill, John Stuart. *Nature and Utility of Religion.* Edited by George Nakhnikian. New York: Liberal Arts Press, 1958.

Munitz, Milton. *Cosmic Understanding: Philosophy and Science of the Universe.* Princeton, N.J.: Princeton University Press, 1986.

Niebuhr, H. Richard. *The Responsible Self.* New York: Harper and Row, 1978.

Nietzsche, Friedrich. *Beyond Good and Evil.* Translated by Walter Kaufmann. New York: Vintage Books, 1966, p. 15.

Oates, David. *Earth Rising: Ecological Belief in an Age of Science.* Corvallis: Oregon State University Press, 1989.

Oelschlaeger, Max. *The Idea of Wilderness: From Prehistory to the Age of Ecology.* New Haven, Conn.: Yale University Press, 1991, pp. 335–36.

Otto, Rudolf. *The Idea of the Holy.* Translated by John W. Harvey. New York: Oxford University Press, a Galaxy Book, 1958.

Pacala, Stephen W., and Simon A. Levin. "The Importance of *Not* Knowing a Thing or Two." *Princeton* (summer 1997): 6.

Peat, F. David. *Einstein's Moon: Bell's Theorem and the Curious Quest for Quantum Reality.* Chicago: Contemporary Books, 1990.

Peirce, Charles Sanders. *Philosophical Writings of Peirce.* Edited by Justus Buchler. New York: Dover, 1955.

Pennock, Robert T. "Naturalism, Creationism and the Meaning of Life: The Case of Phillip Johnson Revisited." *Creation/Evolution* 16:2 (winter 1996): 10–30.

Pope, Alexander. "Summer: The Second Pastoral, or Alexis." In *The Oxford Authors: Alexander Pope*, edited by Pat Rogers. Oxford and New York: Oxford University Press, 1993, p. 10.

Putnam, Hilary. *Pragmatism.* Oxford: Blackwell, 1995.

Rachels, James. *Created From Animals: The Moral Implications of Darwinism.* Oxford and New York: Oxford University Press, 1990.

Randall, John Herman, Jr. *The Making of the Modern Mind: A Survey of the Intellectual Background of the Present Age*, 50th anniversary ed. New York: Columbia University Press, 1976.

Rollin, Bernard E. *The Unheeded Cry: Animal Consciousness, Animal Pain, and Science.* Oxford and New York: Oxford University Press, 1989.

Rolston, Holmes, III. *Environmental Ethics: Duties to and Values in the Natural World.* Philadelphia: Temple University Press, 1988.

———. *Genes, Genesis, and God: Values and Their Origins in Natural and Human History.* Cambridge: Cambridge University Press, 1999.

Ross, Stephen David. *Locality and Practical Judgment: Charity and Sacrifice.* New York: Fordham University Press, 1994.

Rubenstein, Richard L. *After Auschwitz: Radical Theology and Contemporary Judaism.* Indianapolis: Bobbs-Merrill, 1966.

Russell, Bertrand. *A Free Man's Worship.* New York: Simon and Schuster, 1957.

Sahtouris, Elisabet. *Gaia: The Human Journey From Chaos To Cosmos.* New York: Pocket Books, 1989.

Sartre, Jean-Paul. *Being and Nothingness: An Essay on Phenomenological Ontology.* Translated by Hazel Barnes. New York: Washington Square Press, 1966.

———. *Nausea.* Translated by Lloyd Alexander. New York: New Directions, 1964.

Savage-Rumbaugh, Sue, Stuart G. Shanker, and Talbot J. Taylor. *Apes, Language and the Human Mind*. Oxford and New York: Oxford University Press, 1998.

Scheffler, Israel. *Science and Subjectivity*. Indianapolis: Bobbs-Merrill, 1967.

Schleiermacher, Friedrich. *The Christian Faith*. Various translators. Edited by H. R. Macintosh and J. S. Stewart. Edinburgh, U.K.: T & T Clark, 1928.

Schon, Donald. *The Displacement of Concepts*. London: Tavistok, 1963.

Schweitzer, Albert. *The Quest of the Historical Jesus: A Critical Study of Its Progress From Reimarus to Wrede*. Translated by W. Montgomery. New York: Macmillan, 1950.

Shade, Patrick. *Habits of Hope: A Pragmatic Theory*. Nashville: Vanderbilt University Press, 2000.

Slocum, Joshua. *Voyage of the Liberdade*. In *Sailing Alone Around the World and Voyage of the Liberdade*. Edited by Walter Magnes Teller. New York: Collier Books, 1962.

Smart, Ninian. *Buddhism and Christianity: Rivals and Allies*. Honolulu: University of Hawaii Press, 1993.

Smith, Gerald Birney. "Is Theism Essential to Religion?" *The Journal of Religion* 5 (1925): 356–77.

Spinoza, Benedict. *The Chief Works of Benedict de Spinoza*, 2 vols. Translated by R.H.M. Elwes. New York: Dover, 1951.

Stone, Jerome A. *The Minimalist Vision of Transcendence: A Naturalist Philosophy of Religion*. Albany: State University of New York Press, 1992.

Storer, John H. *The Web of Life*. New York and Scarborough, Ontario: New American Library, a Mentor Book, 1953.

Stout, Jeffrey. *Ethics after Babel: The Languages of Morals and Their Discontents*. Boston: Beacon Press, 1988.

Tagore, Rabindranath. *Gitanjali*. In *Collected Poems and Plays of Rabindranath Tagore*. London: Macmillan, 1962, 33. Quoted in Diana Eck. *Encountering God: A Spiritual Journey from Bozeman to Banares*. Boston: Beacon Press, 1993, p. 140.

Thoreau, Henry David. "Walking." In *The Essays of Henry David Thoreau*, edited by Richard Dillman. Albany: NCUP, 1990, p. 131.

Tillich, Paul. *The Courage to Be*. New Haven, Conn.: Yale University Press, 1952.

———. *Systematic Theology*, 3 vols. Chicago: University of Chicago Press, 1951, 1957, 1963.

Viney, Donald Wayne, and Donald A. Crosby. "Free Will and Determinism in Process Perspective." *New Ideas in Psychology* 12:2 (July 1994): 129–41.

Whitehead, Alfred North. *The Function of Reason*. Boston: Beacon Press, 1958.

———. *Modes of Thought*. New York: Capricorn Books, 1958.

———. *Process and Reality: Corrected Edition*. Edited by David Ray Griffin and Donald W. Sherburne. New York: Free Press, 1978.

———. *Science and the Modern World*. New York: Free Press, 1967. (The epigraph to chapter 3 is on p. 187.)

Wieman, Henry Nelson. *Religious Experience and Scientific Method*. New York: Macmillan, 1927.

Wilshire, Bruce. *The Moral Collapse of the University: Professionalism, Purity, and Alienation*. Albany: State University of New York Press, 1990.

Wilson, E. O. *Consilience: The Unity of Knowledge*. New York: Knopf, 1998.

———. *The Diversity of Life*. Cambridge: Belknap Press of Harvard University Press, 1992.

Index of Authors and Titles

Index of Subjects

Advaita Vedanta, 149
afterlife, 129, 180–81n. 5
animals, purposive acts of, 105
artifacts, 110
atheism, 12

Bell's theorem, 45, 175n. 3
Big Bang theory, 39, 43
Big Crunch theory, 39, 43, 173n. 18
Buddhism, 149, 180–81nn. 5, 6

chance, 30, 39, 41, 52
    and causality, 126
Christianity, traditional, 180–81n. 5
consciousness in animals, 94–101
constructivism, radical, 22–24
convictional openness, 7
cosmic epochs, 35, 43–44, 154
cosmocentrism, 149
culture
    of animals, 93
    definition of, 93
cultures, human, 93
    as aspects of nature, 17, 106–107, 141,
        183n. 30
    and language, 108–109
    teaching of, 108–109

death, 85–86, 129
    price paid for life, 82
"Death of God" theologians, 9
determinism, causal, 28–31, 62

ecology, 10–11, 140, 149
ecological crisis, 109

ethics
    ecological, 117, 128, 143–45
    human, 128, 143–45
    platitudes of, 175n. 8
    and religion, 144
evil
    and Book of Job, 8, 147–48
    in human history, 164
    existential problem of, 8, 148
    traditional theological problem of,
        8–9, 147–48, 150, 183n.33
evolution, 39, 173–74n. 2
    biological, 161–62
    cultural, 113
    Darwinian theory of, 10–11
experience
    broad construal of, 49–50
    conceptual interpretation of, 24–26
    and knowledge, 23–26
    perspectival character of, 19
explanation, logic of, 154

facts
    changeability of, in the natural sci-
        ences, 63
    as expressing judgments of values, 64
    as inferences, 63
    nature of 62–63, 76
    not privileged over values, 76
faith, 122
feelings
    as candidates for value, 72–74
    cognitive importance of, 70–74
    and values, 70–74
forgiveness, 129–30